Communications in Computer and Information Science 642

Commenced Publication in 2007
Founding and Former Series Editors:
Alfredo Cuzzocrea, Dominik Ślęzak, and Xiaokang Yang

More information about this series at http://www.springer.com/series/7899

Stefan Gruner (Ed.)

ICT Education

45th Annual Conference of the Southern African
Computer Lecturers' Association, SACLA 2016
Cullinan, South Africa, July 5–6, 2016
Revised Selected Papers

 Springer

Editor
Stefan Gruner
Department of Computer Science
University of Pretoria
Pretoria
South Africa

ISSN 1865-0929 ISSN 1865-0937 (electronic)
Communications in Computer and Information Science
ISBN 978-3-319-47679-7 ISBN 978-3-319-47680-3 (eBook)
DOI 10.1007/978-3-319-47680-3

Library of Congress Control Number: 2016954931

Printed on acid-free paper

This Springer imprint is published by Springer Nature
The registered company is Springer International Publishing AG
The registered company address is: Gewerbestrasse 11, 6330 Cham, Switzerland

This book is respectfully dedicated to the late
Hartmut EHRIG *(*1944 †2016), Professor of*
Theoretical Computer Science and Formal
Specifications at the Technische Universität
Berlin (Germany), who was an outstanding
educator of our discipline. He taught and guided
large numbers of students to their academic
informatics degrees.

Preface

This volume of CCIS contains the revised papers of SACLA 2016, the 45th Annual Conference of the Southern African Computer Lecturers' Association, held in the old diamond mining town of Cullinan (Republic of South Africa), July 5–6, 2016, under the motto: "Achieving Brilliance in ICT Education."[1] This conference was jointly conducted (in mutually beneficial co-location) with the CSERC 2016, the Computer Science Education Research Conference,[2] and the University of the Witwatersrand's JCSE Workshop on ICT Skills Shortage in South Africa.[3]

Over 45 years, Southern African computing lecturers have been holding annual meetings to discuss matters and issues in the context of lecturing computing (computer science, informatics, information technology) in tertiary education. This SACLA series thus has one of the most long-standing conferencing traditions in our discipline world-wide, though the series was internationally not widely known in its earlier years. During the course of its history, the SACLA series evolved from initially very informal gatherings to increasingly formalized and peer-reviewed conferences — although still with a rather regional Southern African character until today. With SACLA 2016, however, the first attempt was made at opening the conference's doors and windows much wider, in order to make the SACLA series henceforth attractive for an international audience anywhere in the world. This move toward internationalization is a rational consequence of the notoriously ongoing globalization of our world, which means that problems —and their solutions— can no longer be contained easily within national or regional borders and boundaries. For this reason also the conference's Programme Committee (PC) was —for the first time— systematically internationalized, with almost half of its members now residing overseas. The call for papers, too, was distributed internationally via various widely recognized communication channels, although the response from overseas was not (yet) as big as (wishfully) expected. What remained, however, constant also at SACLA 2016 (in spite of the new move toward internationalization), is the original motivation of the very first SACLA meetings from more than four decades ago, namely: to provide a forum at which lecturers of computer science and informatics can thoroughly discuss any contemporary issues of lecturing these subjects at a tertiary education level.

With this motivation, SACLA 2016 called for original research papers as well as noteworthy experience reports in all matters concerning the lecturing (teaching) of informatics or computer science (ICS) at institutions of tertiary education (TE) — i.e., classical universities, comprehensive universities, and vocational-technical training colleges. Relevant contemporary topics mentioned in the call for papers included:

---

[1] http://sacla.cs.up.ac.za

[2] https://www.ou.nl/web/cserc/cserc-2016

[3] http://www.jcse.org.za/events/sacla16-ict-skills-shortage-workshop

- ICS massive open online courses (MOOCs)
- Didactics and methods for teaching ICS in TE
- ICS curricula development in TE: scientific-theoretical versus industrial-practical orientation
- Didactic software and educational support tools for ICS in TE
- Program-code plagiarism, ghost-writing, and counter-measurements
- Ethical problems in the teaching of ICS at TE level
- Students' behavior, self-perceptions, plans, and aspirations within their ICS learning environment at TE level
- Deficiencies in literacy, numeracy, logical reasoning, and general study-ability among students of ICS today
- Transition of newly graduated middle-school (secondary school) pupils into their ICS curricula at TE level: factors of success or failure
- Transition of newly graduated ICS students into their post-TE employment environments: factors of success or failure
- Marks/grades inflation and/or assessment standard/quality changes over longer periods of time in the history of ICS-TE
- International comparability of degrees and levels of knowledge/skill/performance among ICS students at TE level
- Effects of the still ongoing massification, egalitarization, and commercial commodification of TE on the ICS teaching and learning environment
- Humboldt's question: separation or combination of teaching and research in small or large ICS departments at TE institutions
- Longitudinal studies in ICS education: past-versus-presence comparisons and plausible future trends
- Social role problems and/or career issues of ICS academics from junior lecturer to emeritus professor at TE institutions
- ICS lecturers' general matters: best/worst practices, success/failure experiences, etc.

Within these themes and topic fields, two types of submissions to SACLA 2016 were possible:

- Full-length research papers or practical experience reports with solid results
- Short papers for interesting and promising work in progress

Submissions in both categories were rigorously reviewed by the Programme Committee for quality in contents and style of presentation. Each submission was assessed by three reviewers, of whom at least one had to be from South Africa and at least one from abroad. All rejection decisions were final, i.e., without any rebuttal phase for the authors after the reviews. Accepted papers had to be discussed at the SACLA 2016 conference *and* thoroughly revised before their inclusion in this CCIS volume, which is the very first (and hopefully not its last) publication of the SACLA series with Springer as its highly esteemed publishing house.

By its closing date, SACLA 2016 had received 30 submissions, out of which (after rigorous review) three (10 %) were accepted as full papers, and another 13 ($\approx$43 %) as 8-page-short work-in-progress papers. All of them appear thematically grouped (regardless of their full- or short-length category) in this CCIS book. The full paper by Serena Coetzee and Victoria Rautenbach —see table of contents— received the conference's Best Paper Award. In addition to these regular submissions, two invited keynote lectures were given by Martin Olivier (day 1) and Bob Travica (day 2): The papers that recapitulate these two lectures are included in this CCIS volume, too. In my role as editor I proposed the invitation of Martin Olivier to the conference's committee while PC member Jan Kroeze proposed the invitation of Bob Travica.

In addition to the "official" members of the conference's Organizing Committee many colleagues and friends contributed to the success of SACLA 2016. Thank you to the regular authors, as well as to the invited speakers, for having chosen SACLA 2016 as the forum for communicating their noteworthy insights and interesting thoughts. Thank you to the members of the PC and their additional reviewers, who all provided insightful and detailed comments well within the stipulated assessment time. Thank you to the representatives of Springer German branch (Alfred Hofmann, Aliaksandr Birukou, Leonie Kunz, Frank Holzwarth) for having provided SACLA 2016 with this CCIS publication opportunity, as well as to the representatives of Springer British branch (Beverley Ford, Wayne Wheeler, James Robinson) for having donated a package of relevant ICS textbooks for further use. Thank you to Peter Csaba Ölveczky for his professional LaTeX advice concerning the structure and the type-setting of this CCIS book. Thank you to the representatives of our financial sponsors: the Department of Computer Science of the University of Pretoria (Andries Engelbrecht) and the IITPSA (Tony Parry), as well as to the organizers of the value-adding co-located events: CSERC 2016 (Marko van Eekelen) and the JCSE workshop on South African IT skills (Barry Dwolatzky, Adrian Schofield). Thank you, last but not least, to Christina Firkins and Joané de Kock for their hands-on help at the conference's registration desk.

After the *45th Annual Conference of the Southern African Computer Lecturers' Association* —and at the end of this preface— I express my hope that this CCIS volume may receive the international recognition that it deserves, and that the herewith-documented success of SACLA 2016 may lead to the further growth and internationalization of the long-standing SACLA conferencing tradition in the not-too-far future.

July 2016   Stefan Gruner

The supporters and sponsors of SACLA 2016 are herewith gratefully acknowledged

Organization

General Chair

Linda Marshall University of Pretoria, South Africa

Local Arrangements and Technical Support

Angela Bekker University of Pretoria, South Africa
Vreda Pieterse University of Pretoria, South Africa
Neels van Rooyen University of Pretoria, South Africa

Programme Chair and Proceedings Editor

Stefan Gruner University of Pretoria, South Africa

International Programme Committee

Aderemi Adewumi University of Kwa Zulu Natal, South Africa
Pieter Blignaut University of the Free State, South Africa
Jürgen Börstler Blekinge Tekniska Högskola, Sweden
Raymond Boute (Professor Emeritus), Belgium
Torsten Brinda Universität Duisburg-Essen, Germany
André Calitz Nelson Mandela Metropolitan University, South Africa
Turgay Celik University of the Witwatersrand, South Africa
Michel Chaudron Chalmers Tekniska Högskola, Sweden
Charmain Cilliers Nelson Mandela Metropolitan University, South Africa
Marijke Coetzee University of Johannesburg, South Africa
Serena Coetzee University of Pretoria, South Africa
Andrea Corradini Università di Pisa, Italy

Carina de Villiers	University of Pretoria, South Africa
Jörg Desel	Fernuniversität in Hagen, Germany
Elize Ehlers	University of Johannesburg, South Africa
Peter Forbrig	Universität Rostock, Germany
Ina Fourie	University of Pretoria, South Africa
Kurt Geihs	Universität Kassel, Germany
Jaco Geldenhuys	Stellenbosch University, South Africa
Stefan Gruner (Ed.)	University of Pretoria, South Africa
Scott Hazelhurst	University of the Witwatersrand, South Africa
Reiko Heckel	University of Leicester, UK
Jan Kroeze	University of South Africa
Herbert Kuchen	Westfälische Wilhelms-Universität Münster, Germany
Michelle Kuttel	University of Cape Town, South Africa
Shaoying Liu	Hosei University, Japan
Philip Machanick	Rhodes University, South Africa
Ernest Mnkandla	University of South Africa
Mohamed Mosbah	Université de Bordeaux 1, France
Susana Muñoz-Hernández	Universidad Politécnica de Madrid, Spain
Sergei Obiedkov	National Research University Higher School of Economics, Russia
Peter Ölveczky	Universitetet i Oslo, Norway
Martin Olivier	University of Pretoria, South Africa
Niels Pinkwart	Humboldt-Universität zu Berlin, Germany
Michael Poppleton	University of Southampton, UK
Markus Roggenbach	Swansea University, UK
Ian Sanders	University of South Africa
Ulrik Schröder	Rheinisch-Westfälische Technische Hochschule Aachen, Germany
Andreas Schwill	Universität Potsdam, Germany
Hussein Suleman	University of Cape Town, South Africa
Matti Tedre	Stockholms Universitet, Sweden
Clint van Alten	University of the Witwatersrand, South Africa
Isabella Venter	University of the Western Cape, South Africa
Willem Visser	Stellenbosch University, South Africa
Gottfried Vossen	Westfälische Wilhelms-Universität Münster, Germany
Bruce Watson	Stellenbosch University, South Africa
George Wells	Rhodes University, South Africa
Janet Wesson	Nelson Mandela Metropolitan University, South Africa
Jim Woodcock	University of York, UK
Albert Zündorf	Universität Kassel, Germany
Olaf Zukunft	Hochschule für Angewandte Wissenschaften Hamburg, Germany

Additional Reviewers

Ade-Ibijola, Abejide
Ajayi, Nurudeen
Chavula, Josiah
Eybers, Sunet
Hagen, Mariele
Huhn, Michaela
Iglezakis, Dorothea
Kapfhammer, Petra

Klein, Richard
Leonard, Awie
Mehner-Heindl,
    Katharina
Niemczyk, Stefan
Padberg, Julia
Phiri, Lighton
Ranchod, Pravesh

Reischmann, Tobias
Rieger, Christoph
Travica, Bob
van der Merwe, Alta
van der Poll, John
Vesin, Boban
Voigtländer, Janis

Contents

Invited Lectures

On the Morality of Teaching Students IT Crime Skills.   3
  Martin S. Olivier

Teaching Informatics in North America: Jugglers Wanted   22
  Bob Travica

Assessment Methods

A Comparison of E-Assessment Assignment Submission Processes
in Introductory Computing Courses.   35
  Melisa Koorsse, Marinda Taljaard, and André P. Calitz

Assessing Programming by Written Examinations.   43
  Ken Halland

Criteria for Evaluating Automated Grading Systems to Assess Microsoft
Office Skills.   51
  Melisa Koorsse, André P. Calitz, and Jaco Zietsman

Towards a Generic DSL for Automated Marking Systems   59
  Fritz Solms and Vreda Pieterse

Instruction Methods

Code Pathfinder: A Stepwise Programming E-Tutor Using Plan Mirroring . . .   69
  Mark S. Durrheim, Abejide Ade-Ibijola, and Sigrid Ewert

Flipping a Course on Computer Architecture   83
  Hussein Suleman

Effective Integration of a Student Response System in An Undergraduate
Computer Science Classroom: An Active-Engagement Instructional
Strategy.   95
  Fani Moses Radebe and Liezel Nel

Teaching Operating Systems: Just Enough Abstraction 104
  Philip Machanick

New Curricula

CS and IS Alumni Post-Graduate Course and Supervision Perceptions. 115
  André P. Calitz, Jean Greyling, and Arthur Glaum

Introducing Health Informatics as an Elective Module in an Information
Systems Honours Degree: Experiences from Rhodes University   123
   Greg Foster and Jane Nash

Towards an Interdisciplinary Master's Degree Programme in Big Data
and Data Science: A South African Perspective   131
   Linda Marshall and Jan H.P. Eloff

Social Skills

Reflections on a Community-Based Service Learning Approach
in a Geoinformatics Project Module   143
   Serena Coetzee and Victoria Rautenbach

Which Are Harder? Soft Skills or Hard Skills?   160
   Vreda Pieterse and Marko van Eekelen

Various Experiences

A Case Study in the Use of the Five Step Peer Evaluation Strategy to
Improve a First Year Computer Literacy Course: An Exercise
in Reflective Evaluation Practice.   171
   Mosiuoa Tsietsi

Enterprise Resource Planning Teaching Challenges Faced by Lecturers
in African Higher Education Institutions   179
   Khadija M. Mahanga and Lisa F. Seymour

Grit and Growth Mindset Among High School Students in a Computer
Programming Project: A Mixed Methods Study   187
   Delia Kench, Scott Hazelhurst, and Femi Otulaja

Author Index   195

Invited Lectures

On the Morality of Teaching Students IT Crime Skills

Martin S. Olivier(✉)

Department of Computer Science, University of Pretoria, Pretoria, South Africa
`molivier@cs.up.ac.za`

Abstract. A superficial introduction to the world of viruses, worms and other malware is often sufficient to get students dreaming about the potential power wielded by those technologies. One needs about a minute to teach them how to build a powerful Trojan Horse, how to distribute such a construction as targeted malware and how to monetise the few minutes they invested in such an effort. Such teaching is rewarding since it is one of the few examples where many students immediately apply their new skills to impress friends. Of course the intention is not to make them criminals, but to gain the deep understanding of issues that would otherwise require them to spent hours with books that discuss abstract concepts that often remains abstract.

The question is whether computing educator should ever even consider teaching students skills that may be abused in this manner.

In this paper I argue that knowledge to harm and knowledge to help overlap in many professional contexts. The lecture argues questions on the morally of imparting potentially malicious knowledge should differentiate between imparting it to those entering a profession and imparting it to the masses. While this does not prevent the professional from abusing knowledge, it is argued that the benefit to society will outweigh the harm. In the non-professional context little benefit is likely to accrue to society, but opportunistic abuse of knowledge already acquired is significantly more probable than the possibility of someone purposefully acquiring and abusing such knowledge.

However, even more important than professionalism is the sense of community. It is argued that meaningful professional communities that are able to use harmful knowledge responsibly are rare in computing. Hence care should be exercised when potentially harmful information is to be taught and self-censorship ought to be exercised in general.

Keywords: Ethics of computing · Professional ethics · Professionalism in IT · *Invited keynote lecture*

1 Thirty Odd Years Ago ...

It was in the late 1980 s when I first got the opportunity to break into a bank. Banks were beginning to realise that some customers required online banking

© Springer International Publishing AG 2016
S. Gruner (Ed.): SACLA 2016, CCIS 642, pp. 3–21, 2016.
DOI: 10.1007/978-3-319-47680-3_1

facilities. At the time the business sector was the online banking target audience. Online banking also did not look as we know it today; since the Internet was not used for commercial services at that time, online banking was not Internet banking. This predated broadband access and any service offered was through dial-up facilities. In some cases a 'portal' (using a term that was not used at the time) was used to connect to the bank; in other cases the bank provided its own modems and select customers could connect to the bank via a direct telephone call: modem to modem.

For banks this was a new mode of interacting with customers and they were understandably weary of the security implications of providing customers such direct access to their systems.

It is in this context that a service provider contacted my employer at the time and the question eventually arrived at my desk. In essence a physical 'key' was created that would uniquely identify the customer and provide access to authorised accounts. Access by using the 'key' would constitute proof that the customer did indeed access the accounts, and the bank could demand to inspect the key at any time, and inspection of the key would, amongst others, reveal when last the key was used. The question that landed on my desk was whether this mechanism —described in even more vague terms than above— was reliable. After signing reams of documents preventing me from ever talking to anyone about the question, I was provided a few more details and a working 'key'. The Achilles heel of the system was clearly the possibility of creating a clone of the 'key', because a clone would enable a user to access accounts, while the original key would not have any indication that it was used and the original key would be indeed be available for inspection at any time.

For me the problem was akin to bypassing copy protection incorporated in many software packages at the time. Nerds like I 'knew' that no copy protection mechanism was infallible and the task at hand did not seem very challenging. The usual tools to bypass copy protection did not work. The next avenue of attack was working through the code that could be accessed on the key. Long story short: It did not take particularly long before the bank was supplied with a duplicate key that unlocked access to the relevant accounts. I do not know whether the bank ever commissioned that particular system; I assumed that the relative ease with which the system could be breached was valuable information for them. I certainly learned quite a few interesting lessons from the process; I gained knowledge that I would have loved to share with others, but those reams of signed non-disclosure agreements kept me quiet for decades and even today I hesitate the share all the details of the adventure.

The knowledge I had of bypassing copy protection schemes hopefully contributed in some small way to make online banking for that particular bank a little safer. Extrapolating from this isolated experience it was obvious that knowledge of how to perform a few morally questionable actions could benefit society in the long run. But, none of my university courses ever hinted at how such morally questionable actions could be performed (or that they may be useful in a positive sense).

Why we had knowledge of ways to bypass copy protection schemes, how we obtained such knowledge and whether we were justified in having such knowledge will be discussed later in this paper.

A year or two after the bank project one of the first computer viruses arrived on our desks because someone's computer occasionally displayed a 'ball' bouncing across the screen. At that time there was no World Wide Web to query and we eventually located the code that displayed this 'bouncing ball', and carving further we eventually realised that we have discovered a computer virus on this computer. At the time there were some rumours about computer viruses, but those rumours did not make sense. But here we had the incarnation of a virus in machine code, and the way that this (then) mythical category of malware operated suddenly started making sense.

Fig. 1. International knowledge sharing prior to wide-scale use of the Internet

We talked about what we discovered and developed software that could remove this virus from an infected machine. Soon a steady stream of new viruses started flowing to our desks. In a relatively short time our skills to locate, isolate, extract and examine such viruses grew to be quite comfortable when confronted with a new possible virus. In some cases we were able to, with authority, say that some incidents were wrongly attributed to viruses. Based on prevalence we discovered why some viruses were 'more viral' than others. We discovered how unintended consequences of viruses were in some instances particularly danger-ous. We even found examples of beauty in viruses where the style of the virus writer was just much more elegant than the norm. We gathered a wealth of knowledge about viruses. This knowledge was used in the fight against viruses or, blowing our own trumpets, 'for the good of humankind'. This time there was no non-disclosure agreement. We could share this knowledge with others; we could teach them a theory of computer viruses. But we did not.

This time there were moral boundaries that we felt we should not cross, because somewhere someone would use the skills that we could transfer for evil. And for many years we talked about viruses in abstract terms —that, almost like the initial rumours we heard, enabled people to talk about the concept, but never to really understand the details— unless, like us, they were willing the acquire the detailed knowledge the hard way.

However, even requests to share copies of viruses were largely ignored. Some-how a small international community formed who became the 'custodians' of viral code and we were only willing to share viruses (as well as analyses and sometimes antivirus software) in that community. Figure 1 reminds one of how information was typically shared in the days before using the Internet became the universal means of communication. This particular photograph shows virus-related software that I received from Fridrik Skúlason *circa* 1989. It serves to emphasise how this community formed and existed prior to the wide adoption of the Internet and other global networking technologies.

My (subjective) experience was that the communities that formed as, ulti-mately, the custodians of malware shared a certain ethic. Similarly, hacking communities sharing a certain ethic, formed. And the ethic of the community had a profound impact on what knowledge was shared when with whom. I doubt that all communities shared the same values, but, rather, that shared values were at the core of communities that did form.

Many years have passed since the days recalled in the paragraphs above. It is time to reflect whether those communities that collected guarded knowledge about malware and hacking acted correctly when they 'guarded' rather than taught such information, and, if they did, whether the same imperatives still apply. Note that the claim is not that all communities guarded potentially dan-gerous information; some shared such information from the very beginning and their decision to share also requires reflection.

2   To Teach or Not to Teach

On the one hand knowledge —*any* knowledge— has value. One only has to look at outcries that result from the burning of books or almost any form of censorship that is imposed. Books are a form of transmitting knowledge, which is effectively a form of teaching. Destruction of books intended to destroy knowledge is an attempt to prevent the information it contains to be transmitted — that is, to be taught. Censorship is a restriction on free speech. It is typically imposed to prevent ideas from spreading; censorship effectively prevents teaching of the censored information.

Note that there is a small class of information that society in general does not condone. The best-known example is the depiction of certain forms of child exploitation. There is general agreement that society should not tolerate such knowledge. However, beyond these very narrow confines open societies usually frown upon most forms of censorship. From this it follows that teaching is, in general, tolerated and the right to teach defended (even when the content of what is taught is disliked).

However, there is often a wide chasm between what ought to be done and what is tolerated. Hence the act of teaching may sometimes be tolerated even when the knowledge taught is deemed inappropriate. At the other extreme, knowledge that is universally valued may make teaching such knowledge an imperative. Of course teaching and knowledge may be tolerated and/or valued anywhere between these two extremes. However, in addition to the freedom to teach (or otherwise), the act of teaching some skill or knowledge invokes at least two other factors, namely the context and the nature of the skills transfer. This triad will be explored in more detail below.

Seen in the abstract, teaching (or education) is deemed valuable. Countries spend huge amounts on education, and individuals seek education to improve their prospects in life. The value of education is captured in the age old proverb *"give a man a fish and you feed him for a day; teach a man to fish and you feed him for a lifetime"*.[1] While the modern-day reader will frown about the gender bias in this proverb, she will agree with the underlying truth: such teaching empowers the learner. It helps the learner to satisfy a basic need. This proverb does not directly impose a moral obligation — it merely compares the utility of two acts: giving and teaching. Teaching has the greater utility due to its multiplicative affect: value for a day compared to value for a lifetime. However, viewed from a utilitarian perspective, confronted with the choice of helping or teaching, teaching is the preferred option. Assuming the obvious fact that satisfying a basic need of a person contributes to the happiness of that person, then teaching may empower many people to help themselves, whereas feeding is limited to the abilities of the one or few who possess the necessary skills or knowledge.

---

[1] One of the earliest occurrences of this proverb used it somewhat differently from the canonical form [13, p. 342]: "I suppose *the Patron* meant that if you give a man a fish he is hungry again in an hour. If you teach him to catch a fish you do him a good turn".

In this sense, teaching facilitates a greater happiness for a greater number of people than feeding would. An overly hasty conclusion at this stage may be that teaching is the most moral activity possible.

However, food is just one of the basic needs. Maslow [7, p. 372] posits that *"it seems impossible as well as useless to make any list of fundamental physiological needs for they can come to almost any number one might wish, depending on the degree of specificity of description"*. And the proverb about feeding does not directly extend to the other physiological needs, such as maternal needs or sleep. As children grow up, maternal skills may be useless unless used to provide care for others' children. In a society the value of such skill is no longer the satisfaction of one's own needs, but the fact that skilled labour can be exchanged for goods or services that satisfy other basic needs. Skilled labour may even be the source of the highest need that Maslow identifies: self-actualisation. However, in any society, retaining skills (and knowledge) is essential, which makes teaching an indispensable part of such a society.

Maslow [7, p. 394], for example, claims that needs form a hierarchy: *"when a need is fairly well satisfied, the next prepotent ('higher') need emerges, in turn to dominate the conscious life and to serve as the center of organization of behavior, since gratified needs are not active motivators"*. This hierarchy is depicted in Fig. 2. Maslow notes that there are exceptions to the order that he describes, but claims that a hierchy of needs still applies in those cases. His hierarchy assigns a conditional value that is assigned to certain skills or knowledge. An individual whose physiological needs are met, will value knowledge about safety. However, when physiological needs are not met, meeting those needs trumps knowledge on how to be safe. From a utilitarian perspective the moral calculus will assign more weight to actions (or skills) that satisfy basic needs than actions (or skills) that guarantee safety [9]. A hungry person may risk safety to acquire food.

In the university context it is not uncommon to assign value to subjects based on their perceived utility. A subject like computer science may be deemed more valuable than, say, philosophy, because the market has more work opportunities

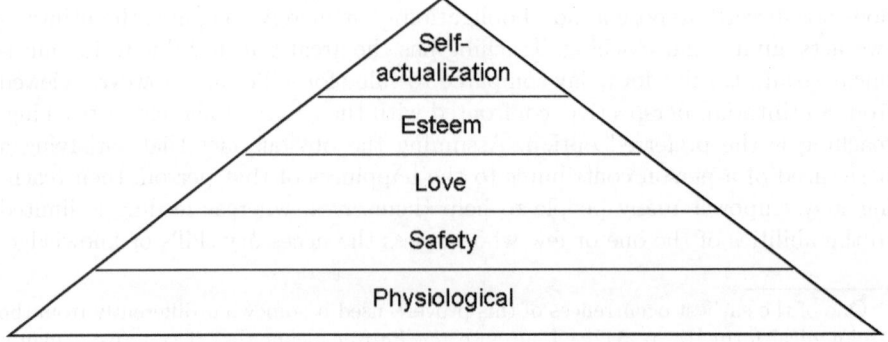

Fig. 2. A depiction of Maslow's hierarchy of needs [7]

in the computing field than it has opportunities for philosophers. Of course there is no generally accepted calculus that weighs all relevant factors to achieve a single correct assessment of the value of any given skill set or knowledge domain.

Note that the notion of utility is inherently instrumental: the utility of something refers to its usefulness to achieve some outcome. Above we alluded to various outcomes, such as career prospects or meeting physiological (or higher-order) needs in Maslow's hierarchy. In utilitarian theories of ethics the desired outcome is the *good* or *happiness* and the utility of a given course of action is the degree to which it achieves such an outcome (for the greatest number of people) [1,9]. Note that such instrumental factors are not unique to utilitarianism: In Aristotelian virtue ethics the virtues are those characteristics that enable a person to best achieve his or her purpose in life.

While knowledge has a 'raw' utility, knowledge does not necessarily have a moral utility. Let us for the time being assume that the moral utility of knowledge depends on its application (and reflect on this assumption later). Hence, we assume here that, for example, nuclear physics is morally value neutral, but applying such knowledge to manufacture an atomic bomb or to build a nuclear power station may have vastly different moral utility values.

The title of this paper uses the phrase *crime skills*. The adjective *crime* was selected over the adjective *criminal* in an attempt to not imbue a moral utility into the skills to be considered. *Criminal skills* would attach a negative moral utility to such skills. By using the phrase *crime skills* we hope to signify skills that may be useful to commit a crime, but not skills that only have criminal applications. A typical example here would be the skills of a penetration tester employed by a facility to test the security of the facility. These skills will be in many ways similar to the skills of the malicious cracker who, on own initiative or as a member of a criminal outfit, attempts to penetrate the facility's defence system for personal gain or to cause harm to the facility. We are therefore firmly positioned in a context where knowledge can be applied for good or evil purposes, and the manner in which it is applied makes all the difference.

The discussion shifted from knowledge to skills in the previous paragraph. To be more specific, the focus of the current paper is on 'how-to' knowledge — knowledge that Aristotle refers to as *techné* [11]. Given that 'how-to knowledge' and skills serve the same purpose we will henceforth use the terms knowledge and skills interchangeably.

Knowledge about harming others seems innate: Hobbes [5] describes the 'natural state of mankind' as one in which all people *"are in that condition which is called warre; and such a warre as is of every man against every man"*. If such knowledge is innate (or easy to obtain) teaching it either is of little additional use to those who want to harm others, or given the general availability of such knowledge it would be hard to object against anyone's actions to share (that is, to teach) such knowledge. Therefore, if any moral objection is to be raised, it can only be raised about knowledge that is neither innate, nor easy to obtain. However, given the ubiquity of the Internet, we live in a time where it seems any knowledge is easy to obtain by anyone. But such an argument is not entirely valid. Consider, say, the theory of general relativity or, as another example, Immanuel Kant's philosophy of reason. In both cases the knowledge is indeed very easy to locate, but usually requires a structured programme of study to acquire. And the guidance provided by dedicated teachers through the prerequisite knowledge and foundations of the theory greatly simplifies the process. In many cases 'pure' knowledge is insufficient to apply, and competency and confidence need to be developed. Presumably not too many people have learned to ride a bicycle from the Internet — training (and often teaching aids such as training wheels) are required. We will revisit the argument that not all knowledge (now explicitly including skills) is available to anyone who wants to master it.

However, the claim that some potentially harmful knowledge may be exceptionally hard to master i(unless taught) seems to be a moot point given that much potentially harmful innate skill (or knowledge that is easy to master) is readily available. Why would anyone with harmful intentions resort to a more complex method to inflict harm if simple methods are available? The answer is arguably that a method becomes attractive when it limits the probability of retribution. If A wants to harm B, A can hit B with a club. However, A may be seen engaging in the act, be caught and be punished. Or B may not be debilitated by the attack and harm A in defence. If A has the option to remotely administer an untraceable toxic substance to B this provides a much 'safer' alternative to A. It also poses a much greater risk to society: In Hobbes's discussion of society the mechanism to avoid a war of each against the other is to *"agree amongst themselves to submit to some man, or assembly of men, voluntarily, on confidence to be protected by him against all others"* [5, p. 106] (emphasis added). Hence this more complex method may not only protect the perpetrator, but also undermine the essence (and stability) of society. And, while this argument was constructed using Hobbes' philosophy, it is rather obvious that it seems to make common sense.

The realisation that people with specific categories of knowledge can abuse such knowledge is an old one. The Hippocratic Oath, for example, implores physicians to use their knowledge to *"to help the sick according to my ability and judgment, but never with a view to injury and wrong-doing"*. Bioethics is often summarised into four precepts, of which non-maleficence is one. This precept is derived from the maxim *first do no harm*, which is often expressed in Latin: *Primum non nocere*. While there is some debate about the origin (and age) of the maxim, it has been used for at least a few centuries [12].

One mechanism frequently applied by society is to regulate those who are entrusted with special responsibilities as professionals. Often it is realised that the safety of society (and/or of individuals) depends on the assumption that such professionals execute their duty responsibly. Masses of people cross bridges on a daily basis with an implied trust that the responsible engineer designed the bridge such that it is safe to use. People are operated on by surgeons with the knowledge that the surgeon has the knowledge (and carries the responsibility) to perform the operation with a very high likelihood of success — an expected outcome that far exceeds the impact of not undergoing such an operation.

In court when one is represented by an advocate or lawyer, that legal professional has an obligation to proceed in one's best interest, or may be held accountable. In fact, responsibility forms the foundation of professional ethics [3]. However, the word *responsibility* encompasses a number of meanings — in particular, *obligation-responsibility*, *blame-responsibility* and *role-responsibility* [3, p. 22].

While such professionals are, in the first place, expected to act in the interest of their clients and/or society, it is obvious that this very notion enables them to act contrary to the expectation. Stated differently, knowledge about safety typically implies knowledge about doing harm. The surgeon's knowledge of how to make an incision that avoids a certain artery or nerve (because damage to the nerve or artery would be catastrophic) implies knowledge about how to precisely target such a nerve or artery and inflict major harm (and this harmful knowledge can be applied outside the normal context of an operating theatre). It is often impossible to teach someone how to avoid harm without, as a consequence, teach that person to inflict harm.

In the context of professionals, these knowledge is typically of such a nature that only professionals are entrusted with a 'licence' to execute such actions in the interest of society. To continue the example of the surgeon, the surgeon is not only provided with the knowledge to perform operations, but also practices such skills — starting with observing, then assisting and finally becoming the person responsible for performing the operation. This provides a 'training ground' that is simply not accessible to anyone else, meaning that only the surgeon is able to perfect his or her technique. Perfect technique provides confidence required to perform operations, but may also provide confidence to inflict harm if a surgeon so wishes. While another person may somehow learn a similar technique, the vast majority of people in society who has such skills, practice them regularly and are arguably in a position to abuse such skills with the least amount of collateral damage, have been taught those skills.

Note that the example of the surgeon is not a unique case: An auditor trained to identify fraudulent entries in a company's books is in an ideal position to insert such entries in a manner that is likely to be overlooked by other auditors. An engineer who knows how, say, the transmission of microwaves ought to be contained, can use that knowledge to inflict harm through common microwave devices. The lawyer who has the knowledge to protect the right of his or her client can draft a contract that denies the other party to a contract any recourse to enforce that party's rights.

There are also examples where skills are taught to cause damage. Engineers may be taught how to implode a building using the least quantity of explosives positioned on the most 'vulnerable' part of buildings. Manufacturers of weapons use knowledge to inflict the most damage possible (within certain constraints). As an example of the latter case, consider a neutron bomb designed to extinguish life, but not damage property, so that it is available for subsequent use by the user of such a weapon.

In summary, teaching potentially (or actual) harmful skills is a regular part of professional education — and has been for centuries: see Fig. 3 for comparison.

Fig. 3. Teaching of potentially harmful skills as part of a professional education: German scythe combat instructions, compiled by Paulus Hector Mair (1517–1579) in the *Opus Amplissimum de Arte Athletica* (≈ 1540), [codex MSS Dresd. C.93/C.94]. Note that a skythe, in contrast to a sword, was a comparatively cheap and widely available agricultural tool in those days

Arguably more benefits than harm accrue to the public from the fact that professionals possess such knowledge (in the vast majority of cases; some cases, such as the neutron bomb, may be a counterexample). If the benefits outweigh the costs a utilitarian argument provides a simple way to justify the teaching of such knowledge.

In cases where the benefits do not outweigh the costs the question arises whether teaching or abuse of such knowledge should be controlled. As an example, vendors often use boilerplate contracts to retain all their own rights, but deny any rights that the customer may have had. One solution in such a case is to promulgate consumer protection legislation that curtails the extent to which such contracts can limit customers' rights.

3   Potentially Harmful IT Skills

An IT skill is potentially harmful if it enables someone to abuse IT in a manner that causes harm to another party. One common example is skills that would enable a criminal to masquerade as some user and withdraw that user's money from his or her bank accounts. On a larger scale such skills may be used to take over or crash a computer system that forms part of a country's critical national infrastructure. The impact from interfering with the operation of systems may range from a minor annoyance to full-scale war. Given that IT is used in almost any modern activity, any such activity may be vulnerable to abuse. For the typical IT-oriented reader of this paper no further elaboration about the impact possible abuses in this sphere is required.

The next question then is why there may be a need to teach such skills. In a nutshell, there are three answers. Penetration testing is an accepted form of testing the security of an organisation's systems. Penetration testers criminals who may want to attack the system need the same (or similar) skills. The digital forensic examiner also fits into this category. Such an examiner needs to know what traces are left by (possibly criminal) actions and can abuse this knowledge to hide his or her own maleficent activities. Secondly, as will be argued below, computer security professionals need a proper understanding of the threats they need to protect systems from, and phantoms of such threats rarely provide sufficient insight. Finally, the vulnerabilities that occur in code are placed there (typically inadvertently) by programmers; they may become more reflective about their coding if they are more familiar with how what they do can be abused. Also this will be reflected on in more detail below.

It may also be possible to justify the teaching of such skills from an educational perspective. From experience I know that students are fascinated by 'hacking', 'cracking' and similar activities. As an example, a lecture about he operation of the Simple Mail Transfer Protocol can be pretty boring. However, showing them how easy it is to spoof sender addresses piques their interest. This also provides an ideal opportunity to bring a discussion of ethics into the lecture. Invariably students then go and send spoofed emails to their friends (hopefully within the ethical limits of such an action). Rather than becoming familiar with the protocol because they *have* to, they suddenly *want* to. And many of them run into situations where simple spoofing does not work and begin to ask questions about technologies such as Sender Protection Framework (SPF) and DomainKeys Identified Mail (DKIM) — topics that they may not have encountered in the curriculum at all. Knowledge of SPF and DKIM limits their confidence about their ability to spoof *any* email address and imposes some restraint on full-scale abuse of this new skill. But even here, with the checks and balances in place, one should reflect on the ethical cost-benefit ratio of inspiring to learn, given the possibility that they will abuse the skill (discounted by the fact that many people using SMTP directly will probably realise its ability for abuse anyway, but then without the benefit of having discussed ethics prior to their own discoveries).

The first reason for teaching students potential harmful skills based on the assumption that they may be employed as penetration testers is valid, but does not scale: An extremely tiny fraction of people will ever work as penetration testers, so teaching the masses such skills is not justified by the few who need the skills to be penetration testers. In addition, to be a penetration tester one needs a natural curiosity and ability to learn from obscure sources; hence acquiring the necessary skills may be part of the genetic makeup of the ideal penetration tester and teaching may add very little to skills they can acquire though their innate curiosity.

The second justification for teaching potential harmful IT skills was the claim that computer security professionals need to properly understand the threats they face. Teaching students about the categories of malware, as an example, gives them a glimpse of that world, but without the ability to construct such malware. Even talking about a Trojan horse, which is trivial to construct in a number of forms, does not seem to give the student the feeling that "I can do that!". While students often tell me about the fun they had sending spoofed emails to their friends, nobody has ever told me after a lecture that discussed Trojan horses about the fun they had building such malware.

How well does a security professional need to know 'the enemy'? To continue with the malware theme, students (and, arguably, professionals) tend to know the categories of malware (viruses, worms, Trojan horses, and so on) and deem them to be fairly similar threats. However, if they are faced with the tasks of creating, say, a Trojan horse and a virus, they will hopefully realise that the first task is trivial and the second not. In terms of a threat assessment it should then be obvious that custom-built Trojan horses present a credible threat from any source; a custom-built virus is very unlikely to originate from an unsophisticated attacker. Hence, depending on the type of organisation, virus scanning may be sufficient mitigation for a virus-based threat, but not for a Trojan horse. A custom-built Trojan attached to a suitable delivery mechanism (such as email) becomes a spearphish. Technical mechanisms are not particularly useful to mitigate this threat. Hence, the standard response tends to be to externalise the cost to the user in a policy that instructs the user not to open any attachments from unknown senders. However, if the pundit of such a policy is able to think how an attacker would deal with such a policy (and hence, how effective such a policy would be), one wonders whether the rational security specialist would still support such a policy. This is a rather simple example, but such policies are ubiquitous.

Many other examples could be provided to show why deep knowledge of a threat is indeed useful to mitigate it. However, there are many more people working as security specialists than penetration testers, it is still a special interest group and arguably insufficient justification to teach the bigger community such skills.

4   The IT Worker — From Hero to Zero

In the introduction an example was provided that illustrated how the values of the community determined who was trusted with knowledge. Arguably that same spirit governs sharing of knowledge amongst penetration testers and many other communities. In the case of the professions such a value system is institutionalised and enforced by professional bodies.

However, the notion of community (whether information or institutionalised) is largely absent from the broader IT workforce. Communities certainly do still exist — see, for example, Himanen's [4] description of the hacker ethic.

Prior to the 1980 s computers were expensive machines housed in climate controlled centres to which access was tightly controlled. It was not uncommon for workers in these centres to wear white coats. This inevitably instilled a sense of community. The scarcity of computers made it necessary to network (in the social rather than data sense), and communities —as groups of people— were linked to one another.

However, over time a culture shift occurred. Many of these older computers were used for corporate management, such as the monthly printing of payslips. However, organisations did not, in general, depend on the operation of its computing facilities. In today's context the organisation often cannot function without its computing facilities.

In a parallel set of events the concept of corporate governance emerged and became increasingly important. Corporations represented the investments of society, the workplace of society and the major sources of impact on society. They no longer were just businesses, but operated at the core of society. And, in such a core function it developed a fiduciary responsibility towards large sets of stakeholders. Various codes (in the form of laws or otherwise) appeared including the Sarbanes-Oxley Act in the US and the King Report on Corporate Governance in South Africa [6]. Over time it was inevitable, given the increasing dependency of corporations on its IT infrastructure, that computing would move from a technical or even scientific context to a management context. The extent to which this has happened is illustrated by the fact that the King III report devotes an entire chapter to IT governance.

In another parallel set of events use of computing facilities broadened to include an ever increasing variety of workers. Initially they used computing through terminals connected to the mainframe, later through personal computers and eventually through a large variety of devices that are connected to a range of services. In contrast to the 'uniformed' centralised specialist IT worker, almost everybody now worked using computing.

Typically a central IT department still exists in the organisation. However, rather than the admired masters of the machine, they are now responsible for maintaining a service where others are the users to be supported. Not only does this new user base need support, but they also need to be controlled as part of IT governance. Effectively the IT department becomes invisible when everything works; users seem self-sufficient. The IT department becomes visible when the infrastructure fails, when new regulations and policies are introduced (and enforced) and (often enough) when the computer is blamed for anything that goes wrong in the organisation. The IT department no longer have a shared technical expertise. It is a mixed group of management and technical skills, with managers who —in contrast to the system or database administrator of an earlier time— may have no technical skills and the technical people living in a foreign world of management. Where the 'technical wizard' was once the person who could solve complex problems, the help desk has become a faceless entity behind an email address or ticket system.

In this world technical skill has become extremely mobile. Expertise is often associated with a project, rather than a system or an organisation [2]. Developers flow from one project to the next. The CV of the typical IT worker is a list of completed projects, with a new employer every 18 months. Much of the IT workforce has become migrant labourers moving to wherever their skills are required for a new project [10]. Of course a part of the workforce still remains stable with people who only work at a few employers (or even a single employer) during their careers. However, in general perpetual motion has become the norm. In many ways we are seeing labour as a commodity more clearly than ever before. Arguably this is, in particular, true for developers whose skills are no longer required once a project has been completed, but where there always seems to be a new project starting somewhere else.

In the context of such migrant labourers it is arguably hard to establish any sense of community. There is little reason to become loyal towards any specific organisation. Project-based work may not be associated with a retirement fund or pension or medical benefits. And in such a context individuals fall out of the system once they are no longer useful. This may be a fertile place where disgruntled insiders (albeit temporary insiders) form. This is a context where an individual sees no way out. In this context the empowered worker may resort to crime to satisfy a basic need (such as to afford medical care for children). There are few social bonds and few professional constraints that prevent such a person from abusing potentially harmful knowledge. There is little reason to believe that the benefit to society will exceed the cost to society if the workforce, in general, has too much potential harmful knowledge.

5   Stratification of Responsibility

Up to this point a sense of community has been posited as one of the major reasons to believe that potentially harmful information will more often than not be used for the benefit of society. The lack of community in the IT sector was raised as the major concern for this sector.

However, in most professions community is not a result from almost identical human beings inhabiting the same space. In the world of medicine, the workforce may consist of various specialists, general practitioners, registered nurses, other nursing staff, ambulance drivers, paramedics, porters and workers in many other roles. In some cases one may encounter mobility, for example, medical students who rotate through various rounds over time. While some roles may have a relatively higher or lower status than other roles, this is not necessarily the case. How does the status of the hospital's general manager, for example, compare to the status of, say, its nursing manager? Both are professionals, but the nursing manager often has a stricter sense of professional responsibility enforced by a professional board. In contrast, the responsibility of the general manager stems from a fiduciary duty towards the hospital's stakeholders. The nursing manager has to be educated to act as a health care worker. Nursing knowledge is an essential part of the nursing manager's duty. The general manager may need a general business acumen and a diverse (but not) specific set of management skills. While the nursing manager reports to the general manager, the general manager cannot make decisions about nursing or patient care, since the general manager is not empowered to be responsible for such decisions.

In the hospital example, the 'culture' or 'community' of one medical specialist may be very different from that of another specialist. These specialists belong to different professional societies that meet, perhaps annually, and in this context a certain sense of community is experienced. However, perhaps more importantly, the responsibilities (and, in particular, accountability) of the roles are clearly defined. To make this example more specific, consider the roles of the surgeon and anaesthetist in an operating theatre. Both are skilled medical doctors, but they have very different responsibilities is each of the three senses of responsibility mentioned earlier (*viz* obligation-responsibility, blame-responsibility and role-responsibility). In such a context, where skills overlap, responsibility and specific accountability is a major factor that ensures smooth operation of the system.

Knowledge is clearly linked to accountability: to be held accountable one needs certain knowledge before accountability makes sense. But accountability also constrains one's abuse of such knowledge.

It seems obvious that such stratification in the IT sector may be meaningful. A developer needs certain skills. A system administrator needs certain skills. This does not imply any hierarchy, but the two roles are clearly accountable in different ways. If such accountability can be enforced, as it is in the medical example, it would be inappropriate for the system administrator to act as a developer (unless the system administrator is indeed also a developer who could be held accountable as a developer). Under these conditions we suggest that workers in certain roles and who are held accountable in those roles can be entrusted with potentially harmful knowledge.

Note that such an enforcement of responsibility does not necessarily reserve jobs for certain people with a certain level of education. Several attempts to professionalise the IT sector have failed; one of the major reasons for such failures is the difficulty to delineate the nature of IT jobs. As a simple example, what would the minimum education be before a person can be a programmer? The problem with asking such a question is the diverse set of people working as programmers. On the one hand someone may be a self-taught programmer who writes simple programs that are useful in his or her business. Another programmer may write code that implements autopilot functionality on a wide-body passenger aircraft. The impact (both positive and negative) of the quality of the work done by each differs significantly. It is unrealistic to expect that both will be expected to have the same qualifications and/or skills. Though these two workers share the same (generic) job title, their professional work is worlds apart. They are most probably not members of the same community in any sense of the word *community*. The programmer working on the autopilot system may be a member of various professional bodies and subject to their codes of conduct; however, such codes are rarely enforced. In the end the engineer who includes the autopilot software into an aircraft is the person who is professionally responsible for its correct operation. In the case of the small-business owner, he or she is responsible to some extent for the code used as business owner, and not as programmer.

It is possible to introduce legislation that limits the type of project a programmer may participate in based on skills and expertise, but the variety of programming tasks and the pace at which technology evolves makes this route unlikely. Add to this variety the fact that code is often reused (including open source code where specific code may not be attributable to a specific programmer), and enforcing stratification by law becomes even more complex. Hence, other options to stratify the IT sector needs to be explored.

One alternative used in a number of professions is the use of insurance to cover professional liability. To return to the medical example, the professional liability of a doctor may be carried by the doctor's employer (such as the state). If not, such a doctor would be foolish to practice without proper medical insurance (and may indeed be required by law to be properly insured). The cost of insurance is typically based on the professional activities the doctor engages in. Even though all doctors are, in principle, able to assist with child birth, the associated risk can be extremely high. This is reflected in the cost of medical insurance for obstetrics. To illustrate, the 2015 cost of insurance for a South African general practitioner who does not perform procedures in operating theatre was almost ZAR 9,000 per year [8]. For such a practitioner who does perform procedures in an operating theatre, insurance almost doubled to ZAR 18,000. The insurance cost for a general practitioner who carries out basic pregnancy care and planned deliveries, insurance costs increased to almost ZAR 120,000 — about 13 times the first premium mentioned above. When the same doctor frequently practices general obstetrics the insurance increased to almost R190,000 per year. The type of work clearly determines the nature of the risk and the associated potential (financial) responsibility in terms of liability. Note that most professionals (who perform professional work) have some form of professional liability insurance, including engineers, lawyers and other health care professionals.

We do not suggest that high insurance premiums keep professionals moral. It may be true that a professional who makes too many mistakes will not be able to find insurance again and thus effectively banned from practicing as a professional, but it is unlikely that this is a major motivation for most professionals to behave in a moral manner. It is far more likely that professionals doing a specific type of work will attend the same conferences, serve on the same committees and generally bond as a community. In this community values will be shared and the norms of the community imprinted on the individuals. Even when the amount of money does not differ, doctors who are interested in treating, say, diabetes (and become known as doctors who are trusted in that particular subdiscipline) tend to form such communities.

Of course similar communities form around other shared interests, such as supporters of a particular football team. In this community values that are shared may be good or evil. Much has been reported about damage caused by some football hooligans, for example. Hence, we posit that the community imbues (and reinforces) certain values. Professional values determine the nature of such values — in particular, whether the interest of society is served by such values.

It has already been argued that the IT workforce is not (or no longer) a community. Some communities do form as special interest groups. However, professional values are hardly ever enforced in such communities. To illustrate, consider a community of security professionals. If a security breach occurs at the institution that employs such a security professional, it is extremely unlikely that the community will reflect or the impact of the personal responsibility of such a member on the breach and vice versa.

One example where exceptions may occur comes from the penetration testing community. Penetration testers typically sign agreements with the owners of systems that are to be tested. The boundaries of the test are explicitly spelled out. As long as the penetration testers operate within those boundaries, the agreement indemnifies them. However, once they exceed those boundaries (for example, by disclosing confidential information to others), they expose themselves to a significant liability in the form of penalty clauses. A penetration tester who does not abide by the values of the penetration testing community will be expelled from the community. Trust of the community is a key element in the sustainability of any business in that community.

As noted, the IT community is, in general, not properly stratified. Exceptions in the form of specific communities exist, but the mere fact that communities exist is not sufficient. Professional responsibility needs to be an inherent part of such a community before it can be trusted as professional.

Unless one teaches such a specific community, it seems prudent to limit potentially harmful knowledge taught to students. If necessary, they will have to acquire such knowledge in the workplace. This does not mean that no such skills should be taught; however, it suggests that the extent to which such skills are taught should be limited so that it does not instil a sense of complete competence in the student. Ideally the student should not be provided with knowledge open to immediate abuse; teaching should stop at a point where much additional knowledge needs to be acquired. One cannot prevent anyone from acquiring knowledge. At best one can ensure that such knowledge is not provided in a sufficiently refined form so that it can be abused to cause harm; if such 'ready' knowledge is provided it will simple be too easy to abuse it without restraint whenever any cause is a sufficient trigger for such abuse.

6 Conclusion

This paper reflected on the extent to which computer crime skills can be taught to IT students from a moral perspective. In many cases IT workers need such knowledge to perform activities that are in the interest of society and that are clearly moral.

It was argued that professionalism is one of the key elements that limits abuse of such knowledge. However, it was also argued that professionalism is not the only determinant of moral behaviour — a sense of community was deemed to be a particularly important part of handling such knowledge with appropriate care. In fact, the description of professionalism deviated from the usual depiction as someone who has been admitted to a profession based on skills (and education); a profession here was rather seen as a context where responsibility is a key concern when workers are assigned specific tasks.

Given the fragmented nature of the IT workforce it was argued that it is inappropriate to trust the general workforce with potentially harmful skills. When such information is taught it should be sufficiently incomplete that it is not possibly to apply the knowledge without further studies.

It remains true that anybody is arguably able to acquire any knowledge. When teaching is limited as argued above, it does not solve the problem of people having or being able to obtain harmful skills. However, it does limit the number of people who have such knowledge and are able to apply it without further work from their side. This limits the abuse of such knowledge in a moment of anger and without some opportunity to reflect. It also speaks to the complicity of the teacher who taught knowledge that is eventually abused.

References

1. Bentham, J.: An Introduction to the Principles of Morals and Legislation. Dover (2007)
2. Fan, Y., Thomas, M., Wang, Y.: Do project managers have organizational career paths? a study of the current state of career development for IT project managers. In: Proceedings International Conference on IS Management and Evaluation (ICIME 2015), pp. 40–48 (2015)
3. Harris, C.E., Pritchard, M.S., Rabins, M.J.: Engineering Ethics: Concepts and Cases. 3rd ed. Thomson Wadsworth (2005)
4. Himanen, P.: Hacker Ethic and the Spirit of the Information Age. Floris Books (1999)
5. Hobbes, T.: Leviathan, or the Matter, Forme, and Power of a Common-wealth Ecclesiasticall and Civill. Andrew Crooke, London (1651)
6. IoD: Third report on corporate governance for South Africa. Institute of Directors, Johannesburg (2009)

7. Maslow, A.H.: A theory of human motivation. Psychol. Rev. **50**, 370–396 (1943)
8. Medical Protection Society: MPS subscription rates. Technical report, MPS0162: 11/14, South Africa (2015)
9. Mill, J.S.: The Basic Writings of John Stuart Mill: On Liberty, the Subjection of Women and Utilitarianism. Modern Library (2002)
10. OCarroll, A.: Working Time, Knowledge Work and Post-Industrial Society – Unpredictable Work. Palgrave Macmillan (2015)
11. Parry, R.: Episteme and techne. In: Zalta, E.N. (ed.) The Stanford Encyclopedia of Philosophy. Stanford University (2014)
12. Smith, C.M.: Origin and uses of primum non nocere – Above all, do no harm!. J. Clin. Pharmacol. **45**(4), 371–377 (2005)
13. Thackeray-Ritchie, A.: Miss Dymond. Elder & Co., Smith (1886)

Teaching Informatics in North America: Jugglers Wanted

Bob Travica[1,2](✉)

[1] Asper School of Business, University of Manitoba, Winnipeg, Canada
btravica@ms.umanitoba.ca
[2] School of Computing, University of South Africa, Johannesburg, South Africa

Abstract. Teaching informatics (information systems) at the university level in North America is challenging. The teacher in Canada and the United States can be compared to a juggler performing before many spectators. The juggler strives to keep in the air multiple balls that cross each other's path. A student-learner ball may collide with a student-customer ball, teacher's needs for new technology and better technological support are countered by funding limitations, while attempts for asserting academic self-identity get confronted by incongruent attributions that the spectators create. Opposed balls come even from the field colleagues when the character of the field and teaching prospects are at stake. The article analyses these tensions and outlines prospects of teaching information systems in North America.

Keywords: Management information systems · Informatics · University teaching · Canada · United States of America · *Invited keynote lecture*

1 Introduction

The following discussion will presents my view of teaching issues in the field of informatics, that is, information systems (IS) in Canada and the Unites States. I have taught in the U.S. for 13 years (accounting for five years of my assistantship during my Master's and Doctoral study) and for 16 years in Canada.

I will use a *circus metaphor* featuring an IS professor in the role of *juggler*. The juggler tries to keep in the air balls that cross the path and may collide. The balls represent opposed forces challenging the juggler. His/her spectators are students, administrators, colleagues within and outside the IS field, academia, business, and government. The show's theme is teaching and related management and governance. Teaching involves course selection, execution, and evaluation.

The discussion will first address the organisation of IS programs. Then, opposed forces will be analysed. Finally, prospects of teaching information systems will be outlined.

2 Organisation of IS Programs

It is important to understand how IS programs are organised in order to grasp the context in which IS professors work and the choices they make in the teaching

© Springer International Publishing AG 2016
S. Gruner (Ed.): SACLA 2016, CCIS 642, pp. 22–31, 2016.
DOI: 10.1007/978-3-319-47680-3_2

process. Different organisational properties set both prospects and limitations to teaching IS in North America.

A North American IS program of study is typically situated in a business school (faculty) that is a part of a larger university. While a business school may give IS teaching a clearer focus, such as managerial decision making, it may also limit the scope of IS subject matter. The latter usually surfaces with new techno-social phenomena residing outside the orthodox management agenda (e.g., the Internet beyond the commercial realm).

An IS program can be organised into a separate department of a business school, IS-exclusive or IS mixed with other areas (e.g., supply chain or decision sciences); please refer to Fig. 1. Optionally, when a business school is centralised and based on study areas rather than departments, an IS program resides within such an area. An area can again be IS-exclusive or IS mixed with other disciplines. The departmentalised model exists in both Canada and the U.S., while the centralised model is deployed only in Canada. In the U.S., there is yet another organisational model in which an IS program resides in a separate school (e.g., Carnegie Mellon University and Syracuse University). A separate pure department model versus a hybrid area model—which make opposed ends on the centralisation continuum—are likely to have implications on the subjects taught.

IS are being taught as a major area of study at the undergraduate level. The number of required (mandatory) courses range from four to over two dozen, Canada being on the lower and the U.S. on the higher. IS are also taught at the graduate level, bestowing the degrees of Master's of Science and Philosophy Doctor (PhD). There is a trend toward specialising graduate degrees in the U.S. (e.g., IS security, or analytics).

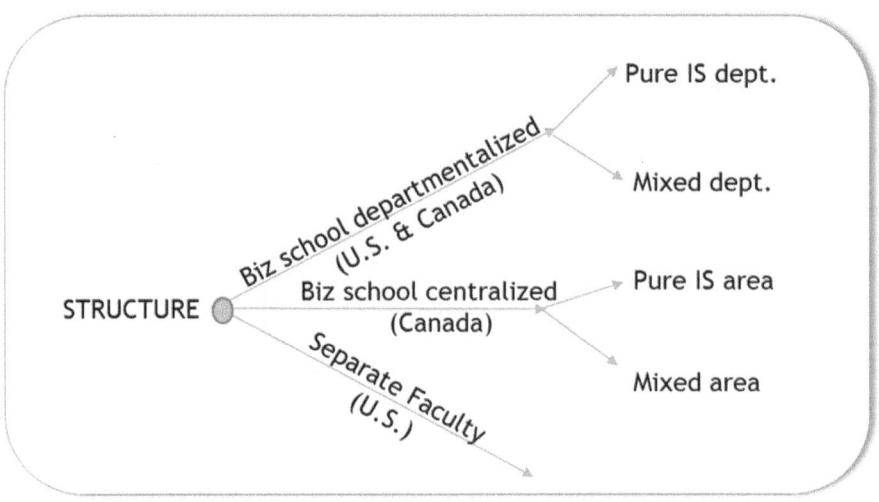

Fig. 1. Organisational models for IS programs

Table 1. IS programs at Canada's top 15 research public universities. Source of ranking: U15 [7].

Characteristic	Finding
Departmentalised: IS program pure model	5
Departmentalised: IS program mixed model	1 (operations, supply chain, innovation, entrepreneurship, accounting, finance)
Centralised: IS mixed model	3 (same as above)
Centralised: IS pure model	3
No IS program	3
Full time tenure-track faculty	3–18
Standard subjects	Databases, systems analysis and design, data communications, programming, enterprise systems/analytics, IS strategy

I investigated a sample of top universities from each country and tabulated results in Tables 1 and 2.

As Table 1 indicates, standard subjects taught in IS programs in Canada include databases, programming, analytics, and IS strategy. In the U.S., the list also includes decision support, process management, and analytics (Table 2). Some IS programs emphasise particular subjects, judging after the course offerings and directions in faculty research. Examples include health informatics, process management/change/innovation, Web user interface, analytics/Data Science, IS security, and more recently social media. In most cases, the U.S. programs are larger than Canadian, with respect to the number of students and full-time tenure-track faculty.

The institution of tenure (permanent employment conferred after a five-year probationary period and a successful evaluation by peers and administrators) exists in both countries. In the U.S., the tenure is usually bundled with promotion from the Assistant Professor rank to Associate, while this is not the case in Canada. The tenure institution ceased to be untouchable in the U.S., with occurrences of laying off tenured full IS professors. This happened when their departments were closed down upon management decisions that were justified by insufficient student enrolments in the IS programs. The 'invisible hand of market' has become quite visible and strong in the period of prolonged recessions since the end of the last millennium. The IS job market in the U.S. is also characterised by a trend of hiring instructors on contract. The hires may fill so-called 'clinical' teaching ranks, contracted for a single academic term or longer periods.

Both in the U.S. and Canada, online course delivery has picked up the speed. Online education may meet several goals, such as expanding markets, increasing convenience for students, filling a gap in a faculty's competences by contracting out. From the perspective of teacher-juggler, however, putting a course online may mean a loss of intellectual property and irreplaceability. An online course

Table 2. IS programs at top 13 universities in the U.S. in 2015. Source of ranking: U.S. News and the World Report [6].

Characteristic	Finding
Departmentalised: IS program pure model	5
Departmentalised: IS program mixed model	5 (decision science, operations, supply chain, management science)
IS College	1
No IS program	2
Full time tenure-track faculty	9–27; trend of contracting teachers
Standard subjects	Databases, systems analysis and design, decision making support (wide range), data communications, programming, enterprise systems, process management, analytics, IS strategy

may be a sag-way to outsourcing educational services and replacing full-time faculty by its part-time counterpart. The tenure and hiring dynamics put pressure on IS professors with regard to what and how to teach.

3   Student-Learner vs. Student-Customer

The drums are beating high, trumpets screaming, the audience's attention is sky-high... The juggler throws up a ball inscribed with 'student-learner' and immediately after a 'student-customer' ball. The balls are flying toward each other and collide. The audience is booing the juggler. What has happened indeed in our metaphorical circus?

An IS teacher faces the situation above every time he/she teaches non-IS major students. Such students are less likely to be motivated for studying topics related to information communication technology (ICT, IT) and its management. And really, why would they? How many drivers in North America have ever opened the hood of a car they drive daily? Do people know how a TV network works or what principles underlie the ubiquitous mobile telephony? Masses of people in North America are consumers interested in using technologies, while caring little about technology principles and workings. Not incidentally did a popular model for studying technology acceptance, which features the ease of use as the key independent variable, come from the U.S. A combination of educational shortcomings and consumerism precludes interest in technology beyond its utility for all but the specialists. Accordingly, non-IS major students in commonly required IS courses often wonder, why do they have to study IS?

Such displeased students tend to turn their customer face toward IS teachers. Strongly encouraged by university administrators, the student-customer role is grounded in notable costs students have to absorb. Study fees in North America range from $5,000 to $50,000 a year (the figures do not account for lodging and other living expenses). American figures are typically two or more times bigger than Canadian equivalents. However, the customer stance can lead the students to a logical impasse: If I am a true customer, why do I have to buy a course I do not want? And they still have to as long as IS courses exist in the required common core.

IS teachers face a permanent challenge of motivating the non-major student-customer. Methods of teaching have to be thought through over and over again. For example, simplifying complex technology topics and spoon feeding students with use procedures may help to get more students to complete planned class activities. Furthermore, teachers may incorporate humor and fun in teaching. (At some universities, course evaluations ask for such a rating.) Next, a popular teacher masters techniques of rewards and gratifications. To satisfy student expectations, everything they do must be scored in some way and built into students' marks (grades). This starts with class attendance and involves the participation in class discussion and other study activities. Applying precisely quantified marking keys against student assignments is also a way of warding off customers' dissatisfaction. These methods make a necessary toolkit for a teacher of less popular subjects, such as IS.

More flexible students may concede to the learner role and get engaged beyond consumerist bounds. Still, their customer face surfaces in a request for 'getting value-for-money'. What more precisely may that value be, remains a question open to subjective assessments. For example, if a teacher instructs students on using some software by the spoon feeding methods cited above, some students may devalue such education ("why come to class when this is so easy?"). At a deeper level, the nature of any knowledge is such that a more objective grasping of its value cannot be assessed up front. New knowledge demonstrates a value only post factum, when integrated with other knowledge or put at practical test. These effects can rarely happen within a single semester. Thus, the request of value-for-money is an empty shell to be filled arbitrarily by each student.

IS teachers are compelled to get good students' evaluations of the courses taught in spite of all these challenges pertinent to teaching technology related subject matter. At the end of every course, these anonymous evaluations are regularly performed. They vary in content, from a few general questions to lengthier surveys with questions grouped and backed by Likert-type scales and possibly open-ended questions. The teacher gets results of course evaluations without knowing who stands behind each – the student-learner or the student-customer. The evaluations have been criticised for subjectivity and even for some statistical problems. Still, they stick as no feasible alternative is available. Mass processing of numerical evaluations is a superb time-saver.

To make things worse, administrators (department heads, deans, and study area directors) take liberty to use these evaluations arbitrarily (e.g., focusing just on some questions, such as those comparing the given course and instructor with all other courses and instructors the student know; or taking rating percentages rather than standard statistical indications of central tendency). Valuing of speed over quality, which characterises North American culture in general, precipitates such quick and dirty measurement. In effect, students' voice is essentially filtered, while teachers may get hurt and left to agonise over achieving what administrators deem good evaluations.

What do students, when planning to take an IS course, look at in course evaluations (provided they can access them)? Only students know that, and variation on the individual basis is plausible. The word of mouth undoubtedly works. The Website 'Rate My Professors'[1] is a side venue that some students embrace. A student can log into it, and after submitting some details rate any course and instructor at a particular university. A quick look at 'Rate My Professors' shows a variety of evaluations from low to high, based on a five point-scale. A professor's name is associated with an average of all evaluations, and individual student comments and evaluations are displayed. There are images of thumb up and down, smiling and sad faces, and of chillies for 'overall hotness'. Clustering of comments around particular courses may indicate the courses that everybody loves or that everybody loves to hate. While the validity of these evaluations is dubious, they can influence the word of mouth. Sometimes, these ratings can even serve as the exclusive informing source on courses and teachers. In reaction to these evaluations, some professors have tried to fight back this method by running Websites for rating students.[2]

4 Technology Wishes vs. Funding Limitations

The IS field is by definition dynamic and innovative. To remain relevant, IS teachers need to keep current their technological knowledge and teaching. New software requires investment and possibly savvy practices of attracting sponsors from the IT industry. Therefore, the teacher-juggler throws up a ball of technology wishes/wants. But its path crosses with a ball of limited funding. Funding for computer laboratories and individual software needs can be random, on a case-to-case basis. The path to money allocations is further complicated by competing software priorities that other business disciplines bring to the table. Altogether, they compete for attention of the Dean's Office that could make allocation decisions on criteria favoring business logic (e.g., student enrolments) rather than technology progress.

Another angle on technology wishes has to do with expert support. It is needed for teaching labs, using third-party systems deployed in courses, running course servers as well as course management systems, content management systems, and communication systems. While efficiency and quality are required, expert support can be suboptimal.

Technological support at North American universities is usually organised by combining a central IS department, which serves both business and teaching needs, and an IS unit internal to a school/faculty. Governance issues are not always clearly defined between these two. Consequently, it may be unclear who

---

[1] http://www.ratemyprofessors.com/.
[2] http://www.rateyourstudent.com/.

is in charge of particular software updates, security, and reliability. In addition, both these organisational levels are often understaffed and overworked. They experience specialisation gaps, which may leave an IS teacher with no option but self-reliance. In the ultimate analysis, deep roots of a sub-optimal technological support are in budget limitations.

5   Self-identity vs. Attributions

The juggler tosses balls inscribed with 'Next-big-thing', 'Visionary', and 'Explorer'. The audience immediately responds by tossing balls that read 'Programmers', 'Techno-freaks', 'Aliens', and just a '?'. This part of the juggling show involves colleagues from other business disciplines, administrators, and the business community. It exposes a remarkable gap between the identity assumptions held by the insiders to the IS field and the attributions made by outsiders. Put another way, the identity of IS programs struggles with misunderstandings that other management disciplines have about it.

Outsiders to the IS field often see the insiders as technology promoters who know little about organisation and management. IS teachers are branded as narrow specialists who can see barely anything beyond computers. It is interesting that even when IT is directly involved in their preoccupations (e.g., digital marketing, supply chain, high-tech innovation, strategy, and entrepreneurship), the colleagues from other management disciplines may view IS teachers almost as some sort of aliens who are unsuitable for collaborative research or graduate student advising.

Inside the IS field, this misunderstanding is sometimes explained by the field's age. But this thesis is rather tenuous. If the IS field is a teenager in comparison with physics or law, it can hardly claim such a status compared with marketing or supply chain management. And yet, hardly would anyone question the identity of these disciplines. Therefore, the problems may be elsewhere, perhaps in the very foundations of the field.

The IS field descended from several parents. Figure 2 depicts relationships between the IS field and subject areas that belong to computer science, operations research, general and special systems theory, and others (the upper left and the middle box). The field has another strong link to organisational and management theory, and weaker links to social and behavioral sciences and some humanities (the upper right box). This complex background enables broad horizons for research and teaching. However, it has some disadvantages, one being incomplete differentiation.

The IS field has never differentiated itself clearly from computer science. Some teaching subjects are simply duplicated and tweaked to a management perspective. Also, the field borrows from the associated disciplines rather arbitrarily and mechanically (for example, from telecommunications and psychology). The field has never defined a basic vocabulary. Thus, the agreement on core concepts stops with their selection (information, data, information system, information technology), while definitions are formally weak and undifferentiated from the

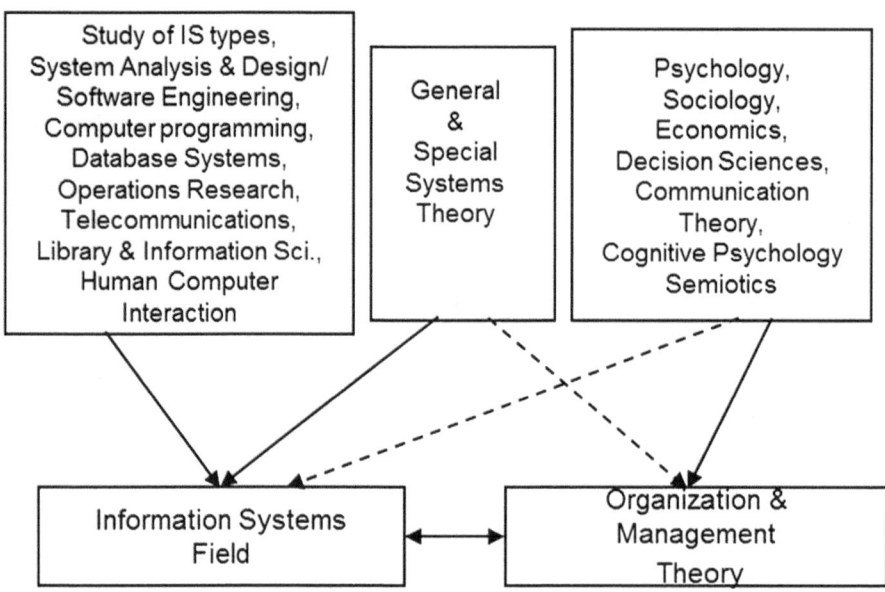

Fig. 2. Relationship between IS field and cognate disciplines (Adapted from Travica [5])

jargon of the IT industry or even everyday talk. Contrary to the thesis that such an openness creates opportunity for an open minded inquiry, the fact is that the field operates with a fuzzy subject of research. This aggravates communication with and recognition by other disciplines.

The shaky foundations influence a lack of development directions in both research and teaching. Running after the next-big-thing confines the field to a stand-by, reactive mode. The field is incapable of marking its targets unless the IT industry rolls out a new product. Sometimes, a new technological development extends an existing subject; an example is Big Data that adds to the Analytics topic and the broader decision making subject. At other times, such a smooth transition is missing; an example is the social media topic that initially appears disconnected from traditional management study, except in the area of marketing. At any rate, the lack of focus influences prospects of teaching IS in North America.

The lacking focus may have to do with the evolution of IT role in North American society. About five decades ago, IT was envisioned as a 'strategic weapon' and a main lever for development and success. Today, IT is increasingly treated as a commodity that does not necessarily bring strategic advantages. The trend of expanding rental solutions, such as Cloud Computing and particularly Software as a Service, reinforces this trend in the business domain. After the glorious start, IT has been tested in the economic and social turmoil, and practitioners treated it consistently just as a cost centre rather than a productivity and development engine. During a recession, IT spending gets quickly onto the chopping board. IT purchases slow down. A decreasing demand for IT professionals follows the suit. Finally, academia gets hit as well, and student enrolments into IS programs go down. This is business reality.

From the theoretical perspective, IT ceased to be scarce or prohibitively expensive any longer, thus resembling any other commodity [2]. According to theory of competition, these properties define a precious asset whose possession brings a strategic competitive advantage. Contributions of IT to the macro-economic productivity in the U.S. have also been questioned in the literature focused on 'IT productivity paradox' [1,4]. All these developments suggest that IT has lost the capabilities of strategic weapon in a developed economy. However, this change should not obscure the fact that new IT-related jobs and even larger scale IT-related economic developments have emerged (think of e-commerce and electronic supply chains). One should also acknowledge the vitality of IT in enhancing the management and professional work (think of advances in analytics for decision making, which currently are expanding into the domain of Big Data). IT is (and will be) necessary for doing successful and sustainable business. This premise creates a realistic platform for prospects of the IS education in North America.

6   Teaching Prospects

The discord among IS scholars regarding the subject of study has a complement in differing development visions. From time to time, these surface in discussions within the field [3]. In my own phrasing, there is a *next-big-thing* approach that is a legacy of independent IS departments in the U.S. It still has a strong following. As noted above, this in fact is a reactive rather than proactive approach. The IS field is not more than a wagon attached to the locomotive of IT industry. In other words, it does not have its own research agenda but depends on the IT industry for it. Although this approach carries benefits of autonomous building of a teaching (and research) agenda, it deepens the gap between IS and academia.

The alternative is an *integrationist* approach that looks for multiple and stronger relationships with cognate disciplines. This approach also has a following in the IS field and it is encouraged by university administrators who expect bigger student enrolments. If properly based on a lasting interest fit and methodological congruence, the integrationist approach may engender durable partnerships, and expand the teaching subject and proactive capability.

Although there may always be a '*next-big-thing*', this does not mean that the survival of an academic field is assured by claiming allegiance to this notion. Theoretical and practical relevance of an academic field matter. If the integrationist approach has a better chance of achieving these, this thesis brings us back to the question of appropriate organisational models. It stands the reason that models that mix IS with other disciplines offer more nurturing conditions for development than pure IS department models. This model does not imply that juggling disappears. It just introduces new balls.

7 Conclusion

I argued that teaching IS in Canada and the U.S. resembles juggling with multiple balls that move along collision paths. The balls symbolise opposed forces related to students, technology and support for teaching, identify of the IS field, and development directions. Different organisational models for IS programs provide the context, opportunities and limitations to the subject matter taught. The models are evolving. Prospects of teaching IS will also depend on the interplay between market forces and resolutions in the IS field's search for self-identity and development directions.

References

1. Attewell, P.: Information technology and the productivity paradox. In: Organizational Linkages: Understanding the Productivity Paradox, pp. 13–53 (1994)
2. Carr, N.G.: IT doesn't matter. Educause Rev. **38**, 24–38 (2003)
3. Looney, C.A., Firth, D., Koch, H., Cecez-Kecmanovic, D., Hsieh, J.P.A., Soh, C., Valacich, J.S., Whitley, E.A.: The credibility crisis in IS: a global stakeholder perspective. Commun. Assoc. Inf. Syst. **34**(1), 1175–1189 (2014)
4. Roach, S.: No productivity boom for workers. Issues Sci. Technol. **14**(4), 49–56 (1998)
5. Travica, B.: Examining the Informing View of Organization: Applying Theoretical and Managerial Approaches. IGI Global, Hershey (2014)
6. U.S. News, the World Report: Management information systems rankings (2016). http://colleges.usnews.rankingsandreviews.com/best-colleges/rankings/business-management-information-systems
7. U15: Group of Canadian research universities (2016). http://u15.ca/

Assessment Methods

A Comparison of E-Assessment Assignment Submission Processes in Introductory Computing Courses

Melisa Koorsse[✉], Marinda Taljaard, and André P. Calitz

Department of Computing Sciences, Nelson Mandela Metropolitan University,
Port Elizabeth, South Africa
{melisa.koorsse,marinda.taljaard,andre.calitz}@nmmu.ac.za

Abstract. Students completing university education programs are generally required to complete an Introductory Computing Course (ICC) in their first year of study. Introductory Computing, also referred to as Computer Fundamentals or End User Computing, are theoretical and practical in nature. Due to the large number of students completing the ICCs, institutions are introducing and increasingly utilising e-learning systems and e-assessment systems. Research generally focuses on e-assessment from an educator or instructor's perspective. In this study, the students' perceptions of e-assessment were evaluated, exploring different options with regards to the submission and assessment of MS-Office documents as part of the ICC. The study identified the best method of submission from a students' perspective considering various factors and comparing three different submission methods. The results highlighted suggestions for improving the on-line submission system. The results could assist educators and instructors utilising e-assessment systems in improving the submission and marking processes, in any course where files are required for submission.

Keywords: Introductory computing courses · E-assessment systems · Automated grading system · Assignment submission

1 Introduction

Presenting Introductory Computing Courses (ICCs) to a large number of students requires educators to utilise effective educational practices in today's modern classrooms [6–8]. Tertiary institutions presently are experiencing large enrolment numbers for ICC. An increase in the number of students also means a linear increase in the number of assignments and tests that need to be graded [9].

Introductory Computing Courses, also referred to as Computer Fundamentals or End User Computing, present their own challenges with students from different backgrounds and a vast difference in skill levels, from complete novices to experienced students. Student content retention can be positively reinforced by increasing the number of exercises, problems and assignments completed by the students

© Springer International Publishing AG 2016
S. Gruner (Ed.): SACLA 2016, CCIS 642, pp. 35–42, 2016.
DOI: 10.1007/978-3-319-47680-3_3

in an ICC [9]. However, increased assignments result in increased workloads for instructors as the amount of work to grade assignments increases [6].

E-assessment and the use of Automated Grading Systems (AGSs) can assist with the grading and feedback provided to students. These systems are generally researched from the perspective of instructors, e-learning experts and educational technologists, however there is limited research that focuses on the students' perception of e-assessment [5]. The Department of Computing Sciences at the Nelson Mandela Metropolitan University (NMMU) is exploring different options with regards to the submission and marking of MS-Office documents as part of the ICC, called the Computing Fundamentals Module (CFM). The need was identified to determine the best method of submission from a student's perspective.

The research problem investigated in this research study was that educators are not aware of the issues that need to be addressed when considering an assignment submission method, from a student's perspective. The main research objective of this study was to compare three different submission procedures for submitting MS-Office assignments in the CFM. The focus was thus on student perceptions of the method used to submit assignments assessing their MS-Office skills and to provide feedback on the effectiveness and efficiency of the different methods.

The research context and research methodology for the study is presented (Sect. 2) and followed by the discussion of the research results (Sect. 3). The paper concludes with findings, recommendations and future work (Sect. 4).

2   Research Study

The research was carried out with students enrolled in the Computing Fundamentals Module (CFM) presented by the Department of Computing Sciences at NMMU in February 2016. This section first describes the current method of practical submission (Sect. 2.1). This was one of the three methods included in the study (Sect. 2.3). The research methods used to conduct the study are explained (Sect. 2.2) as a prelude to the results presentation (Sect. 3).

2.1   Current Situation

Students enrolled in the CFM are required to submit weekly practical assignments requiring students to format and/or adapt a document, spreadsheet or powerpoint file based on a set of instructions. Students need to submit the assignment file by saving it in a special network folder for the purpose of module submissions.

There are over 1000 students enrolled in the module, with the result being that the task of marking the assignments that may be required for submission weekly, is impossible for lecturers. Students receive assistance and feedback from student assistants in practical sessions or if they approach the lecturers. However, they do not receive any feedback about the accuracy of their documents after submission. Feedback on whether or not the method of saving documents in the submission folder is preferred by students, would be useful.

2.2 Research Methods

The research study used the survey research approach. The use of surveys incorporating Likert scale questions, attitudes and feelings can be quantified [5] in order to make generalisations and inform decision making [4].

The research aimed to compare three different systems. A survey specifically designed for the evaluation of system usability is the System Usability Scale (SUS). SUS enables a researcher to get a measure of the perceived usability of a system [1]. The SUS questionnaire consists of 10 Likert scale items or statements related to system usability in terms of effectiveness, efficiency and satisfaction [2]. In this study, the 5-point Likert Scale was used, where one was Strongly Disagree and five Strongly Agree.

It was decided to use an assignment that was due for submission. Participation was voluntary. In total, 45 students agreed to participate in the study. The participants were required to submit the assignment using the first method, then complete the SUS survey for that method before moving to the next method and doing the same. Once all three methods were completed the participants were also asked to directly compare methods with each with regards to the following statements:

1. More likely to use in future,
2. Easier to use,
3. Learn more quickly,
4. More confident using,
5. Allows to work efficiently,
6. Allows to work effectively,
7. Marks more accurately,
8. More confident that submitted,
9. More satisfied that submitted, and
10. Provides better marking feedback.

For each of the statements, participants were asked to choose between Method 1 and Method 2, Method 2 and Method 3, and Method 1 and Method 3. Participants could also indicate no difference. The order of the methods were changed to avoid bias in the results due to learnability.

2.3 Methods of Submission

Three methods of submission and grading were evaluated in this study, namely the submissions folder method, the use of Moodle, and an online system. Essentially the only difference between each was the method of submission. All three used the same AGS to grade the assignments and provide participants with a mark report.

The submissions folder method was the method currently used by students. Each student is allocated a folder on the network for assignment submissions. They simply have to save their assignment files in this folder for submission purposes. For the purposes of the study, participants were required to indicate once this task had been completed so that the submitted file could be graded immediately. Once the marking process was completed an email was sent to the participant with the mark report as an attachment.

The Moodle submission method required participants to sign into the NMMU Learn site (a Moodle learning site) and submit their assignment. Participants were familiar with using the Moodle site for module quizzes and to download module information. Participants were provided with instructions on how to upload and submit their assignment files. Participants had to indicate once the file was submitted so that the marking process could be initiated manually. A mark report was emailed to the participant as an attachment.

The online submission method required participants to navigate to an online site where they could upload the file they wished to submit. The online system was able to check that files are named correctly, informing participants if the file name was not correct. The online system initiates the marking of the assignment file and, once complete, indicates to participants that the file was successfully submitted and provides a link to download the mark report.

The same marking system was used to grade the assignments submitted in all three methods. Originally the study planned to also evaluate the marking system by comparing the new system to the system used previously, namely the SAM assessment system [3]. However, the timeline for the study was delayed and SAM was no longer licensed for use at the time of the surveys.

3   Data Analysis and Results

The SUS surveys for the three methods were analysed by looking at the overall mean score for each method as well as considering the mean response for each statement. Table 1 indicates that the submission folder method obtained the highest SUS score. Both the submission folder method and the online system method scores were above average, where average is a score of 68 [2]. The Moodle submission method scored just below average.

Considering the different statements individually and comparing the responses for the three methods (Fig. 1), it can be seen that participants rated the submission folder method more highly. The difference between the online system and the Moodle system was small, however, participant responses indicated

Table 1. Mean SUS scores for each method ($n = 45$)

Submission	Online	Moodle
78.7	70.6	66.5

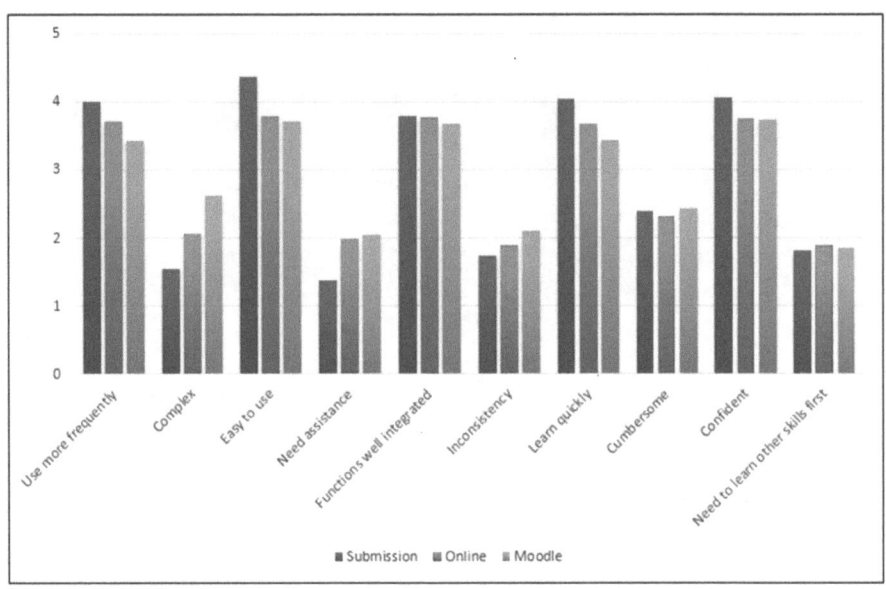

Fig. 1. SUS responses

that the online system was less complex to use, quicker to learn and they would use it more frequently.

The participants' selection of which method was preferred in response to the 10 statements listed in Sect. 2.2, was analysed by calculating the amount of times each method was selected overall for each item (Fig. 2). An interesting trend to note in the graph of the items is the high percentage of selection of the submission folder method for items two to six. Participants indicated that they found it easier to use and learn and indicated that it was more efficient and effective for submitting assignments, supporting the results of the SUS survey items. However, participants also indicated that they were more confident using the Moodle system than the online system. This contradicts the responses from the SUS survey, where the means were the same ($\mu = 3.75$).

The results indicate that participants would be more likely to use the online method in future. This differs from the results of the SUS survey to use the system more frequently. The submission system mean score ($\mu = 4.00$) was higher than that of the online system ($\mu = 3.72$).

The results of the last four items indicate that participants preferred the online submission method. The online system was the only method providing feedback to participants that the file had been successfully submitted. Most of the participants did not indicate completion of the submission folder and Moodle tasks during the study, thus not receiving emailed marked reports. Not receiving the emailed mark reports may be the reason for the low ratings for marking accuracy and feedback responses for the Moodle and submission folder methods.

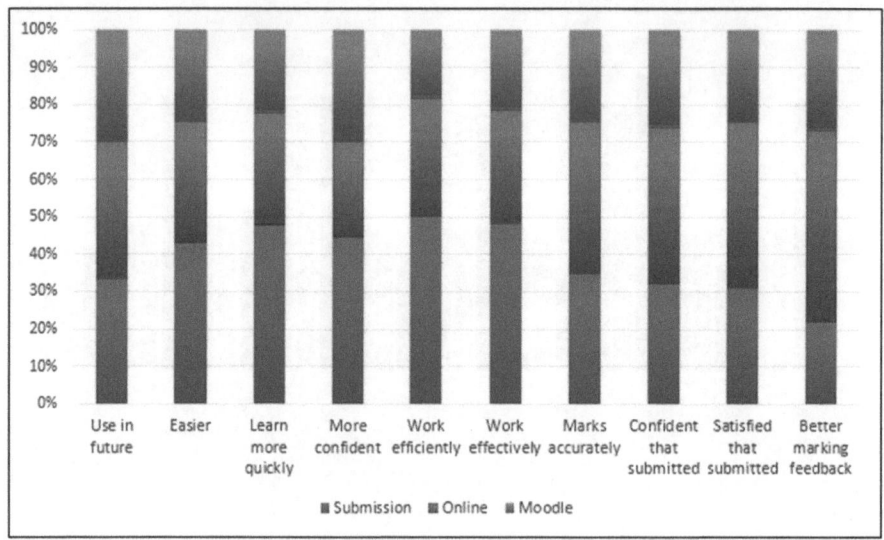

Fig. 2. Comparison of the methods

Participants were also encouraged to provide comments related to their experience of the system. Only nine of the participants provide any comments. Two participants commented on the difficulty of the URL for the online system. No link was provided for participants to click on and participants had to type the URL in after reading it on the instruction sheet (paper-based).

Participants $(n = 2)$ also commented that the Moodle system was *"long and complicated"*. Participants had to sign in to the Learn site, navigate to the module page, navigate to the link for the survey, select to upload a file, provide details for the file and then save the information, in order to upload the file. One of the participants commented that it was *"easier to save in the submissions folder as you can see that it is saved"*. This also alludes to the need for some form of confirmation that the file has been submitted. One participant commented on the feedback provided in the mark report. In particular that the report only indicates that a task was done incorrectly but not how to correct it.

4   Conclusions and Future Work

The aim of the study was to identify students' attitudes towards the different methods of submitting assignment documents. Although the assignments were specifically for the CFM as part of an ICC at NMMU, the results are useful for any course where files are required for submission.

The overall results indicated a preference towards the submission folder method. This method, according to participants, is easy to use, effective and efficient. However, the online submission system provided participants with a greater level of satisfaction that the file had been submitted successfully. Overall, participants preferred the simplicity of the submission folder method, while wanting feedback that the file had been submitted (online system). A process that requires too many steps in order to submit the file (Moodle method) is not efficient or desirable for participants to use.

The immediate feedback provided by the online submission system resulted in participants being more satisfied with the marking accuracy and feedback of the online system. The only difference between the mark reports provided by the three submission methods is that, for the Moodle and submission folder methods, the marking was manually initiated, which many participants failed to do.

The study also revealed that an AGS would be beneficial if feedback could be provided to students regarding weekly assignments. Many students participating in the study enquired whether other assignments, not part of the study, could be submitted for assessment so that feedback can be received. In addition, if assignments are assessed on a weekly basis, the scores could be used for summative assessment and instructors would have feedback on whether or not students were achieving the learning outcomes or lacking in certain skills. Feedback provided to students on how to correct errors or at least more detail regarding what the problem may be, would also be beneficial.

It is acknowledged that it would be expected that students would prefer the submission folder method as they have used it more often, and that the results could be anticipated. This would be from an educator/researcher perspective. The purpose of the study was to determine student views on the preferred submission method. Additional information regarding the different submission methods was revealed from the study which will be beneficial for future work.

The study was unable to evaluate the accuracy of different marking systems and was restricted to feedback provided by participants attending a weekly lab session. Future work would further investigate which methods are more effective and efficient when working off-campus, especially when considering the use of virtual private networks to use the submission folder method. In addition, it would be beneficial to determine if students prefer downloading the mark reports themselves or if they would like to receive an email with the mark report as an attachment. The detail provided by the mark report could also be investigated further.

There is also scope in the future to evaluate improvements to the online submission and marking system, including sign in screens, user accounts keeping track of assignments and allowing students to submit assignments on a weekly basis for assessment. Results from this study have indicated that the system should be kept as simple and easy as possible, while providing useful feedback.

References

1. Brooke, J.: SUS: a 'quick and dirty' usability scale. In: Jordan, P., Thomas, B., Weerdmeester, B., McClelland, A. (eds.) Usability Evaluation in Industry. Taylor and Francis, London (1996)
2. Brooke, J.: SUS: a retrospective. J. Usability Stud. 8(2), 29–40 (2013)

3. Learning, C.: SAM: Skills Assessment Manager (2016). http://www.cengage.com/sam/

4. Cohen, L., Manion, L., Morrison, K.: Research Methods in Education. Routledge (2007)

5. Dermo, J.: E-assement and the student learning experience: a survey of student perceptions of e-assessment. Brit. J. Educ. Technol. **40**(2), 203–214 (2009)

6. Kay, D.G.: Large introductory computer science classes: strategies for effective course management. ACM SIGCSE Bull. **30**(1), 131–134 (1998)

7. Kovačić, Z.J., Green, J.S.: Automatic grading of spreadsheet and database skills. J. Inf. Technol. Educ. **11**, 53–70 (2012)

8. Murphy, M., Sharma, A., Rosso, M.: Measuring assurance of learning goals: effectiveness of computer training and assessment tools. Inf. Syst. Educ. J. **10**(5), 87–94 (2012)

9. Murray, T.: Authoring knowledge based tutors: tools for content, instructional strategy, student model and interface design. J. Learn. Sci. **7**(1), 5–64 (1998)

Assessing Programming by Written Examinations

Ken Halland[(⊠)]

School of Computing, University of South Africa, Johannesburg, South Africa
hallakj@unisa.ac.za

Abstract. This position paper discusses the assessment of programming courses by means of written examinations. It describes the various learning outcomes of programming that should be covered, and then discusses how well they can be covered in a written examination.

Keywords: Learning outcomes · Assessment methods · Assessment of programming

1 Introduction

This paper discusses the use of written examinations for the assessment of programming courses. It is a position paper [7], so no data has been collected or analysed. Rather, experiences are described and arguments provided in support of the position that the valid assessment of many learning outcomes of programming can be achieved by means of written exams. The intention is to encourage discussion of this issue.

As lecturers, we feel increasingly under pressure to exclusively use practical forms of assessment such as projects and practical exams to assess programming. This pressure comes from students, university administrators, and even colleagues who are not involved in teaching programming. A common argument is that "Programming is a practical skill, so it must be assessed practically". At my institution, we are also under pressure to use so-called "non-venue-based" assessment, i.e. not administered in exam halls. Unmanageable student numbers seem to be the main reason for this policy.

The purpose of this paper is therefore to show that written exams still have a place in the assessment of programming and that in certain respects they have an advantage over other forms of assessment.

This paper is structured as follows: Sect. 2 provides a literature review of aspects of assessment. Section 3 describes various learning outcomes for programming and the methods that are commonly used for assessing them. Section 4 discusses the suitability of the methods for assessing the learning outcomes, and the suitability of written exams in particular detail. Section 5 states our position about the suitability and necessity of written exams and provides some concluding remarks.

© Springer International Publishing AG 2016
S. Gruner (Ed.): SACLA 2016, CCIS 642, pp. 43–50, 2016.
DOI: 10.1007/978-3-319-47680-3_4

2   Literature Review

Assessment: This is the attempt to certify and measure the extent to which learning has taken place [6]. It includes reflection or self-assessment [3].

Learning Outcomes: These are the knowledge, understanding, skills, attitudes and habits of mind which form the objectives of a learning unit (or course) [6].

Quality of Assessment: Three characteristics of good assessment are identified internationally [2] and endorsed by the South African Qualifications Authority [5].

> **Validity:** Are all and only the stated learning outcomes of the learning unit assessed?
>
> **Reliability:** Is the assessment repeatable or replicable?
>
> **Fairness:** Are all individuals being assessed, treated equally?

Security of Assessment: Breaches of security can be in the form of leaked exam papers, as well as cheating and plagiarism. This affects the integrity of the assessment since the individual who gets the mark is not the same individual whose work is being assessed [8].

Formative and Summative Assessment: Assessment that occurs during the learning period is formative, whereas assessment at the end is summative. Formative assessment often includes detailed feedback to enable students to gauge their progress and so that corrective action can be taken. Summative assessment however is merely intended to evaluate whether learning has taken place [6].

Assessment Methods: The most common methods for assessing the attainment of learning outcomes are assignments, projects, portfolios, quizzes, tests and exams [9]. Exams generally test all the learning outcomes of a course and are used for summative assessment.

3   Assessment of Programming

In order to discuss the suitability of written exams for the assessment of programming, we need to specify the learning outcomes of programming, and the various methods that can be used to assess programming.

3.1   Learning Outcomes of Programming

Each institution (or Computing department) probably has its own list of learning outcomes for its programming courses. The most definitive is provided in the ACM Computer Science Curricula 2013 (CS2013) [1]. We have adapted and unpacked the outcomes specified for Software Development Fundamentals in CS2013 as follows.

Basic Constructs: Ability to form working programs by combining

> **Variables, values and types:** data types, literal values, variable declarations, scope of variables, operators and expressions, memory allocation, stack and dynamic memory access;

Statements: declarations, assignments, control structures and subprogram calls;

Subprograms: functions or procedures, parameter passing mechanisms

Standard data structures: strings and arrays, standard classes and objects.

Syntax: Knowledge of the syntax of the basic constructs of the programming language to be able to use the construct correctly; able to look up the correct usage of functions, classes and methods in a language reference.

Operational Semantics: Understanding of the meaning of expressions, statements and constructs, i.e. how they work; their effect on variables and other objects.

Problem Solving: Ability to understand a problem and conceive of a solution in terms of the constructs available in the language; able to apply standard techniques for solving similar problems.

Algorithms: Ability to think and plan algorithmically, i.e. come up with a general plan to solve a larger class of problems; awareness of standard algorithms of Computer Science and be able to adapt and apply them appropriately.

Data Structures, ADTs and Classes: Ability to use appropriate complex data structures (like linked lists, trees, etc.) for the purposes of a programming problem; able to define appropriate ADTs, or in the case of an object-oriented programming language, to define appropriate classes, and use them correctly to solve a problem.

Principles: Understanding and ability to apply various programming principles appropriately in code, e.g. robustness, reusability, extensibility, separation of concerns, etc.

Design: Ability to come up with a sensible design in terms of the programming constructs, algorithms, data structures and principles mentioned above.

Style: Appreciation of good style, and use such consistently in programs.

Precision: Understand the precision required by the syntax of the language and the semantics of the constructs.

Paradigms: Understanding of different programming paradigms, i.e. procedural, object-oriented, declarative or functional, and use them correctly and appropriately.

Testing: Ability to test code thoroughly, and do so for their programs.

Debugging: Ability to identify and fix errors in code, including simple syntax errors, errors that cause a program to crash, and complex errors that are only apparent in special circumstances.

Documentation: Ability to document code sensibly, both in the form of comments within the code and as a separate document.

Comprehension: Ability to read and understand code to debug it, or to maintain or add features to it; ability to explain what the purpose of code is, or what code achieves or does not achieve.

Cooperation: Ability to work with others, either in pairs or in bigger teams.

3.2 Assessment Methods for Programming

This section lists and briefly describes the various mechanisms that can be used for assessing the learning outcomes of programming.

Assignment: This involves writing a program ranging in difficulty from simple to complex. Students may be allowed to solve the problem whichever way they can, or they may be given hints, guidelines or requirements about how it should be solved. Students may also be given a partial solution which they have to complete.

Project: A project is really a large assignment, except that it is often more open-ended in that the problem to be solved may be negotiable or broadly defined. A project also generally tests a wider range of learning outcomes. A project often requires the student to provide some sort of documentation with the software artefact in the form of a user guide, or a description of the process that was followed, or problems that were experienced, etc.

Portfolio: This is a loose conglomeration of evidence that a student compiles to show that they have attained the learning outcomes of a course. For programming, this will most likely consist of a number of software programs that the student has developed.

Test: This can range from a quiz, to a set of multiple choice questions (MCQs) to a longer set of questions. However, it is not as comprehensive as an exam. It only covers a limited number of learning outcomes, and may require students to perform short programming tasks.

Practical Exam: Students are given programming tasks which they have to complete in a limited amount of time. The programs have to be implemented on a computer, and students must have access to compiler or interpreter software to develop and test their programs.

Oral Exam: This is where a student is interviewed personally. The student may be required to make a presentation of software that they have developed, followed by questions that need to be answered about it. The student may also be required to answer questions about other code, or about various aspects of coding.

Written Exam: This is an examination written by hand, or typed on a computer using word-processing software. For the purposes of this paper, we particularly exclude the use of compiler or interpreter software to compile, run or test program code during a written examination.

3.3 Other Issues

Orthogonal to the different methods of assessing programming listed above, other decisions need to be made about how to organize such assessments.

Choices of who does the marking include expert assessment (lecturer, tutor or marker), peer assessment, self-assessment or automated assessment. Then there is the issue of individual versus team-work. Finally, there is the issue of controlled conditions: When students are in an examination hall or in a computer laboratory, there is a measure of control that can be exercised on what sources of assistance they can and do make use of. For example, one can control the access to physical or online documents, including language references, example code, etc., as well as assistance from friends or other experts. Working at home or in an unmonitored environment are considered as uncontrolled conditions.

4   Suitability of Assessment Methods

4.1   Suitability Matrix

Table 1 represents an attempt to evaluate the suitability of the various assessment methods identified in Sect. 3.2 for assessing the various learning outcomes identified in Sect. 3.1.

Table 1. Suitability of assessment of programming outcomes

Topic	Assignment	Project	Portfolio	Test	Practical exam	Oral exam	Written exam
Basic constructs	4	2	2	3	3	3	4
Syntax	4	3	3	3	2	2	3
Operational semantics	3	2	2	3	2	3	3
Problem solving	3	4	4	3	4	3	3
Algorithms	4	4	4	3	3	2	3
Data structures, ADTs, Classes	4	3	3	3	3	3	3
Principles	4	4	4	3	4	3	4
Design	4	4	4	3	3	3	3
Style	4	4	4	4	4	2	4
Precision	3	3	3	3	3	2	4
Paradigms	3	2	2	3	2	4	4
Testing	4	3	3	3	4	3	3
Debugging	4	4	4	3	3	2	3
Documentation	4	4	4	3	4	2	3
Comprehension	4	2	2	4	3	4	4
Cooperation	4	4	4	2	3	2	2

The values in Table 1 represent the following levels: (1) unsuitable, (2) partially suitable, (3) suitable, and (4) extremely suitable. These values should not be taken particularly seriously. They were determined by a few moments reflection on the author's experience. The reader might find it an interesting exercise to think what values he/she would fill in various positions in the table.

What should be taken seriously are the values in the final column, since they are pertinent to our position.

4.2 Suitability of Written Exams

We now discuss how each of the learning outcomes identified in Sect. 3.1 can be assessed by means of a written exam in particular:

Basic Constructs (4): Questions requiring students to write code in the form of short programs or fragments of programs that require the use of a small number of the basic constructs, can test students' understanding and mastery of them. The fact that students do not have access to a compiler and reference material means that one can more effectively assess whether these constructs and concepts have truly been internalized by students.

Syntax (3): Since students do not have access to a compiler to check and correct their syntax, a written exam can better test whether students really know and understand the syntax of the language.

Operational Semantics (3): Without being able to run the program to test whether it does what it should, students have to have a better grasp of the meaning and effect of the expressions, statements and constructs that they use. It forces them to have a mental model of what is happening in the memory and to the state of the program. They cannot hack the code until it works.

Problem Solving (3): Access to a compiler gives no advantage for demonstrating this higher-level, cognitive skill, so this outcome can be tested well using a written exam. In fact, access to a compiler is often a disadvantage since the necessity to get the program to compile correctly and produce the correct answers distracts the student from concentrating on the more conceptual level of problem solving. A disadvantage is that the limited time available in an exam often means that only simple problems can be realistically solved.

Algorithms (3): Students can be required to explain an algorithm, or write one in pseudo code. This can test their understanding and ability to think algorithmically, without having to implement a program and get it to run on a computer.

Data Structures, ADTs, and Classes (3): Once again, questions that involve the writing of short programs, or the implementation of ADTs or classes that have a particular purpose, can effectively test these outcomes.

Principles (4): Students can be required to answer questions about principles, or to write code that applies the principles.

Design (3): In a written exam, students can be required to explain a design without attempting to implement it. With a practical assessment method, good design can only be inferred from its implementation.

Style (4): The code that students write in a practical exam can easily be assessed for good style. In addition, questions can be set about why good style is important.

Precision (4): The fact that students do not have access to compiler software to check and fix their syntax errors, writing code by hand demonstrates students' understanding of the need for precision more clearly.

Paradigms (4): Theory questions about paradigms, and which would be the most appropriate for a given problem, can be posed in a written exam.

Testing (3): Although students can't practically test their programs during a written exam, they can be asked about the importance of testing, and be required to explain how they would test a piece of code.

Debugging (3): Since students are unable to compile or run their programs, it makes it difficult to assess the use of a debugger by means of a written exam. However, faulty code can be presented to students in a written exam, where they may be required to identify and/or fix the bugs.

Documentation (3): Students can be required to add comments to code, or to write part of the documentation for some code during a written exam.

Comprehension (4): Students can be given code that they have to change or complete. To be able to do this successfully, they need to be able to read and understand the code properly. Written exams are particularly suitable for getting students to explain their own code, or code that is provided to them. This is more effective than a practical assignment, test or exam.

Cooperation (2): Written exams are not suitable for assessing teamwork. At best, students can be required to write about their experiences, or about aspects of teamwork that are important.

5   Our Position

If you agree with the explanations of how the learning outcomes of programming can be assessed by means of a written exam as provided in Sect. 4.2 above, then you should agree that written exams can be used to assess some learning outcomes of programming well, and others less well.

However from Table 1, it would appear that there is no advantage to using written exams over other assessment methods. In fact, some other methods are better suited to assessing certain outcomes. Some authors have even argued that there are drawbacks to the exclusive use of written exams [4].

As stated in Sect. 2, for assessment to be fair, all individuals being assessed must be treated equally. Fairness is related to security, because if students are allowed to cheat, then they are being allowed to get marks that they don't deserve.

Plagiarism and other forms of cheating are perennial problems in assessing programming. We are aware of people who advertise to do the assignments, portfolios and projects for students for payment. Software that is designed to detect plagiarism in program code cannot detect this form of cheating. Even if it is possible to implement measures to detect and punish some forms of cheating, a far more effective way is to prevent it from happening in the first place. And the only way to do that is in controlled conditions, as described in Sect. 3.3.

A related issue is whether students should be required to work individually or as a team. Teamwork is important if one wants students to learn the outcome of cooperation properly. But it is problematic if all assessment is via teamwork, because one can never be sure that the mark that each member receives correctly reflects their individual mastery of the learning outcomes. Again, this is unfair. At best, teamwork should be used with at least one of the other assessment methods.

The only other summative assessment methods that manage to avoid these problems are practical exams and, to a certain extent, oral exams. We believe that practical exams work well except when the numbers of students make it practically impossible.

An oral exam can be problematic when part of the evidence is produced in uncontrolled conditions. However, in most cases it is not difficult to determine whether a student was the actual (and sole) programmer who produced some software. Probing questions about details of the code often reveal whether the student really understands the code. A disadvantage is that oral exams cannot be administered effectively when student numbers run into the hundreds.

The following issues flowing from this paper could be investigated in future: Gather qualitative and quantitative data on the effectiveness of written exams for assessing the various learning outcomes of programming. Do a study on what mix of methods can be used to assess all the learning outcomes of programming reliably, validly and fairly, while maintaining an acceptable measure of security.

It is hoped that this position paper will generate reflection and discussion.

References

1. ACM: CS2013 Computer Science Curriculum 2013: Final Report. Technical report (2013)
2. AERA, Apa, NCME: Standards for educational and psychological testing. AERA Publications, Washington, DC (2014)
3. Desjarlais, M., Smith, P.: A comparative analysis of reflection and self-assessment. Int. J. Process Educ. **3**(1), 3–18 (2011)
4. Haghighi, P., Sheard, J.: Summative computer programming assessment using both paper and computer. In: Proceedings ICCE 2005, pp. 67–75. Singapore (2005)
5. SAQA: National policy and criteria for designing and implementing assessment for NQF qualifications and part-qualifications and professional designations in South Africa (2015). http://www.saqa.org.za/list.php?e=Policy
6. Suskie, L.: Assessing Student Learning: A Common Sense Guide, 2nd edn. Jossey Bass, San Francisco (2009)
7. Tucker, K., Derelian, D., Rouner, D.: Building the case: Position papers, backgrounders, fact sheets, and biographical sketches. In: Public Relations Writing: An Issue-driven Behavioral Approach, pp. 79–85. Prentice Hall, Upper Saddle River (1997)
8. U.S. Department of Education: Testing Integrity Symposium: Issues and Recommendations for Best Practice (2013). http://nces.ed.gov/pubs2013/2013454.pdf
9. Western Carolina University: Handbook for program assessment in administrative/educational support units (2007). http://www.wcu.edu/WebFiles/PDFs/AssessmentHandbook_AES.pdf

Criteria for Evaluating Automated Grading Systems to Assess Microsoft Office Skills

Melisa Koorsse[(✉)], André P. Calitz, and Jaco Zietsman

Department of Computing Sciences, Nelson Mandela Metropolitan University,
Port Elizabeth, South Africa
{melisa.koorsse,andre.calitz,jaco.zietsman}@nmmu.ac.za

Abstract. Higher Education Institutions (HEIs) generally require first year students to attend and complete an Introductory Computing Course (ICC). The topics covered include basic skills in word-processing, spread sheets, power-point presentations and database management systems. Initially ICCs were presented by means of lectures, practicals and tutorials. Increasingly HEIs are utilising e-learning environments to facilitate teaching and learning in ICCs due to the large number of students required to complete the courses and acquire the required IT skill sets. The use of an Automated Grading System (AGS) can significantly enhance the learning process of computer literacy skills in ICCs and make the grading process manageable and provide more thorough assessment. Criteria for the development and selection of an AGS have been provided in literature studies. This paper builds on previous research and provides a detailed set of criteria that was utilised to evaluate the features, benefits and limitations of three commercially available AGSs.

Keywords: E-assessment · Automated grading systems · Introductory computing courses

1   Introduction

Students at Higher Education Institutions (HEIs) are required to complete an Introductory Computer Course (ICC) to provide them with the required IT skills for use in other courses as well as to equip them with IT skills needed in the workplace after graduating [6]. Productivity in the workplace can be negatively impacted if staff do not have the computing skills required to effectively perform their jobs [1,6].

HEIs require computer literacy training for STEM (Science, Technology, Engineering and Mathematics) majors. ICCs focus mainly on the use of productivity software applications such as word processors, spreadsheets, presentation software and database applications. Some institutions require an assessment of the basic skills, whilst others require the assessment of more advanced IT skills [12,14].

The enrolment numbers at many institutions for ICCs can be large where the ICC is a pre-requisite to other courses and programmes [9]. The increase in the

© Springer International Publishing AG 2016
S. Gruner (Ed.): SACLA 2016, CCIS 642, pp. 51–58, 2016.
DOI: 10.1007/978-3-319-47680-3_5

number of student enrolments implies an increase in the number of assignments
and tests to be graded [15].

E-assessment and Automated Grading Systems (AGSs) can significantly
enhance the learning process [12] and are being used to make the grading process
more manageable and provide a more thorough assessment [9]. E-assessment is
defined as the process whereby technology is used for the presentation of the
assessment activity and the recording of responses, which includes the assessment process [11].

There is a difference between assessment and grading. Grading simply evaluates the learning and performance of students [3,10]. Assessment provides
detailed feedback for every question and can provide reasons for any incorrect solutions or answers, thus helping to improve student learning. Automated
assessment systems is as a subset of AGSs and in this paper, referring to AGSs
will also include automated assessment systems.

Various research studies have been dedicated to developing AGSs for evaluating programming assignments [8]. There has, however, been limited research
focusing on automated grading for MS-Office applications [8,10]. A review of
existing systems has shown that current AGSs have advantages as well as shortcomings.

More research is needed to identify the requirements of AGSs for the grading
of MS-Office application documents. This research evaluates existing systems to
identify common features and compare the functionality provided by commercial
systems using, and extending, the criteria identified by Matthews et al. [12].
The research objective is to identify features and functionality that should be
considered when developing or selecting an AGS for ICCs.

A summary is provided indicating whether the evaluated commercial systems
(Sect. 3) meet each of the features, techniques and limitations identified. An
overview of the popular approaches used and the trade-offs between different
features is provided. Conclusions and future research are discussed in Sect. 4.

2   Literature Survey

AGSs should support specific learning and/or teaching goals (Sect. 2.1). Thus,
there are different types of AGSs (Sect. 2.2) using different approaches that can
be positive, but also have shortcomings.

2.1   E-Assessment

Different techniques are used in classrooms, labs and online to effectively present
large introductory courses [9,10,14]. The challenge of ICCs is having students
from different backgrounds with a vast difference in skill levels from experienced students to complete novices. Student learning can be positively reinforced
by increasing the number of problems, assignments and exercises completed by
students [15].

Research has shown that students' learning can be increased where students are able to identify where they have made an error [7,12]. Feedback on student assignments is beneficial for students. However, it is difficult to provide timely feedback to students, specifically in modules with large student numbers [9]. There is a need to find a balance between assignments that can challenge students but that would also be easy to grade and provide feedback.

Distributing the work could reduce the workload [12]. However, it may lead to inconsistencies in student performance and what they are learning. The grading task may also be shared between multiple people, but this may lead to inconsistencies in the grade and feedback provided [9,12]. Grading rubrics are faster to grade, consistent and lead to increased student satisfaction.

Instructors are choosing to use learning management systems and AGSs [10] to handle the increase in student numbers. Learning management systems, such as Moodle and Blackboard [11] are improving the student learning experience.

Reasons for the adoption of AGSs and e-assessment systems in particular, include a cost-effective means of grading [18], rapid feedback in the form of marks and comments and being able to provide quality feedback to the student [19]. AGSs makes it easier for instructors to handle large student numbers and improve objectivity and consistency in marking.

Students also believe that e-assessment adds value to learning [5]. E-assessment supports e-learning and feedback provided can add value to the learning experience. If a system is constantly available to assess work, students would be able to check their understanding of topics more frequently [19]. Quality feedback would encourage reflection and allow them to take control of their own learning.

2.2   Types of Automated Grading Systems

Electronic program submission and automated testing of correctness can make the grading process more manageable and provide a more thorough assessment [9]. There are grading systems currently available that can support increased assignments to improve learning but each has its own advantages and limitations [12].

AGSs are categorised into three different types by Matthews et al. [12]. The first two types are also identified by Zhu and Shen [20]. The first type is a project-based auto grader where the system provides a set of cases or projects that are challenging and realistic that the student completes in the application package. The grading system will thus analyse the resulting document [20]. This type is easier to develop, maintain and extend than the second type. A disadvantage of this method is that there may be partial analysis of some of the MS-Office objects resulting in restrictions on what may be examined.

Instructions are provided on how to format and change the original document, which may be blank. Once complete, students upload the file and the document is graded. Feedback is instantaneous and based on incorrect responses. Instructors generally do not create their own cases. These systems are usually commercial systems associated with textbooks to complement the ICCs. Examples are CaseGrader (for Office 2007) which seems to have been replaced with projects within SAM [2]. SNAP [16] allows students to work in the application while the instructions are visible together with helpful tips as they work. MyITLab [17] allows the instructors to select projects or create their own.

The second type of grading system is procedural-based grading. These applications use simulators and respond to the procedure followed by students in terms of their responses (key strokes and mouse-clicks) to complete a task [12,14]. Simulation tools have proven to be an effective means of training and assessing large numbers of students. The system can either be an actual simulator program or simply record the operating steps of the users while working in the document using a macro recording function [20].

The drawbacks are that constructing a simulation system is time-consuming and difficult to update resulting in poor adaptability. Macro recording functions have low accuracy as certain steps might be missed. Simulation environments may not completely prepare students to apply the skills learned to other tasks and projects [14]. These programs do not always include all methods of answering a problem and they do not allow instant changes or customised tests by the instructor.

Tools that provide simulation functionality include SAM [2], MyITLab [17] and SimNet [13]. Training using project-based systems, where students work in the actual software package, can be time-consuming to assess, particularly where there are large numbers of students. A combination of simulation training and in-application training is thus recommended [14].

The third type of system is a multiple choice system, but may also include fill-in-the-blank and paragraph or open-ended questions. This type of automated grader does not allow skill-based assignments or assessments. Many of the commercial systems, such as SAM [2], SNAP [16] and MyITLab [17], also include multiple-choice assessments.

2.3 Summary of Requirements

Different systems identified in literature were reviewed and each indicate the different methods and techniques that can be used to develop an AGS for MS-Office application documents. The different systems also highlighted certain aspects that needed to be taken into consideration during the grading process, such as catering for incorrectly named worksheets and formulae that are equivalent but not an exact string match. The different systems also vary with regard to user involvement. Some systems require users to indicate what to grade where others may automatically determine differences by comparing two documents.

Matthews et al. [12], when developing their system, identified several features (Table 1) and limitations (Table 2) used to evaluate their system and compare their system to project-based, procedural and test-bank AGSs. In addition, the review of different systems identified several additional features and limitations, thus extending the list of Matthews et al. [12]. The additional features are prefixed with an asterisk (∗) in the respective tables.

Three features were added to the list of Matthew et al. [12], namely, in-document feedback or comments, allowing the instructor to specify the marks

Table 1. System benefits and features

Benefits and features	Commercial
Challenging, real-world problems	ALL
Automated grading	ALL
Consistent grading	ALL
Instant feedback	ALL
Customized feedback	MyITLab, SAM
Web interface/portal	ALL
Multiple skills assessed concurrently	ALL
Hands-on experience	ALL
Smaller one-skill problems	ALL
Question/assignment library	ALL
Reduced preparation time	ALL
Availability of student reporting	ALL
Expandable answer banks	MyITLab
Repository for file submissions	ALL
Plagiarism detection	MyITLab
Provide rubric/instructions *	MyITLab
In-document feedback *	MyITLab
Specify mark weightings *	ALL
Security (sign in) *	ALL

allocated to items being assessed and providing a rubric or instruction list of what to mark. Indicating what to mark allows the instructor to customise the questions and feedback. However, setting up this rubric could be time-consuming depending on how the particular grading system has implemented this process. Instructors may need to spend additional time setting up the paper or assignment for assessment. Other limitations include the system only being able to assess a small set of skills or Office application document types. AGSs should further aim to minimise instructor intervention.

Other system issues are also included in the list of features and limitations. Matthews et al. [12] included consistent grading, web interface/portal and plagiarism detection in their list of features, while installation of additional software was included in the list of limitations. Security, in terms of authentication, is added to the list of features. The next section (Sect. 3) combines all the features, limitations and techniques (Sect. 2.2) and summarises the different systems reviewed to determine trends with regard to how AGSs are developed.

3   Recommended Features

This section summarises the discussion from the previous sections, identifying the features and/or benefits supported by commercial systems, as well as the limitations. The commercial systems that were included are only the three systems that are capable of project-based grading, namely, SAM [2], MyITLab [17] and SNAP [16]. All these systems also support simulation or procedural-based assessment.

All the systems allow students to work in the application package, thus allowing students to work on real-world problems and providing a hands-on experience. Multiple skills can be assessed concurrently or students can work on smaller one-skill problems, depending on the project assignment. All systems provide automated grading that is consistent. It was decided that if instructors were required to provide rubrics or instructions for the system to use in assessment, then preparation time would not be reduced. Thus only systems comparing the document structures or that provided a test bank of projects to use, would reduce the preparation time. MyITLab is the only commercial system that meets all criteria, including the facility to allow instructors to create their own assignments.

Limitations of AGSs (Table 2) were also identified by Matthews et al. [12]. Exact match answers is difficult to evaluate as there may be certain skills that will match exactly, especially where string matching is performed on text, whereas, alternatives may be allowed with regards to formulae. Cases or projects are limited where the instructor is not able to create their own assignments. The commercial systems provide simulation environments but only SNAP does not also project-based grading. Limited skills or functionality are evaluated by many AGS systems when considering that the applications are capable of much more.

MyITLab is the only commercial system allowing customisation of assignments or projects, requiring instructors to set up a rubric or list of skills to be assessed on the system as part of the grading process. The commercial systems

Table 2. System limitations

Limitations	Commercial
Answers must be exact matches	ALL
Limited number of cases	SAM, SNAP
Textbook/supplemental required	ALL
Software must be installed	
'Simulated' environment	ALL
Other purchases required	
Limited number of criteria to assess *	
Instructor intervention required *	
Setting up marking rubric/system *	MyITLab

all have textbooks that are very closely aligned to the systems. However, the systems can be used without the textbooks.

4 Conclusions

Criteria for the development and selection of AGSs have been provided in literature studies. This research study identified common features and compared the functionality provided by these AGSs using and extending the criteria identified by Matthews et al. [12]. The study provided an extended set of criteria that was utilised to evaluate three commercially available AGSs, namely SAM [2], MyITLab [17] and SNAP [16].

HEIs can utilise the research findings to assess and evaluate current and new AGSs. Commercial AGSs are expensive. An affordable option may be to consider local (SA) AGS systems, such as SMARK [4], which includes support for Word, Excel, PowerPoint and Access.

Future research will further investigate if there are other techniques that could be used to improve the marking accuracy while reducing educator workload. The use of intelligent techniques in the development of an AGS will also be investigated further.

References

1. Bunker, B.: A summary of international reports, research and case studies of digital literacy including implications for New Zealand of adopting a globally-recognised digital literacy standard. Technical report, Knowledge Weavers NZ (2010)
2. Cengage Learning: SAM: Skills Assessment Manager (2016). http://www.cengage.com/sam/
3. Chorana, A., Lakhdari, A., Cherroun, H., Oulad-Naoui, S.: XML-based e-assessment system for Office skills in open learning environments. Res. Pract. Technol. Enhanced Learn. **10**(1), 1–17 (2015)
4. Convert.ToCode: SMARK (2016). http://www.converttocode.com
5. Dermo, J.: E-assement and the student learning experience: a survey of student perceptions of e-assessment. Br. J. Educ. Technol. **40**(2), 203–214 (2009)
6. Gibbs, S., Steel, G., McKinnon, A.: Are workplace end-user computing skills at a desirable level? A New Zealand perspective. End-User Information Systems, Innovation and Organizational Change (2015)
7. Heinrich, E., Milne, J., Moore, M.: An investigation into E-Tool use for formative assignment assessment – Status and recommendations. Educ. Technol. Soc. **12**(4), 176–192 (2009)
8. Hill, T.: Excel grader and Access grader. ACM SIGCSE Bull. **36**(2), 101–105 (2004)
9. Kay, D.G.: Large introductory computer science classes: strategies for effective course management. ACM SIGCSE Bull. **30**(1), 131–134 (1998)
10. Kovačić, Z.J., Green, J.S.: Automatic grading of spreadsheet and database skills. J. Inf. Technol. Educ. **11**, 53–70 (2012)
11. Malmi, L., Korhonen, A., Saikkonen, R.: Experiences in automatic assessment on mass courses and issues for designing virtual courses. In: Proceedings of the 7th Annual Conference on Innovation and Technology in Computer Science Education (ITiCSE 2002), vol. 34, pp. 55–59 (2002)

12. Matthews, K., Janicki, T., He, L., Patterson, L.: Implementation of an automated grading system with an adaptive learning component to affect student feedback and response time. J. Inf. Syst. Educ. **23**(1), 71–83 (2012)
13. McGraw Hill Education: SIMnet (2016). http://successinhighered.com/cit/simnet/
14. Murphy, M., Sharma, A., Rosso, M.: Measuring assurance of learning goals: effectiveness of computer training and assessment tools. Inf. Syst. Educ. J. **10**(5), 87–94 (2012)
15. Murray, T.: Authoring knowledge based tutors: tools for content, instructional strategy, student model and interface design. J. Learn. Sci. **7**(1), 5–64 (1998)
16. Paradigm Education Solutions: SNAP (2016). http://www.snap.2016.com/
17. Pearson: MyITLab (2016). http://www.pearsonmylabandmastering.com/north america/myitlab/index.html
18. Swithenby, S.: E-assessment for open learning. In: The 6th International Conference on Education and Information Systems, Technologies and Applications: EISTA 2008, Orlando, FL, USA (2008). http://oro.open.ac.uk/27481/
19. Whitelock, D., Brasher, A.: Developing a roadmap for e-assessment: which way now?. In: Danson, M. (ed.) Proceedings 10th CAA International Computer Assisted Assessment Conference, pp. 487–501. Professional Development, Loughborough University, Loughborough, UK (2006)
20. Zhu, Y., Shen, F.: An Office automatic marking system research and implementation. J. Theor. Appl. Inf. Technol. **47**(1), 242–245 (2013)

Towards a Generic DSL for Automated Marking Systems

Fritz Solms[✉] and Vreda Pieterse

Department of Computer Science, University of Pretoria, Pretoria, South Africa
fritz@solms.co.za, vpieterse@cs.up.ac.za

Abstract. The automated static and dynamic assessment of programs makes it practical to increase the learning opportunities of large student classes through the regular assessment of programming assignments. Automatic assessments are traditionally specified in tool-specific languages which are closely linked to the functionality and implementation of a particular tool. This paper considers existing specification languages for assessments and proposes a generic and extensible domain-specific language for the specification of programming assignment assessments.

Keywords: DSL · Syntax · Automated assessment · Software testing

1 Introduction

In undergraduate programming courses it is particularly important to request students to regularly complete programming assignments so that they can be graded and be given meaningful feedback. At institutions such as the University of Pretoria, many of these undergraduate courses have many hundreds of students and manual assessment by teaching assistants is resource intensive, time-consuming, tedious and bound to be inconsistent. Consequently there has been a quest to develop automated grading systems and to evolve them so as to provide more meaningful assessments and improved feedback to students [1,14–16].

The computer science department at the University of Pretoria uses an in-house developed automatic marking system, *Fitchfork*, to mark *C* and *C++* programming assignments for first-year computer science students [14]. The instructor specifies a set of test cases beforehand. Students then upload their source code and any supporting artefacts onto a Linux server where the source is unpacked into a sandbox where it is compiled and executed. The output of a students' program is matched against the expected output for each given test case.

One critical aspect of such systems is the assessment specification which the instructors must develop. The specification includes information on how the programming assignment will be processed (e.g. compiled and executed), how it will be assessed, how marks are aggregated and the feedback that will be given to the students. It is vital that the specification of such assessment should be intuitive, efficient and not prone to errors.

© Springer International Publishing AG 2016
S. Gruner (Ed.): SACLA 2016, CCIS 642, pp. 59–66, 2016.
DOI: 10.1007/978-3-319-47680-3_6

It has been found that informally specified languages tend to become excessively complex and error prone as systems evolve so as to perform more complex assessments [17]. For this reason, researchers have been exploring the possibility of developing more robust specification languages for assessments, which can be formally verified and for which one can easily develop supporting tools.

Domain-specific languages (DSLs) are commonly introduced to provide simple, consistent domain-centric languages which are easy to use and easy to process [8]. The availability of DSL work-benches [9] simplifies the task of developing and verifying a domain-specific language and of enriching the language with tools such as language-aware editors, and transformation tools.

We are currently developing an *assessment-specification language* (ASL) for the specification of a generic and extensible assessment process. What differentiates our language from the languages developed for other tools is (a) a semiformal specification of the semantics using a metamodel. This model can be transformed into an ontology for verifying language qualities. Other features are (b) the ability to support different textual and diagrammatic concrete syntaxes; (c) extensive tool support for generating syntax-aware textual and diagrammatic editors, model validation, model transformation and code generation, and (d) the language is tool-independent so that its scope is constrained to the specification of what is required to be done, not how a particular tool would perform the assessment. The final feature is (e) one can write an adapter layer which aggregates the assessment across different assessment tools, i.e. by transforming aspects of an assessment specification which can be handled by a particular tool to the specification that can be processed by that tool.

In principle, the use of such an ASL will enable memoranda which were specified for one tool to transported to another tool, contributing to simplifying the sharing of assessments across platforms and tools.

Section 2 discusses a few existing automatic assessment systems in terms of their contribution to the types of assessments that should be specifiable using the ASL we propose in this paper. We also refer to other authors who have proposed DSLs similar to the ASL we propose. Section 3 lists the objects that may be used by an automatic assessment tool—these constitute the semantic scope for the proposed ASL. We also discuss its quality requirements. In Sect. 4 we describe how we developed our ASL. We justify the tools we used, show the abstract syntax we developed using a UML class diagram and discuss our design decisions. Methods to transform this abstract syntax to concrete syntaxes are briefly mentioned. In the final two sections, we summarise what we have achieved, highlight the benefits of having our ASL and discuss future work to improve this ASL and promote its use.

2 Related Work

Wilcox provides a survey of the testing strategies used to grade programming assignments [19]. He discusses (a) *textual output comparison,* (b) *output analysis* which performs further processing of the output to, for example, assess whether the output is internally consistent, (c) *stream control* which is used to interleave input and output in order to drive a particular program flow, (d) *testing* against an API in a way similar to unit testing, (e) *source code analysis*, (f) *issue detection* used to observe the issues encountered during the assessment process and the occurrence of compilation or execution issues (e.g. non-termination).

A tool for automatically analysing and assessing the programming style of C++ programs was implemented by Ala-Mutka *et al.* [3]. They claim that its use improved the quality of their coursework and that students learned to pay better attention to their coding practices. Ponženel *et al.* [15] acknowledge that the addition of white-box testing (i.e. structural evaluation) to the predominant black-box testing (i.e. functional testing) applied by most systems is essential for the pedagogically sound and fair evaluation of student programs. For example, the AutoLEP system [18] combines static analysis with dynamic testing when evaluating student programs. Static analysis includes syntactic and structural checking. Similarly, eGrader [2] uses JUnit for dynamic analysis and a static evaluation based on a graph representation of the program.

Fonte *et al.* [7] illustrate the need to allow the identification of partially correct programs with semantic errors. Fitchfork [14] achieves this by comparing the output of a program with the known output that a program would produce if it contained an anticipated semantic error. The detection of such expected wrong output enables us to give the student feedback about the semantic error in the program.

Lately there has been a move toward developing DSLs to describe assessments [7,17]. Fonte *et al.* [7] propose a DSL they call OSSL which supports the semantic specification of expected program output. They use extension modules to specify the integration between the Oto grading system and external tools such as a compiler, and JUnit. Insa and Silva [12] developed an assessment Java library with abstraction methods for verifying the properties of code and a DSL built on top of it for assessment templates.

The manual specification of assessments for automatic assessment tools is likely to be tedious. The specification can be simplified when using an ASL. The reduced complexity will probably contribute to improving the quality of the assignments that are specified in this manner.

3   Requirements for the Proposed DSL

This section discusses the requirements of the generic ASL we intend to specify. Firstly, we identify the semantic scope of the ASL in terms of the essential elements one should be able to specify when using the proposed ASL. We then discuss the critical quality requirements for the ASL.

3.1   Semantic Scope

The ASL needs to be an open language whose scope can be extended with add-on modules. The language core should contain the essential elements needed by all assessment tools. We have identified that such core should include: (a) the specification of process steps and the dependencies between process steps, (b) the concept of an assessment which can be extended with specific assessment types, (c) the basic infrastructure for specifying mark allocation and aggregation and (d) the infrastructure to identify error scenarios in the assessed code in order to give the students insightful feedback on ways of improving their programs.

Many existing assessment tools assess the output of program execution. To accommodate these, we decided that this type of assessment should be included in the core language specification. Therefore the ASL should have means to specify simple text output assessments which can be used to assess the output of a program's execution. This type of assessment can be employed to assess the output of other kinds of processing steps, for example the compilation process. It can even be utilised to perform a static assessment of the code by assessing the output of a file search evaluating the presence of some constructs in the code.

3.2   Quality Requirements for the ASL

The ASL can only be expected to be widely adopted if it meets standard usability requirements such as learnability, efficiency, effectiveness, reliability and satisfaction. Dumas and Reddish [6] emphasise that the people who use a product should be able to accomplish their tasks quickly and easily. These must accommodate users who may have different levels of technical skills varying language backgrounds. It is important for users to be able to extend the language in order to specify more specialised processing, assessment and mark aggregation requirements. Assessment specifications must be verifiable against the semantic rules of the language. The ASL should be portable across platforms (e.g. operating systems) as well as across assessment systems. It is expected that one can transform the subset of an assessment to a tool-specific assessment specification for a tool which can be used for that aspect of the assessment. The language must be published as an open public standard so that it is accessible and usable by different assessment tool developers and the users of these tools.

4   The Domain-Specific Language

Domain-specific languages can be developed in a variety of technologies. One of the options is that of using the technology support specified by OMG's *Model-Driven Architecture* standard. The advantages of using these standards are that (a) the standard is reasonably mature and it evolves in a controlled way, (b) there are multiple concrete tool implementations for the standard and (c) there are extensive auxiliary tools such as transformation tools and tools for generating language editors [9].

In particular, we separated the abstract syntax (introducing the semantics) from the concrete syntax (used by instructors to specify assessments). This separation facilitates (a) concrete syntax-independent verification of a specification against the semantics of the language, (b) the development of different concrete syntaxes for users with different levels of technical skills and different home languages and (c) the transformation of an assessment specified in any of the concrete syntaxes to an abstract representation which is independent of the concrete syntax used, hence allowing the uniform processing of assessment specifications across different concrete syntaxes.

4.1   Abstract Syntax

Here we introduce the ASL. It is specified using *Ecore* which is an implementation of *EMOF* provided by the *Eclipse* foundation [9].

Figure 1 shows a diagram of the abstract syntax of the core language. The language allows for the specification of a process of multiple processing steps. The order in which the steps are to be executed is specified only indirectly through the dependencies between steps. This simplifies the specification of assessment processes, makes them more maintainable and allows for the concurrent execution of steps which do not have dependencies on one another.

Each processing step optionally specifies a command which is executed as well as zero or more assessments. The commands for example may be to extract an archive, compile the source code, execute the program with specified test data sets, or to execute a unit test. The resources (memory, time/CPU, networking, etc.) which a command can consume may be constrained via one or more resource constraints.

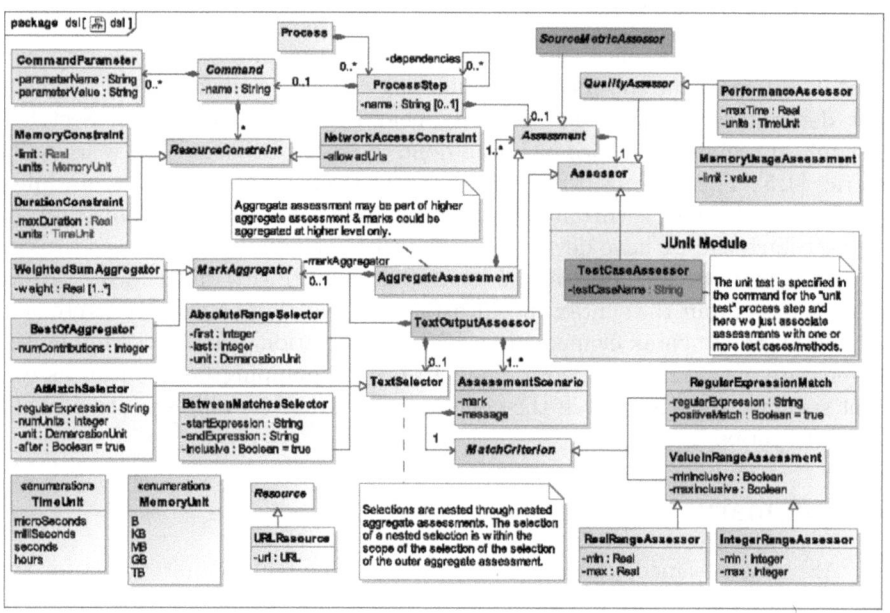

Fig. 1. The abstract syntax of the DSL for programming assessments.

The central concept of the language is the abstract concept of an assessment. Assessments can be recursively aggregated into aggregate assessments using different ways to aggregate the marks of the assessment components by selecting appropriate mark aggregators. The language is extensible, allowing additional assessors to be specified in extension modules. Figure 1 illustrates how a *JUnit* extension module is added to the language.

The core language includes the specification of *TextOutputAssessor*s. It is crucial for students to receive insightful feedback on the errors they make. For this reason, *TextOutputAssessor*s allow for the assessment of different output scenarios resembling several variations of correct, partially correct and incorrect solutions, each with their own mark and their own feedback message. Scenarios are identified by matching the output text selection to a particular output pattern. The feedback message associated with a scenario is meant to give the students insights into solution deficiencies and improvement options. To further enrich the assessment, the language allows for multiple scenarios to contribute toward the mark for the assessment. Though one can simply use a "BestOfAggregator" to select the scenario with the highest mark, one can also specify more complex aggregators which reward or penalise certain aspects of a solution, i.e. the same mark aggregators used to aggregate marks across assessments can be used to aggregate the marks accumulated across scenario assessments. The default for aggregating across aggregate assessments is simple-sum aggregation. The default for scenario aggregation is to select the best scenario mark.

4.2   Concrete Syntaxes

A domain-specific language allows for the specification of multiple concrete syntaxes. It is largely the specification of different concrete syntaxes of the language that determines the language usability characteristics discussed in Sect. 3.2. A significant amount of work has been done to design DSLs guided by usability metrics [4,5]. The rigorous development of a concrete syntax guided by usability metrics is work which is currently in progress. This will enable us to illustrate the abstract language we have developed so far with a simple English-based syntax.

An example text syntax can be developed in *EMFText* [11] which is a tool which gets as input the syntax specification as a mapping between concrete syntax and abstract syntax elements in a BNF-like notation. *EMFText* can be used to generate a syntax-aware editor and to do the mapping between an assessment specification specified in the concrete syntax and its representation in the abstract syntax.

5   Summary

The ASL was designed while keeping in mind the quality requirements for the language. In particular, the language supports the specification of extension modules within which it is possible to provide the semantics required to specify different types of processing commands, assessments and marks aggregation algorithms.

When new elements are being developed, our generic ASL assessment specification must be mapped onto tool-specific assessment specifications for such element to ensure the portability of the language across assessment tools.

Since this is an ecore-based DSL, a wide variety of declarative and imperative model-to-model [10,13] and model-to-text [9] transformation tools are available. Furthermore, transformation can also be specified implicitly by specifying the tool language as a concrete syntax for our ASL. In cases where the assessment specification requires concepts not covered by our ASL, the ASL needs to be extended. Such an extension should only be required to increase the scope of the language, not for technical reasons such as to allow mapping to a tool-specific assessment specification. Any technical enrichment should be made during the mapping transformation.

We have generated a language-aware editor which verifies a concrete assessment specification against the language rules. Further qualities of the language can be specified as static constraints against the language metamodel. This can be done using the *Object Constraint Language* and the *Eclipse OCL libraries* [9].

The usability of the language will be determined by the development of concrete syntaxes for the language and will therefore be the subject of future work.

6   Conclusions and Future Work

We have introduced an extensible domain-specific language for the specification of program assessments. The specification of such a language as a domain-specific language has the advantages of being able to specify a variety of concrete syntaxes for different user groups and of having a rich tool set available for generating language-aware editors, assessment validators and transformations for transporting onto tool-specific assessment formats. The focus of our work will now shift to specifying a concrete syntax based on usability guidelines and on assessing such languages by measuring their usability metrics and by performing in-field user testing. We will then specify transformations onto tool-specific assessment specification formats, which will include that of our in-house developed system. Different aspects of assessment (e.g. assessment of source code and dynamic metrics) are expected to be covered and specified in extension modules.

References

1. Ahoniemi, T., Reinikainen, T.: Aloha: a grading tool for semi-automatic assessment of mass programming courses. In: Proceedings of the 6th Baltic Sea Conference on Computing Education Research: Koli Calling 2006, Baltic Sea 2006, pp. 139–140. ACM, New York (2006)
2. Al Shamsi, F., Elnagar, A.: An intelligent assessment tool for students' Java submissions in introductory programming courses. J. Intell. Learn. Syst. Appl. 4(1), 59–69 (2012)
3. Ala-Mutka, K., Uimonen, T., Järvinen, H.M., Knight, L.: Supporting students in C++ programming courses with automatic program style assessment. J. Inf. Technol. Educ. 3, 245–262 (2004)

4. Albuquerque, D., Cafeo, B., Garcia, A., Barbosa, S., Abrahão, S., Ribeiro, A.: Quantifying usability of domain-specific languages: an empirical study on software maintenance. J. Syst. Softw. **101**, 245–259 (2015)
5. Bariic, A., Amaral, V., Goulão, M.: Usability evaluation of domain-specific languages. In: Eighth International Conference on the Quality of Information and Communications Technology (QUATIC), pp. 342–347, September 2012
6. Dumas, J.S., Redish, J.C.: A Practical Guide to Usability Testing. Intellect Bks, Portland (1999)
7. Fonte, D., da Cruz, D.C., Gançarski, A.L., Henriques, P.R.: A flexible dynamic system for automatic grading of programming exercises. In: 2nd Symposium on Languages, Applications and Technologies, SLATE 2013, Porto, Portugal, pp. 129–144, June 2013
8. Fowler, M.: Domain Specific Languages, 1st edn. Addison-Wesley Professional, Boston (2010)
9. Gronback, R.C.: Eclipse Modeling Project: A Domain-Specific Language (DSL) Toolkit, 1st edn. Addison-Wesley Professional, Boston (2009)
10. Guduric, P., Puder, A., Todtenhoefer, R.: A comparison between relational and operational QVT mappings. In: Sixth International Conference on Information Technology: New Generations, ITNG 2009, pp. 266–271, April 2009
11. Heidenreich, F., Johannes, J., Karol, S., Seifert, M., Wende, C.: Model-based language engineering with EMFText. In: Lämmel, R., Saraiva, J., Visser, J. (eds.) GTTSE 2011. LNCS, vol. 7680, pp. 322–345. Springer, Heidelberg (2013)
12. Insa, D., Silva, J.: Semi-automatic assessment of unrestrained Java code: a library, a DSL, and a workbench to assess exams and exercises. In: Proceedings of the 2015 ACM Conference on Innovation and Technology in Computer Science Education, ITiCSE 2015, pp. 39–44. ACM, New York (2015)
13. Jouault, F., Allilaire, F., Bézivin, J., Kurtev, I.: ATL: a model transformation tool. Sci. Comput. Program. **72**(1–2), 31–39 (2008). http://dx.doi.org/10.1016/j.scico.2007.08.002
14. Pieterse, V.: Automated assessment of programming assignments. In: Proceedings of the 3rd Computer Science Education Research Conference on Computer Science Education Research, CSERC 2013, pp. 4:45–4:56. Open Universiteit, Heerlen, Open Univ., Heerlen, The Netherlands (2013). http://0-dl.acm.org.innopac.up.ac.za/citation.cfm?id=2541917.2541921
15. Poženel, M., Fürst, L., Mahnič, V.: Introduction of the automated assessment of homework assignments in a university-level programming course. In: 38th International Convention on Information and Communication Technology, Electronics and Microelectronics (MIPRO), pp. 761–766, May 2015
16. Tremblay, G., Guérin, F., Pons, A., Salah, A.: Oto, a generic and extensible tool for marking programming assignments. Softw. Pract. Exper. **38**(3), 307–333 (2008)
17. Tremblay, G., Lessard, P.: A marking language for the Oto assignment marking tool. In: Proceedings of the 16th Annual Joint Conference on Innovation and Technology in Computer Science Education, ITiCSE 2011, pp. 148–152. ACM, New York (2011). http://0-doi.acm.org.innopac.up.ac.za/10.1145/1999747.1999791
18. Wang, T., Su, X., Ma, P., Wang, Y., Wang, K.: Ability-training-oriented automated assessment in introductory programming course. Comput. Educ. **56**(1), 220–226 (2011)
19. Wilcox, C.: Testing strategies for the automated grading of student programs. In: Proceedings of the 47th ACM Technical Symposium on Computing Science Education, SIGCSE 2016, pp. 437–442. ACM, New York (2016)

Instruction Methods

Code Pathfinder: A Stepwise Programming E-Tutor Using Plan Mirroring

Mark S. Durrheim[✉], Abejide Ade-Ibijola, and Sigrid Ewert

Department of Computer Science and Applied Mathematics,
University of the Witwatersrand, Johannesburg, South Africa
570169@students.wits.ac.za, researcher@abejide.com,
sigrid.ewert@wits.ac.za

Abstract. A significant problem in Computer Science Education is introducing students to programming. Many novice programmers show difficulties in mastering the basics of writing programs. Many students may abandon their study of Computer Science due to these problems. Intelligent Tutoring Systems have been developed to provide guidance and feedback to students. Previous systems require the instructor to prepare extra documentation for the software to function. This creates more work for lecturers who wish to implement such a system. We have developed an Intelligent Tutoring System that will guide a student step-by-step through the writing of simple programs in the language of C++. It will also provide feedback on any mistakes they make. This system will require only a correct version of the code for it to develop its feedback scheme.

Keywords: Automatic tutoring · Narrations · Plan mirroring

1 Introduction

In Computer Science Education, teaching novice programmers to code has been a challenge for many years [8]. Intelligent Tutoring Systems have been developed to assist in teaching novices basic programming skills. These often give feedback and instructions in syntax-free forms [8,10]. This makes it easier for students who are not well versed in programming to understand the instructions.

We have developed an Intelligent Tutoring System that uses a correctly written program to create all of the instructions and feedback for the student. The students are guided to reproduce the instructor's program line by line.

The rest of the paper is structured as follows. Section 2 presents the background to the project. It provides definitions of terminology used in the document as well as a review of previous work related to this project. Section 3 outlines the problem which we wish to address with our system. Section 4 describes the methods used to achieve the system's key functions. Section 5 details the implementation of the system and our results. Section 6 discusses the limitation of our program. Section 7 summarises the results and contributions of the project.

© Springer International Publishing AG 2016
S. Gruner (Ed.): SACLA 2016, CCIS 642, pp. 69–82, 2016.
DOI: 10.1007/978-3-319-47680-3_7

2   Background

2.1   Definitions

Below are definitions of terminology used in this paper.

Intelligent Tutoring Systems: Software designed to emulate the impact of human tutors on a student. They engage students in sustained reasoning activity. Interactions with the student are based on a deep understanding of the students behaviour [4].

Novice programmers: Students who are being exposed to programming for the first time [6].

Novice programs: The sort of programs that a student will encounter when they start learning to program [1,3].

Plan: An abstracted form of a procedure in an algorithm that represents the intended function of a piece of code [7]. Plans can consist of a single operation or a composition of multiple plans [6].

Program narrations: Detailed, syntax-free representations of an algorithm. They are presented in natural language and describe the steps taken by the program [1,3].

Program alphabet: The collection of all semantic tokens used in a program [1,2].

Plan similarity: Two distinct plans x and y are similar if these conditions are met:

1. both plans contain exactly the same characters, or
2. the following three conditions are true:
   (a) the number of tokens in x is the same as in y and
   (b) every token in plan x is of the same literal category as the token in the same position in plan y, e.g.: both are identifiers, keywords, or numeric values.
   (c) if there is a numeric literal in the same position in both plans, the floating value of both literals must be the same, i.e.: $6 = 6.0$, but $6.2 \neq 6.0$.

Conditions 2a, 2b and 2c must be satisfied for plans to be similar, except when Condition 1 is true [1].

Plan equivalence: Two plans x and y are equivalent if:

1. both plans contain the same number of tokens.
2. all tokens, except for identifiers, are exactly the same.
3. for each identifier a in plan x there is the identifier b in the same position of plan y, where b is the equivalent identifier to a between the two program alphabets [1].

2.2   Plan-Oriented Teaching

There have been studies on the effectiveness of how content in an introductory programming course is presented. It has been investigated which areas of knowledge are the most problematic, as well as which areas are foundational to others, and hence the order in which they should be presented. The concepts present in the understanding of programming can be classified into two broad categories: language constructs and plan composition [5]. Language constructs refer to the knowledge of how to use the syntax of the language to produce correct code. Plan composition refers to the ability to construct algorithms that will perform a task. Studies have been conducted to investigate how these two concepts should be taught in relation to each other.

One study found that students struggle with understanding the syntax of the language and that they tend to focus on the implementation rather than problem solving [6]. It was suggested that focussing first on abstract plan composition and then teaching how to implement plans would be effective. A second study found that the order in which concepts are taught does not significantly change the amount a student learns [8]. It was found that teaching syntax before program planning is more efficient in that it places less strain on the students. Yet another study found there to be a strong link between the aptitude in both language constructs and plan composition [5]. This suggested that skills in language constructs and plan composition reinforce each other, thus showing the importance of developing both. While it is not conclusive which area should be taught first, it is clear that a good understanding of both language constructs, plan composition, and the relation between the two is important in teaching novice programmers.

2.3   Intelligent Tutoring Systems

Intelligent Tutoring Systems are software that aid students in the mastery of skills and concepts. These programs provide this by responding to the actions of the student. They identify problems in the student's work and give feedback to help correct the misunderstandings that caused that error.

Students who can interact one-on-one with human tutors often score significantly higher in tests than students who do not [10]. An Intelligent Tutoring System can provide natural language feedback to a student which should hopefully provide a level of improvement as well. This could prove highly useful in institutions where there are not the resources to provide one-on-one attention to all students.

A tutoring system called ProPL [10] emulated the interactions with a human tutor through the use of natural language in a text-based chat system. The system interacts with the student as they work through a set of problems. The system tries to encourage the student to think through their problems, rather than explain how to correct their mistakes. The results of the study of ProPL suggest that interacting with a tutoring system in this manner resulted in the students engaging with problems at a higher level of abstraction. ProPL requires the structure of *Knowledge Construction Dialogues* to be manually specified for each problem [10]. These are scripted conversations designed to guide the student's reasoning to solve the problem.

Another tutoring system (PROUST [7]) is able to detect bugs in Pascal code and provide natural language explanations of errors. PROUST requires a brief describing the goals of the program to be written for each problem [7].

Automatic Feedback Generator [11] is a tutoring system for the Python programming language. It is suggests corrections to a student's code so that it satisfies the requirements of the exercise. For each task the lecturer provides a template solution and possible corrections in the form of an Error Modelling Language. This requires the lecturer to predict specific errors that the students are likely to make and how those will make their code differ from the template.

An unnamed system uses a Model-Based Reasoning approach [9]. Approaches the problem in a very different manner to the other tutoring systems mentioned here. It does not look for mistakes in the student's code. It creates C++ code with bugs and tests whether the student can identify the errors. This is done by taking a template piece of code and creating variations of it. The system knows which errors will be created with each variation, so the questions for the student can be generated by the system as well.

Almost all of the systems mentioned here require the instructor to provide some documentation. The content and format varies greatly, but all are for providing guidance to the system about what to teach.

2.4   Program Narration

A system called NOPRON [3] processes C++ code and provides a detailed, syntax-free explanation of the algorithm followed. The system does this by decomposing the program into its most basic operations and identifying the plans that are represented by those operations. These plans are stored in an abstract manner and are later expressed using natural language with pre-defined templates.

2.5   Basis for a New Intelligent Tutoring System

Many students fail their first programming course [8]. While there are systems designed to assist novice programmers [10], there is no system that specifically guides a student in translating tasks to their syntax.

Using natural language descriptions of the algorithm, as seen in NOPRON [3], could provide simple step-by-step sets of instructions to students for writing a novice program. The abstracted structure representing these plans could also function as the template for error checking that a system such as PROUST [7] requires. This reduces the work that an instructor needs to do to set up a programming exercise with the tutoring system.

3   Problem Statement

For novice programmers, two basic skills are language constructs (i.e., writing valid code) and plan composition (i.e., designing algorithms) [5]. These skills are considered key to novices learning to program [5,6,8]. Can we develop a system that helps students learn the syntax of C++ as well as reinforce the connection between its plan and implementation?

Natural language instruction shows promise as an effective technique for interacting with the student [10]. Many Intelligent Tutoring Systems require instructors to write the documentation for these applications to produce instructions and feedback to students [7,10]. However, the technique of narration allows natural language explanations for a program to be produced exclusively from its source code. It is possible for us to create an Intelligent Tutoring System that provides natural language instruction and feedback based entirely on the provided code?

We require that the student write code that achieves the same result as the instructor's solution i.e. follows the same plan. We, however, do not require that they produce the exact same code. The name of a variable for instance has no bearing on its function. Can we then create a system that evaluates whether the code written by a student is equivalent to that of the instructor?

4   The Tutoring System

In this section we discuss the structure of our Intelligent Tutoring System. We will refer to our program as `Code Pathfinder`. This name refers to how the student is guided through the writing of programs. Figure 1 provides an outline of the flow of `Code Pathfinder`.

4.1   Role of Narrations

The method for producing narrations from source code is the same as was done in NOPRON [3]. Some pre-processing is done first before the actual narration process.

We require that each line of code to perform only one action. Multiple tasks on one line can happen when declaring variables or sending values to the standard output. We can identify cases where the lecturer has done this and split those into multiple lines.

We also strip all leading and trailing white space, as well as comments from the code.

We have written regular expressions that can identify the various tokens of the C++ language. Combinations of these tokens are used to define regular expressions that are used to identify lines of code that match a particular plan. These regular expressions can also be used to extract information from a line of code, such as the variable names used.

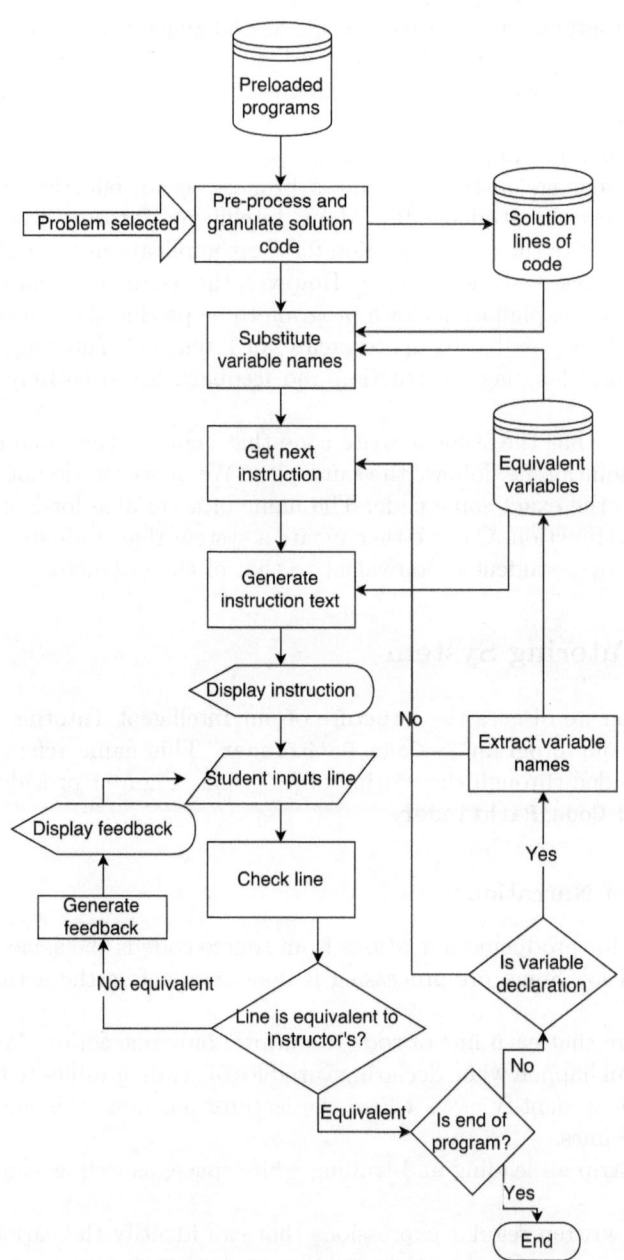

Fig. 1. Structure of Code Pathfinder

4.2   Plan Mirroring

`Code Pathfinder` gives the student instructions for individual lines of code. The student must give an equivalent line of code before they can proceed. If the line that they write is not correct then feedback is provided to them based on their mistakes. The instructions use the variable names that the students have declared.

4.3   Equivalent Variables

We do not specify to the student what to name the variable that we ask them to declare. We do this to provide some element of choice to the student. Since the system works on line-by-line plan mirroring, variables declared on the same line of the student's code and the lecturer's code will be equivalent. We keep track of which variable names are equivalent between the student and instructor's programs. This is essential for the creation of instructions and feedback, both are discussed below.

4.4   Creating Instructions

We wish to give instructions that use the variable names that the student declared. This is done by determining the code that the student is required to write. The narration of this line of code is used as our instruction to the student. To determine the required line of code we replace all the variable names from the lecturer's line with the equivalent variables from the student's code. This is not needed for variable declarations, as explained above. The narration of this line is used as the instruction given to the student. The system uses regular expressions to identify the plan for that line as well as other relevant information, such as variable names, to incorporate in the instruction. For each line plan we have written a function that describes the action of that plan as a task for the student to perform.

4.5   Checking the Line

To check whether the student's line of code is correct we run several checks. First we check for syntax errors. This is done by checking if a plan is recognised by one of our regular expressions. All valid lines of code with structures within the scope of our system are recognised. We then check if the student's and instructor's codes have similar plans. By our definition, this means that the two lines of code are using the same plan, but possibly have different tokens. We substitute all variable name tokens in the instructor's line of code with the equivalent ones from the student's program. We then normalise the lines of code to have the same spacing. These lines should match character-to-character for the student's code to be equivalent to the instructor's.

4.6   Producing Feedback

Feedback for the student is generated based on which of the above checks succeed. Failure to identify a matching plan indicates a syntax error; while being similar to the instructor's code, but not equivalent, suggests the use of the wrong variable name. Using regular expressions we can check specific parts of the lines of code to identify the location of the mismatch. For example, we can check the type of variable declared and whether it is the same between the student and instructor. We have functions written for each type of error that will inform the student of what they have done wrongs.

4.7   Available Problems

We have included the following problems for demonstration: next integer, average problem, factorial problem, and Fahrenheit to Celsius conversion. Some of these programming problems have been used to demonstrate functionality of Intelligent Tutoring Systems in the past [3,5,7].

5   Implementation and Results

Code Pathfinder has been implemented as a Windows application using regular expression and text-to-speech libraries of the .Net Framework provided by Microsoft Corporation. We have also used the Fast Colored TextBox component [12] to display the instructions and provide the student's code editing space.

For each problem below we display two listings: one which contains the source code for a problem, and the other which contains the complete set of instructions provided to the student to produce the associated code.

5.1   User Interface

A screenshot of Code Pathfinder can be seen in Fig. 2. The left text box provides instructions and feedback to the student. The right text box is the space where the student writes their code. The code editor provides syntax highlighting and auto-indentation. Feedback on errors is provided in bars below the instruction for the current action. All feedback is available in audio form using text-to-speech. This can be disabled by the user if they want to do so. The user cannot go back to change already written code.

5.2   Next Integer

Code Pathfinder has successfully provided instructions and feedback for the next integer problem. The program should take in an integer and output the next number. Listing 7.1 shows the instructions given by Code Pathfinder. Listing 7.2 gives the complete code written to satisfy the program. Note that the instructions use the variable name chosen by the student.

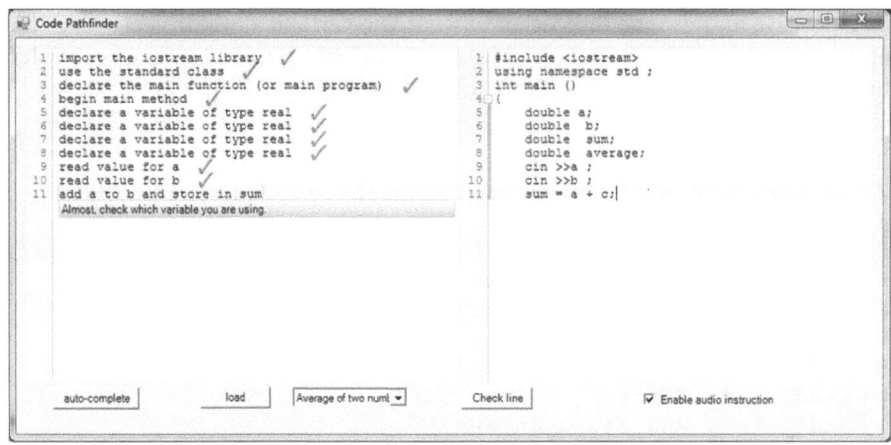

Fig. 2. Screenshot of `Code Pathfinder`

```
 1   import the iostream library
 2   declare the main function (or main program)
 3   begin main method
 4   declare a variable of type integer
 5   read value for k
 6   increment k by 1
 7   display the value of k
 8   terminate the main function
 9   end main method
10   Program complete. Good job!
```

Listing 7.1. Instructions for next integer problem [3]

```
1   #include<iostream>
2   int main()
3   {
4       int k;
5       cin >> k;
6       k += 1;
7       cout << k;
8       return 0;
9   }
```

Listing 7.2. Code for next integer problem [3]

5.3   Average of Two Numbers

In Listings 7.3 and 7.4 we can see similar functionality to that in the next integer problem. What is clear as well is that the instructions for `declare a variable` get repetitive and give no indication of what the variable does. It is possible that future variations of this system could suggest variable names or even specify what the variable is for. This possibility is discussed in Sect. 7.2.

```
1  import the iostream library
2  use the standard class
3  declare the main function (or main program)
4  begin main method
5  declare a variable of type real
6  declare a variable of type real
7  declare a variable of type real
8  declare a variable of type real
9  read value for x
10 read value for y
11 add x to y and store in sum
12 divide sum by 2.0 and store in average
13 display the value of average
14 terminate the main function
15 end main method
16 Program complete. Good job!
```

Listing 7.3. Instructions for average of two numbers [3]

```
1  #include <iostream>
2  using namespace std;
3  int main()
4  {
5      double x;
6      double y;
7      double sum;
8      double average;
9      cin >> x;
10     cin >> y;
11     sum = x + y;
12     average = sum / 2.0;
13     cout << average;
14     return 0;
15 }
```

Listing 7.4. Code for average of two numbers [3]

5.4   Factorial Problem

The factorial problem requires the program to calculate the factorial of a given positive integer. The factorial is the product of all integers from one to the number. There are many ways in which this could be programmed. Our example uses a while loop.

```
 1 | import the iostream library
 2 | use the standard class
 3 | declare the main function (or main program)
 4 | begin main method
 5 | declare a variable of type integer
 6 | read value for maxVal
 7 | declare a variable of type integer
 8 | set factorial equals 1
 9 | declare a variable of type integer
10 | set i equals 2
11 | make a loop that repeats while i is less than or equal
        to maxVal
12 | begin while loop
13 | multiply factorial by i and store in factorial
14 | increment i by 1 after this line has been executed
15 | end while loop
16 | display the value of factorial
17 | terminate the main function
18 | end main method
19 | Program complete. Good job!
```

Listing 7.5. Instructions for factorial problem

```
 1 | #include<iostream>
 2 | using namespace std ;
 3 | int main ()
 4 | {
 5 |     int maxVal;
 6 |     cin >> maxVal;
 7 |     int factorial;
 8 |     factorial =1;
 9 |     int i;
10 |     i = 2;
11 |     while (i <=maxVal)
12 |     {
13 |         factorial = factorial * i;
14 |         i++;
15 |     }
16 |     cout << factorial;
17 |     return 0;
18 | }
```

Listing 7.6. Code for factorial problem

5.5 Fahrenheit to Celsius Conversion

Converting between units of temperature is a classic task for students taking their first course in programming. The program is given a temperature in degrees Fahrenheit and must return the equivalent value measured in degrees Celsius.

```
 1 │ import the iostream library
 2 │ use the standard class
 3 │ declare the main function (or main program)
 4 │ begin main method
 5 │ declare a variable of type real
 6 │ read value for temp
 7 │ subtract  32 from temp and store in temp
 8 │ divide temp by 1.8 and store in temp
 9 │ display the value of temp
10 │ terminate the main function
11 │ end main method
12 │ Program complete. Good job!
```

Listing 7.7. Instructions for Fahrenheit to Celsius conversion

```cpp
 1 │ #include<iostream>
 2 │ using namespace std;
 3 │ int main()
 4 │ {
 5 │     double temp;
 6 │     cin >> temp;
 7 │     temp = temp - 32;
 8 │     temp = temp / 1.8;
 9 │     cout << temp;
10 │     return 0;
11 │ }
```

Listing 7.8. Code for Fahrenheit to Celsius conversion

5.6　Feedback Examples

If the student is given the instruction `declare a variable of type real`, then the following lines of code from the student will elicit their corresponding responses as seen in Table 1. Similarly, if the student is given the instruction `read value for b`, then their answers will be given responses as per Table 2.

Table 1. Examples of feedback for `declare a variable of type real`

Code	Response
`int a;`	Wrong variable type
`double while;`	That name is a reserved word in C++, please use a different name
`double a`	Syntax error, check your code
`a = 2;`	That's not what you should be doing
`double x;`	Correct, well done

Table 2. Examples of feedback for `read value for b`

Code	Response
`cin >> a;`	Almost, check which variable you are using
`cin > b;`	Syntax error, check your code
`cin >> b;`	Correct, well done

6   Limitations

In this section we discuss what `Code Pathfinder` cannot do. In the previous section we demonstrated that `Code Pathfinder` can handle the basic structures of the C++ language. `Code Pathfinder` does not handle all structures provided by C++. For example, `Code Pathfinder` cannot handle multiple operations on one line, nor can it process definitions of new data structures. There are many cases where the order of tokens in a line of code would not change its result, adding two values for example. `Code Pathfinder` does not allow for this type of line equivalence. `Code Pathfinder` requires that only one thing is done per line of code. Common practices like declaring multiple variables on one line or initialising a variable on its declaration line cannot be done by the user. The instructor's code may use these methods, but our preprocessing breaks these into multiple lines. `Code Pathfinder` provides no explanation as to the purpose of a variable. This means that the student does not know what the variable will be used for, so they cannot give it a descriptive variable name.

7   Conclusion and Future Work

We have demonstrated that our system, `Code Pathfinder`, is capable of providing instructions and feedback to novice programmers for simple C++ programming problems.

7.1   Key Contributions

Feedback generation: We have developed a method where we can use the source code of a problem to generate feedback for a tutoring system.

Plan mirroring: We have developed a system that can convert the variable names of one program to those of another program that follows the same plan.

7.2   Future Work

Multi-line instruction: We have demonstrated that we can provide line-by-line instructions for novice programs. Can we generate instructions and feedback for code segments spanning multiple lines? Could this handle variations of the order of lines and the number of operations done on a line? Could variations of high-level plans be handled? For example, different sorting algorithms being accepted as a sort plan.

Variable name guidance: Can we provide a description of what a variable is used for by analysing the instructor's code? This could be done by using the lecturer's variable name as a suggestion, or using comments from the instructor's code. Alternatively, could Program Comprehension be used to identify the purpose of the variable? Counter variables and flags could possibly be identified by the operations used on them.

References

1. Ade-Ibijola, A.: Automatic novice program comprehension for semantic bug detection. PhD Thesis, University of the Witwatersrand, Johannesburg (2016)
2. Ade-Ibijola, A.: Definitions of plan similarity. In: Personal Communication (2015)
3. Ade-Ibijola, A., Ewert, S., Sanders, I.: Abstracting and narrating novice programs using regular expressions. In: Proceedings of the Annual Conference of the South African Institute for Computer Scientists and Information Technologists (SAICSIT 2014), pp. 19–28 (2014)
4. Corbett, A.T., Koedinger, K.R., Anderson, J.R.: Intelligent tutoring systems. Handbook of Human-Computer Interaction, pp. 849–850 (1997)
5. Ebrahimi, A.: Novice programmer errors: language constructs and plan composition. Int. J. Hum. Comput. Stud. $41(4)$, 457–480 (1994)
6. Ebrahimi, A., Schweikert, C.: Empirical study of novice programming with plans and objects. ACM SIGCSE Bulletin $38(4)$, 52–54 (2006)
7. Johnson, W.L., Soloway, E.: PROUST: knowledge-based program understanding. IEEE Trans. Softw. Eng. 3, 267–275 (1985)
8. Kranch, D.A.: Teaching the novice programmer: a study of instructional sequences and perception. Educ. Inf. Technol. $17(3)$, 291–313 (2012)
9. Kumar, A.N.: Model-based reasoning for domain modeling in a web-based intelligent tutoring system to help students learn to debug C++ programs. In: Cerri, S.A., Gouardères, G., Paraguaçu, F. (eds.) ITS 2002. LNCS, vol. 2363, pp. 792–801. Springer, Heidelberg (2002)
10. Lane, H.C., VanLehn, K.: Teaching the tacit knowledge of programming to novices with natural language tutoring. Comput. Sci. Educ. $15(3)$, 183–201 (2005)
11. Singh, R., Gulwani, S., Solar-Lezama, A.: Automated feedback generation for introductory programming assignments. ACM SIGPLAN Notices $48(6)$, 15–26 (2013)
12. Torgashov, P.: Fast colored textbox for syntax highlighting. http://www.codeproject.com/Articles/161871/Fast-Colored-TextBox-for-syntaxhighlighting

Flipping a Course on Computer Architecture

Hussein Suleman[✉]

Department of Computer Science, University of Cape Town,
Rondebosch, South Africa
hussein@cs.uct.ac.za

Abstract. This paper reports on an experiment with a flipped class-room for a Computer Architecture course. In a flipped classroom, students access content out of the classroom and then engage in a discussion in-class, rather than the other way around. This seemed like an ideal strategy for a course that can easily focus on the minutiae of architectural details and computer history. The results showed that students liked the interactive and practical aspects of the course but were particularly negative about pre-lecture readings. These results suggest that students need to learn how to learn in different ways, and move away from the exclusive strategy of in-classroom, content-centric lectures.

Keywords: Flipped classroom · Computer architecture · Low resource environments

1 Introduction

In traditional lectures, a lecturer will stand before a class and recite a paper that contains all that is considered important for the class to know, maybe resorting to use of the chalkboard [2]. As technology evolved, this model changed to use presentation cues in Microsoft Powerpoint slides visible to all rather than in notes used only by the lecturer. However, the predominant mode of verbally exposing information to the students remained. This model has been criticized because of its assumption that dissemination of content is the primary purpose of a classroom. It has been argued that, instead, such content is better learnt on an individual basis and the classroom is better utilized as a space for discussion and active engagement with the content [10]. This could lead to higher levels of understanding than if classrooms are used purely for presentation of the content to students.

These arguments are part of the motivation for flipped or inverted class-rooms. A flipped classroom is one where students acquire content knowledge outside the classroom, and use the classroom as a space for discussion instead of lectures [10]. This has been used extensively in teaching and learning in various disciplines, including Computer Science. The traditional format of a flipped classroom includes out-of-classroom video instruction and in-classroom discussions. Students are expected to watch the videos before coming to class to gain

© Springer International Publishing AG 2016
S. Gruner (Ed.): SACLA 2016, CCIS 642, pp. 83–94, 2016.
DOI: 10.1007/978-3-319-47680-3_8

the content knowledge and be prepared to engage in discussion about the topics of the videos.

The flipped classroom approach is arguably a good technique because of the following reasons:

- Each student is able to learn at his or her own pace.
- Students are able to learn without explicitly being taught.
- Lectures are more engaging when there is discussion rather than exposition of content.
- Higher levels of understanding are possible if there is greater discussion and interrogation of the content.

This paper reports on an experiment to use the flipped classroom technique in a Computer Architecture course. This course is typically dense in factual content, often leading to traditional forms of lectures. There is little problem-solving and large amounts of technical and historical information. While there is opportunity for debate and discussion, this requires an in-depth knowledge of the content first. Thus, it appeared that this course would be ideal for the flipped classroom approach and this experiment was conceived.

The rest of the paper presents related work, then the design of the course and its various elements, followed finally by an evaluation of the experiment and conclusions.

2   Literature Review

The core idea of an inverted or flipped classroom is presented by Lage et al. [10], where it is defined as the inversion of activities conducted within the classroom and outside the classroom. Specifically, the format of multimedia or video lectures is presented as a vehicle for the content, with the aim of providing learners with flexibility in their approaches to learning. This simple inversion is often accompanied by an expansion of the range of activities, to supplement the inversion model [3].

In Computer Science, various experiments have been conducted with flipping of courses on different topics, with many recent studies on introductory programming courses.

Campbell et al. [4] compared a flipped classroom approach to a first year programming course against a traditional version of the same course and demonstrated improvements in the experience of students. They did not mandate compulsory attendance but suggested using in-class quizzes in future years. Latulipe et al. [11] extended the flipped programming course model for a lab-based course, by adding elements of lightweight teamwork and gamification. Their results showed positive feedback from students, although they did not individually test the effect of each intervention as Campbell et al. did. Lacher and Lewis [9] tested the effect of pre-class video quizzes on student performance in a controlled study and discovered no significant effect. They postulate that while these quizzes before the class make students engage with the content, there is no deep learning taking place for most students, especially those with lower marks.

Computer Architecture was taught using a flipped classroom approach by Gehringer [7]. He taught both a graduate and undergraduate version of the same course and recorded the lectures in one for use in the other, to maximize reuse of content. In comparisons of student performance, the flipped class students fared worse. However, there were only 8 students and there were many differences between the classes so these results are unlikely to have much significance.

In this paper, an alternative approach to a Computer Architecture flipped class is presented, based on the positive lessons learnt, and with adaptations for a specific environment and cohort of students.

3 Outline of Computer Architecture Course

Computer Architecture is the study of computer hardware and the design decisions and choices that affect computer hardware. This course is studied either from the perspective of designers of hardware or designers of software. The former study architecture to understand how to design hardware while the latter study architecture to build better software systems.

This course was aimed at the latter group of students, in the second year of their degree, but included a mixture of Computer Science and Computer Engineering students in the classroom as the course was required for both degrees.

The content of the course followed the popular textbook by Patterson and Hennessy [12], with some contemporary modifications, such as the inclusion of an Open Hardware topic for relevance. The topics included in the course in 2015 were as follows:

- Introduction to computer architecture,
- RISC and CISC CPU architectures,
- MIPS assembly language,
- Pipelining,
- Multicore CPUs,
- Cache architectures,
- Virtualization,
- Performance and benchmarks,
- Memory / SDRAM,
- Secondary storage: hard drives, solid-state drives and RAID,
- USB,
- General purpose GPUs,
- Open Source Hardware: Arduino,
- Summary and concluding remarks.

There were 14 classroom sessions in total. This is a very short course compared to offerings elsewhere so the focus of the course was on carefully selected high-level design concepts rather than the intricate details of any one section. Each topic in the list above was the subject of a single classroom session in the course.

175 Students were enrolled in 2014 and 179 students were enrolled in 2015. The course was run in 2014 and 2015, with similar content and structure in both years. The following section describes the various elements of teaching and learning used in the classroom sessions.

4   Learning Design

4.1   Flipping on the Cheap

At the beginning of the course it was decided that this new approach would have to be low-cost. The flipped classroom approach, in general, requires a large financial and time investment, especially for the creation of lecture videos. In addition, any interactive experiential learning in class may require additional staff, such as tutors and teaching assistants where groupwork is needed.

Many universities simply do not have the resources available to conduct such experiments. There are typically no funds for producing pre-recorded videos. Also, students would be required to have access to written content such as a textbook and, realistically, not all students purchase these books. Further, it is not clear that such an approach will work for any given course so the risk factor is high and many universities cannot afford such risks. Finally, costs are divided into fixed costs, such as producing videos once for an entire group, and proportional costs, such as additional tutors to mark more assessments. For a course to be scalable, proportional costs must be managed so that flipping a classroom does not increase the cost of offering a particular course.

For the reasons above, it was decided that the cost of converting and running the course as a flipped classroom course needed to be minimal. Each element discussed below takes this cost reality into account in its design.

4.2   Content Videos

Every classroom session had an associated video clip that students were required to watch before the session. Each video clip was approximately 10 min in length. The videos were made available through a Youtube playlist [5], with links created on the Learning Management System (LMS) used at the university (see Fig. 1). In addition, all videos were downloaded and made available for download via the LMS so students would not need external Internet bandwidth to access the videos.

In the particular case of Computer Architecture, there is a large number of videos from primary sources available online, such as an interview with John Hennessey on RISC. It was decided that these would be appropriate as primary sources of information. The first lecture was an overview of the course and this was recorded and put online.

The purpose of the videos was to create excitement about topics that might otherwise be considered dull. All of the videos were chosen because they focused on very specific and fundamental ideas students should be familiar with.

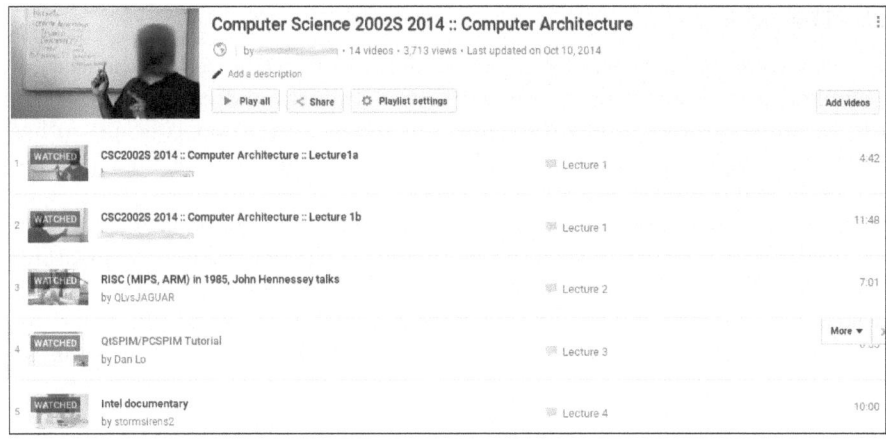

Fig. 1. Youtube playlist for class videos

For example, the video for the Performance topic was of a hardware reviewer demonstrating side-by-side timing of mobile phones running a popular benchmark suite. Students ought to identify with such examples more so than the theoretical benchmarking of hardware they do not have access to.

4.3 Readings

Videos by themselves do not contain sufficient technical information on which to base a discussion on Computer Architecture. Thus, it was decided that there would be accompanying readings. Some of the readings came from popular articles and extracts from the textbook [12] — the entire RISC/MIPS section had been made available for free by the publisher as the definitive guide to this topic. Most of the readings, however, were selected sections of articles from Wikipedia. Popular wisdom is that Wikipedia articles have poor quality, but some formal studies [8] have shown that the quality of Wikipedia articles is comparable to, for example, the carefully curated Enclopaedia Brittanica.

Wikipedia was selected in many instances because of many reasons, as outlined below:

- It is free and easily accessible on all devices.
- It is arguably the most current source of formal information in a rapidly-changing field like computer architecture.
- It is carefully checked and cross-referenced by the authors.
- Information can be either in-depth or span a breadth of subtopics.
- Links are provided to navigate to related topics (this is simply not possible in traditional textbooks).

4.4   Discussion

Each classroom session included a general discussion, facilitated by the lecturer. A number of questions were presented to the students and each was discussed in turn. Some questions were designed to highlight important concepts, others were to raise questions about the application of concepts while the final questions were often about a critical analysis of concepts.

Discussions were open-ended and could veer off into directions chosen by the students or lecturer. The lecturer served as more of a chair than a commentator. Some students were confused by this role, expecting the lecturer to provide the answers to all questions but, if that were to happen, there would be no real discussion within the class any longer. Figure 2 shows a typical set of discussion questions.

Introduction to Computer Architecture

1. What is the purpose of a Graphics Processing Unit?
2. What is better: integrated or dedicated cards?
3. How do we measure the performance of a GPU?
4. What is better: DirectX or OpenGL?
5. How can we improve on current GPUs?

Fig. 2. Discussion questions for a session

4.5   Quizzes

Every classroom session included a quiz on the assigned reading and video. These were to ensure that all students did in fact read and view the assigned work before participating in the discussion. Students were given 5 multiple-choice questions on key facts from the assigned work. These were flashed on the screen in a timed manner such that each question and its options were only visible for 30 seconds.

The answers were filled in on a computer-readable form that could be scanned and automatically graded afterwards. This system was adapted for this course from one built for a previous course. No special equipment was needed — a common photocopier was used to scan the documents. The answer sheets (see Fig. 3) were also produced on a photocopier or printing press, with varying skew and scale. Image processing automatically compensated for these issues, automatically generated a mark for each student, uploaded these marks to the LMS and made the answer sheets available to students as downloadable PDF files.

Most approaches used for in-class quizzes use mobile devices or laptops. However, those approaches require that the wireless network is operational and this cannot always be guaranteed. In addition, students could easily search for answers online if they are using a laptop. The integration of paper answer sheets into an otherwise digital workflow makes the system both scalable and robust, without increasing the technology requirements for students in the classroom.

Department of Computer Science

Quiz

Student Number   :

Name (optional)   :

Course   :
CSC 2002S

Date   :
07/10/2010

Instructions:

a) Fill out the details above.

b) Shade in your student number in the block to the right.

c) Shade your answers in the block below.

d) Use a dark pencil (so you can erase the mark if you make a mistake).

ANSWERS:

Question	1	2	3	4	5	6	7	8	9	10	11	12	13	14	15	16
Answer a																
b																
c																
d																
e																
f																
g																
h																
i																
j																

Fig. 3. Quiz answer sheet

4.6   Demonstrations

Demonstrations were included in almost all classroom sessions to create a stronger link between theoretical concepts and practical implementations. This was not, however, always possible because of some topics did not naturally lend themselves to realistic demonstrations e.g., pipelining. Many topics could easily be demonstrated, such as benchmarking software, virtualization (using VirtualBox) and open source hardware (using a Google Cardboard VR device). The remaining demonstrations were on current topics that were deemed useful to students at this level, such as the use of a Raspberry Pi computer.

Fig. 4. Demonstration using laptop webcam

Cost is always a factor in designing appropriate and feasible demonstrations. In order to demonstrate the Raspberry Pi in-class, a USB video frame grabber was used along with frame grabber preview software to simulate a display for the device and have this reflect on the screen students were looking at. Figure 4 shows a mobile device being demonstrated to students using the lecturer's laptop webcam. These techniques allow for demonstrations with small devices to be used in a classroom without the need for additional staff — as long as the data projector's screen is viewable by all students, these demonstrations are scalable to the size of the class.

Finally, some demonstrations used software emulation of hardware devices. For example, a robotic arm that connected via USB would only work on an older computer so this was simulated using virtualization. This allowed for a wide range of hardware experiments to be conducted in class without having to haul additional equipment to the classroom.

5   Evaluation and Analysis

In all classes, students provide feedback as a matter of course. In this course, students were asked for additional feedback on elements of the flipped classroom model used. These, as well as the regular feedback, are discussed next.

5.1 Quantitative Feedback

In 2014, students were asked to indicate either a positive, negative or neutral reaction to each of the elements introduced in the course. Feedback was kept to a minimum because students were also providing feedback on the lecturer in a separate exercise. Table 1 displays the summary of student responses.

Table 1. Student perceptions of aspects of flipped classroom experiment

Feedback	Readings	Videos	Quizzes	Demos	Discussions
Positive	19	46	31	58	49
Neutral	25	21	30	15	22
Negative	32	9	15	3	5

Videos, demonstrations and discussions were considered to be mostly positive by students. It was expected that students would prefer to watch videos, given that students consume more video than ever before. Discussions were previously well received by students in 4th year, so students confirmed that even earlier in their degree they appreciate in-class discussions. Demonstrations got the most positive response, possibly because students were presented with a more practical view of the course than they would get in other courses.

Readings and quizzes were, as expected, not well received by students. Students were more negative about readings than positive, suggesting that the majority of students did not want to read before class. While many students were negative about quizzes, the results lean towards the positive. It may be that some students disliked the constant assessment (and the fact that quizzes were conducted at the beginning of the lecture) while others appreciated being forced to do the readings diligently.

This quantitative evaluation exercise was not repeated in 2015 because lectures were disrupted by student protests precisely as the course came to an end.

5.2 Qualitative Feedback

When asked for feedback on the experimental elements of the course, students were also asked for general comments. Some of the comments are listed below:

- "the theory was too much and it is difficult to understand without having done the things practically",
- "some pre lecture readings took quite a long time to go through the day before a lecture",
- "needs to give better notes and not just wikipedia pages",
- "I feel like no effort was put in with making our readings wikipedia pages ... And the fact that it was wikipedia was slightly off-putting".

Students made similar comments in the lecturer evaluations in 2014 and 2015.

A major focus of the comments was the readings. Students made every conceivable argument against reading anything before class. The only argument that could be considered valid is that students have difficulty if English is not their first language. However, at an English-medium university, students more than halfway through a Bachelors degree ought to be able to read technical literature.

The elements of the course with positive quantitative feedback were not commented on by students.

5.3   Lecturer Evaluation

Students in both years submitted lecturer evaluations for the course. In both cases, the numerical scores indicated that the lecturer was considered 'above average' for effectiveness. This is in stark contrast to the written comments on how the readings were 'horrible' or deemed completely inappropriate. When asked about the overall experience, students appeared to assess the overall experience but, when asked to provide general feedback, they only honed in on their issues with the readings.

This was an unexpected disconnect between evaluating the complete experience and evaluating a single aspect that had a profound impact on the students.

5.4   Analysis

From the various forms of evaluation and discussions with students, it is clear that students have an expectation that courses will be taught in a manner they are familiar with. In this case, students voiced strong opinions on how they think the course should be taught, what they think the content should be and how the content should be presented. They were asked if any of them had ever looked at any textbooks on the subject, and none of them ever had. These expectations are a cause for some concern, as it is clear that students are in a comfort zone from which they do not wish to be disturbed. The flipped classroom presentation of this course was more of a disruption than they had expected.

Reading is the biggest challenge for the future. Students made it clear that they do not read and do not wish to read. This is not a new challenge but Computer Science is changing and students cannot simply get a degree on the basis of mathematical skills — they now need soft skills like reading, writing and speaking or presenting. If students have difficulty in reading at second year level, maybe it is a sign that they need to do more reading from the beginning of the degree. Traditionally, the early part of the degree is focused on programming skills but maybe that needs to change.

Feedback from students also makes it clear that they have learnt particular ways of learning. A flipped classroom expects students to learn in a different way and students appear to have difficult in learning how to learn differently. This too may need to be addressed by exposing students to different ways of learning earlier rather than later in their studies.

Finally, students were given original unsolved problems to address in their final examinations. The vast majority of students were able to provide cogent arguments to support design decisions they would make in designing original computer hardware. Their specific answers, and a high level of achievement in general, suggest that students learnt not only the content that was expected but the critical thinking skills they were expected to learn. Thus, the goal of the course was achieved — students learnt precisely the skills they were supposed to learn. The only downside is they did not all enjoy the process of this learning. This outcome correlates with the study by Amresh, et al. [1], who also found that student performance in such a course improved but possibly at the expense of the student experience.

6   Conclusions and Future Work

This paper has reported on an experiment to use the flipped classroom metaphor in teaching a second year course in Computer Architecture. Many different elements of the course were changed to support this mode of teaching and do it without incurring additional costs. Some aspects were specifically chosen because of the nature of the specific course. The flipped classroom metaphor was mostly successful and addressed all the needs of the course, without increased cost. In future, this approach could be applied to various similar content-heavy courses or replicated to verify the outcomes and allow for deeper analyses.

Student feedback in various forms has indicated that students appreciated most aspects of the course, but were strongly opposed to reading. This is where the next level of intervention may need to take place. Writing across the curriculum [6], and indeed reading as well, may need to be adopted as a general strategy to train Computer Science graduates with new age skills that go beyond algorithms and logic. This will have the dual effect of creating graduates with broader skills and creating a student cohort that is able to learn effectively using a wider range of teaching and learning modalities. While it may be argued that these skills ought to already be in place by the time students arrive at university, it is clearly still a problem that needs to be addressed.

Acknowledgments. This research was partially funded by the National Research Foundation (NRF) of South Africa (Grant numbers: 85470 and 88209) and University of Cape Town. The author acknowledges that opinions, findings and conclusions or recommendations expressed in this publication are that of the author, and that the NRF accepts no liability whatsoever in this regard.

References

1. Amresh, A., Carberry, A.R., Femiani, J.: Evaluating the effectiveness of flipped classrooms for teaching CS1. In: Frontiers in Education Conference, pp. 733–735. IEEE (2013). http://dx.doi.org/10.1109/FIE.2013.6684923
2. Becker, W.E., Watts, M.: Chalk and talk: A national survey on teaching undergraduate economics. Am. Econ. Rev. **86**(2), 448–453 (1996). http://www.jstor.org/stable/2118168

3. Bishop, J.L., Verleger, M.A.: The flipped classroom: A survey of the research. In: Proceedings of 120th ASEE Annual Conference and Exposition, ASEE (2013)
4. Campbell, J., Horton, D., Craig, M., Gries, P.: Evaluating an inverted CS1. In: Proceedings of the 45th ACM Technical Symposium on Computer Science Education (SIGCSE 2014), pp. 307–312. ACM (2014). http://dx.doi.org/10.1145/2538862.2538943
5. Suleman, H.: Computer Science 2002S 2015 : Computer Architecture (2015). https://www.youtube.com/playlist?list=PLElBQiaE5ZyFj2RLERYwH-vsF3lz EaM_h
6. Fell, H.J., Proulx, V.K., Casey, J.: Writing across the computer science curriculum. In: Proceedings of the Twenty-Seventh SIGCSE Technical Symposium on Computer Science Education (SIGCSE 1996), pp. 204–209, ACM (1996). http://dx.doi.org/10.1145/236452.236540
7. Gehringer, E.F., Peddycord III., B.W.: The inverted-lecture model: a case study in computer architecture. In: Proceeding of the 44th ACM Technical Symposium on Computer Science Education (SIGCSE 2013), pp. 489–494, ACM (2013). http://dx.doi.org/10.1145/2445196.2445343
8. Giles, J.: Internet encyclopaedias go head to head. Nature **428**, 900–901 (2005). http://dx.doi.org/10.1038/438900a
9. Lacher, L.L., Lewis, M.C.: The effectiveness of video quizzes in a flipped class. In: Proceedings of the 46th ACM Technical Symposium on Computer Science Education (SIGCSE 2015), pp. 224–228. ACM (2015). http://dx.doi.org/10.1145/2676723.2677302
10. Lage, M.J., Platt, G.J., Treglia, M.: Inverting the classroom: A gateway to creating an inclusive learning environment. J. Econ. Educ. **31**(1), 30–43 (2000). http://doi.org/10.2307/1183338
11. Latulipe, C., Long, N.B., Seminario, C.E.: Structuring flipped classes with lightweight teams and gamification. In: Proceedings of the 46th ACM Technical Symposium on Computer Science Education (SIGCSE 2015), pp. 392–397. ACM (2015). http://dx.doi.org/10.1145/2676723.2677240
12. Patterson, D.A., Hennessy, J.L.: Computer Organization and Design: The Hardware/Software Interface, 5th edn. Morgan Kaufmann, Prentice Hall (2014)

Effective Integration of a Student Response System in An Undergraduate Computer Science Classroom: An Active-Engagement Instructional Strategy

Fani Moses Radebe[1]([⊠]) and Liezel Nel[2]

[1] Department of Computer Science and Informatics, University of the Free State, Phuthaditjhaba, South Africa
[2] Department of Computer Science and Informatics, University of the Free State, Bloemfontein, South Africa
{radebefm,nell}@ufs.ac.za

Abstract. Classroom learning experiences are often hindered by a lack of student participation and superficial interactions with the course content. Student engagement is essential in ensuring that students take an active role in their own learning experiences. A student response system (SRS) is an educational technology that has proven valuable in increasing student engagement. In this study, an active-engagement instructional strategy was devised to guide the effective integration of an SRS as part of classroom activities. A case study was then conducted to investigate the impact of the instructional strategy on student engagement in an undergraduate Computer Science classroom. Analysis of the collected data indicates that the integration of the SRS supported active learning and increased students' motivation to participate in classroom activities. The instructional strategy served as an effective guide for instructional activities and helped to identify instances that could sabotage the facilitation of student engagement.

Keywords: Student engagement · Student response system · Teaching practices · Active learning · Motivation

1 Introduction

Classroom learning is often hampered by passive, unmotivated students and low attendance rates [22]. Student engagement is a popular catalyst of teaching and learning that has the potential to ensure equal involvement of all students in learning processes [15]. In order to enhance student engagement, educators can employ motivational and active learning strategies to cultivate positive behavior and meaningful participation in learning processes [2]. Additionally, the integration of educational technologies into the learning environment has the potential to facilitate pedagogical goals and stimulate interest in learning [24]. However,

© Springer International Publishing AG 2016
S. Gruner (Ed.): SACLA 2016, CCIS 642, pp. 95–103, 2016.
DOI: 10.1007/978-3-319-47680-3_9

the challenge remains to devise instructional strategies that will enable the effective use of educational technologies inside classrooms. A student response system (SRS) is an educational technology that has proven valuable in increasing students' engagement, attention and attendance [5,6]. SRSs, also known as clickers, enable the polling of students' understanding through classroom quizzes [4]. Although numerous studies identify best practices for the integration of SRS questions as part of face-to-face lectures [4,6], there are no definite directives guiding the overall restructuring of such class sessions to ensure the effective use of SRSs in a student-centered classroom environment aimed at enhancing student engagement.

The aim of this paper is to evaluate the effectiveness of a tailor-made active-engagement instructional strategy that was devised to facilitate the integration of an SRS in an undergraduate Computer Science (CS) classroom. Specific attention will be given to the manner in which an SRS can be integrated as part of an overall instructional strategy.

2   Perspectives from Literature

2.1   Student Engagement

Student engagement is defined as involvement in educationally effective practices in the classroom that result in desired learning outcomes [16], and the quality of efforts that students devote while they participate in these educationally meaningful activities [2]. Kolb and Kolb [15] state that learning is a process of constructing knowledge, which can be improved by focusing on engaging students in processes that enhance learning. Students learn more by being engaged in learning activities that allow for the creation of connections between current knowledge and experience [21]. This way of learning enables students to think critically about learning content. Instructors and students have a joint responsibility to invest quality time and effort in order to achieve these goals.

The distinctive part of student engagement is that it helps all students, especially underserved students, to learn actively [3]. Underserved students are those who do not have adequate access to learning facilities such as computer laboratories; their only hope for learning is through engaging lectures. In such learning environments, instructors are tasked with devising innovative teaching and learning strategies that borrow essential parts from other learning modes in order to enhance student engagement.

2.2   Active Learning and Motivation

Active learning is an essential ingredient of student engagement. Allen and Tanner [1] define active learning as the acquisition of new information, constructing meaning thereof, and having the opportunity to reiterate it to others. This form of instruction emphasizes interaction between students, their peers and the instructor. Instead of passively listening to a lecture, students have numerous opportunities to participate in classroom activities and receive immediate feedback [9]. A learning activity can only be classified as 'active' when each student is actively engaged in the learning activity and applies constructed knowledge, skill, and attitude in order to make meaning of the learning content [18]. This type of learning environment enables students to relate new facts to the information and skills that they already possess.

One of the most important psychological concepts in education is motivation [2]. According to Williams and Burden [23], motivation consists of various facets involving arousal of interest, sustaining that interest, and investing time and effort to achieve a specific goal. Motivated students are more likely to engage in learning and complete learning activities [10]. Motivation, therefore, helps to sustain students' interest and enjoyment of learning [2]. However, students will not automatically be motivated to learn. Instructors need to provide students with learning activities that support motivation. Motivation to learn is therefore closely tied to student engagement — as a driver for sustaining students' devotion and effort to learn through active learning activities.

2.3   Student Response Systems

Low levels of student participation during face-to-face classes remain one of the major concerns of higher education instructors [11]. This lack of participation can often be attributed to a lack of student engagement and motivation. Cain, Black and Rohr [4] found that the integration of educational technologies, such as SRSs, increased participation and motivated students to attend class. Further, the interactive natures of such technologies enable students to learn actively.

SRSs typically consist of hand-held keypads and a receiver. Students respond to in-class quizzes by keying in their responses on the hand-held keypads, which relay the information to the receiver that aggregates the question responses. The instructor can then, through a data projector connected to the receiver, display the results of the student responses (typically in the form of graphs) on a presentation screen [13]. Although SRSs are typically used to collect individual responses from students, it can also be used in a collaborative learning environment, where students have the opportunity to discuss the quiz questions with their peers before they submit their individual answers [14]. Such a collaborative strategy could assist in further enhancing reported SRS benefits related to increased participation and engagement; increased quantity and quality of class discussions; and improved feedback [5].

In one of the few research studies focusing on effective teaching practices for the integration of SRSs, Lee and Shih [17] identify "four crucial SRS teaching practices", of which three are relevant to the context of this study:

1. The inclusion of ungraded pre- and post-lecture SRS questions to evaluate students' prior knowledge and level of comprehension of the lecture content;
2. The use of SRS questions to guide student classroom discussions in order to enhance active and participatory learning; and
3. The use of SRS activities to link theory and practice in order to improve students' understanding of theoretical concepts.

An instructional strategy that incorporates these SRS practices is more likely to result in an interactive classroom atmosphere [17] that promotes active learning and student motivation.

3 Instructional Strategy

As part of this study, the researcher (the first author) identified SRSs as a promising educational technology that could potentially assist in enhancing student engagement in his classrooms. Due to a lack of institutional resources, the researcher was, however, forced to consider more affordable SRS options. He therefor developed a custom mobile phone-based SRS that uses Bluetooth® communication technology to enable students to respond to classroom quizzes via mobile devices, such as mobile phones and laptops. This section presents the design of a tailor-made active-engagement instructional strategy (see Table 1) that the researcher followed in an attempt to effectively integrate the SRS as part of classroom activities.

In line with Lee and Shih's [17] "SRS teaching practices", this instructional strategy made provision for the asking of pre- and post-lecture SRS questions as well as the creation of a collaborative learning environment where students could work in groups to discuss possible answers to the SRS quiz questions. Where applicable, SRS activities also focused on establishing links between theory and practice. In devising this new instructional strategy, Gagné's [8] nine events of instruction were used as a guide to construct a six step lesson structure — including descriptions of the activities, activity rationale and media. The summary of the proposed instructional strategy is presented in Table 1.

Step 1 ran for five minutes in an attempt to capture students' attention with pre-lecture questions. In Step 2, the instructor used 15 min to explain the topics and concepts with Microsoft© PowerPoint slides. The slides were made available on the institutional learning management system (LMS) prior to the lectures so that students could focus on the lesson without being concerned about taking notes. Step 3 allowed the instructor to pose questions that probed the students' understanding of the lecture content. The students were first asked to discuss the questions with their peers and then respond individually via the SRS. Step 4 allowed the instructor to explain/re-explain topics and concepts if any misunderstandings were identified during Step 3. Alternatively, the lecture continued to new topics. If time was up, the questions were postponed to the next lecture to serve as a prior knowledge probe. In Step 5, the closure of the lecture, slides containing the topics to be covered in the next session were presented to the students. Students also had access to these slides on the LMS after the conclusion of the lecture (as part of Step 6) so that they could use it, in conjunction with their textbooks, to prepare for the next lecture.

4 Methodology

A case study research design was used to evaluate the effectiveness of the proposed instructional strategy in facilitating the integration of the SRS to support

Table 1. Active-engagement instructional strategy for effective SRS integration

Timeline	Activities	Activity rationale	Media
Step 1 (5 min)	*Instructor*		
	Ask reading questions	Draw attention	SRS
	Probe prior learning	Probe prior knowledge	SRS
	Students		
	Answer reading questions	Focus into the lecture. Recall prior knowledge	SRS
Step 2 (15 min)	*Instructor*		
	Display picture or video	Visualize concepts	Picture Video
	Explain new concepts	Clarify topics and concepts	Slides
Step 3 (5 min)	*Instructor*		
	Ask new skill questions	Confirm learning	SRS
	Facilitate group discussions	Reinforce learning	SRS
	Clarify concepts	Clarify topics and concepts	Slides
	Students		
	Participate in group discussions	Students learn from one another	SRS
	Answer questions individually	Confirm understanding	SRS
Step 4	Repeat Steps 1 to 3 (if time available), or conclude with Step 5		
Step 5	*Instructor*		
	Review topic(s) for next lecture	Conclude lecture	Slides
Step 6	*Students*		
	Complete homework	Prepare for next lecture	Textbook Slides

student engagement. Case studies are deemed suitable to describe the intervention as well as the real-life context in which the intervention took place [25]. The population for this study included all 23 students enrolled for a 13-week undergraduate CS course at the rural campus of a South African university. This course had three 50-min lecture sessions per week. The sampling strategy can be regarded as convenient [11] since the researcher was also responsible for teaching this particular course. Of the 23 students who participated in the study, 19 (83 %) were male and four (17 %) were female. This paper shares information from a larger study (conducted over a 13-week semester) and will only focus on the 5-week period directly related to the initial implementation and evaluation of the proposed active-engagement instructional strategy.

The data was collected by means of participant observations and a group interview. The researcher recorded his observation notes in a journal at the end of each class session. The notes contained information about the effectiveness of the instructional strategy, students' interaction with the SRS, and interactions between students during the in-class group discussions in order to find answers to the quiz questions. At the end of the study, students were invited to participate in a group interview to reveal more insights regarding their experiences. Six students volunteered to participate in the group interview. Content analysis was employed on the narrative data collected from the group interview to condense responses to a series of canonical quotes so that each quote represented a phrase [12]. The observation notes were used to supplement the group interview data.

5   Reflection on Instructional Strategy

The main objective of the instructional strategy as set out in Table 1 was to provide an overall structure for the effective integration of an SRS in a classroom environment aimed at enhancing student engagement. The inclusion of pre-lecture SRS questions not only provided the students with an opportunity to evaluate their prior knowledge [17] but also gave the instructor a better idea of the problematic concepts he should focus on during the mini-lecture to follow [19]. This strategy also allowed the instructor to dedicate more time to helping students develop their understanding with less time spent lecturing. After the mini-lectures, students were given opportunities to apply and demonstrate what they had learnt by answering post-lecture SRS questions. Students received immediate feedback on their responses and, where necessary, more clarification was provided if some students gave an incorrect answer to a specific question. The strategy also provided students with some structure for their homework as they knew exactly what content to prepare for the next class. By making the lecture slides available on the LMS prior to the lecture session, students could pay more attention during the mini-lectures since they did not have to take detailed notes in class.

As Morice et al. [20] noted, students are more engaged when they can interact with one another to exchange ideas and solutions for their answers to quiz questions. Students were therefore encouraged to discuss the SRS questions before submitting their individual responses — enhancing both active and participatory learning. The strategy also allowed for a balanced time allocation between discussing and answering SRS questions and conducting other lecture activities.

The incorporation of a variety of timed learning activities (SRS quizzes, discussions and mini-lectures) during one class session helped to keep the students motivated and engaged, enabling them to learn more during each lecture [7]. The inclusion of pictures and videos as part of the mini-lectures and as introductions to some of the SRS questions also helped the students to form a link between theory and practice — improving students' understanding of theoretical concepts. This variation of learning activities also made learning possible for both verbally adept students and those who are more comfortable with anonymous participation [6].

The implementation of the proposed instructional strategy was not without challenges. In setting up the SRS quizzes the instructor had to make sure that the individual quiz questions were properly aligned with the focus of the lecture. He also had to anticipate which concepts students were more likely to struggle with so that these could be covered in the questions. The instant feedback he received regarding students' understanding of concepts (through their responses to the SRS questions) also required him to change the instruction focus on the fly [4].

Overall, the instructional strategy helped to segment each lecture session into manageable sub-sections and supported the easy facilitation of student engagement activities. Students were regularly motivated to pay attention and participate in active learning by discussing and finding answers to quiz questions.

6   Conclusions

This paper reports on how a tailor-made active-engagement instructional strategy was used to facilitate the effective integration of an SRS in an undergraduate CS classroom. The instructional strategy helped to segment lecture sessions into manageable chunks of activities aimed at enhancing student engagement. The SRS served as an effective stimulus to support student engagement, particularly, by motivating students to participate in active learning activities and answer quiz questions. For future research, similar studies can be conducted to validate these findings and refine the proposed instructional strategy, in particular studies that include large class sizes and/or populations from different academic disciplines and course levels. Although specific details regarding the custom mobile phone-based SRS used in this study falls outside the scope of this paper, it proved to be an invaluable tool in supporting the enhancement of student engagement during face-to-face class sessions. However, further research is needed to investigate the impact that the 'mobile' nature of the SRS used in this study could have on the proposed instructional strategy.

References

1. Allen, D., Tanner, K.: Infusing active learning into the large-enrollment Biology class: seven strategies, from the simple to complex. Cell Biol. Educ. **4**(4), 262–268 (2005)
2. Barkley, E.: Student Engagement Techniques. Jossey-Bass, San Francisco (2010)
3. Bergtrom, G.: Content vs. learning: an old dichotomy in science courses. J. Asynchronous Learn. Netw. **15**(1), 33–44 (2011)

4. Cain, J., Black, E.P., Rohr, J.: An audience response system strategy to improve student motivation, attention, and feedback. Am. J. Pharm. Educ. **73**(2), 21 (2009)
5. Cubric, M., Jefferies, A.: The benefits and challenges of large-scale deployment of electronic voting systems: University student views from across different subject groups. Comput. Educ. **87**, 98–111 (2015)
6. Efstathiou, N., Bailey, C.: Promoting active learning using audience response system in large bioscience classes. Nurse Educ. Today **32**(1), 91–95 (2012)
7. Freeman, S., Eddy, S.L., McDonough, M., Smith, M.K., Okoroafor, N., Jordt, H., Wenderoth, M.P.: Active learning increases student performance in science, engineering, and mathematics. Proc. Natl. Acad. Sci. **111**(23), 8410–8415 (2014)
8. Gagné, R.: The Conditions of Learning and the Theory of Instruction, 4th edn. Holt, Rinehart and Winston, New York (1985)
9. Gleason, B.L., Peeters, M.J., Resman-Targoff, B.H., Karr, S., McBane, S., Kelley, K., Thomas, T., Denetclaw, T.H.: An active-learning strategies primer for achieving ability-based educational outcomes. Am. J. Pharm. Educ. **75**(9), 186 (2011)
10. Green, M., Sulbaran, T.: Motivation assessment instrument for virtual reality scheduling simulator. In: Reeves, T., Yamashita, S. (eds.) Proceedings of E-Learn: World Conference on E-Learning in Corporate, Government, Healthcare, and Higher Education, pp. 45–50. Association for the Advancement of Computing in Education (AACE), Chesapeake (2006)
11. Greenstein, T.N.: Methods of Family Research. Sage Publications, Thousand Oaks (2006)
12. Hall, R.H., Collier, H.L., Thomas, M.L., Hilgers, M.G.: A student response system for increasing engagement, motivation, and learning in high enrollment lectures. In: Proceedings of the Eleventh Americas Conference on Information Systems (AMCIS), p. 255. Curran Associates Inc., Omaha (2005)
13. Han, J.H.: Closing the missing links and opening the relationships among the factors: a Literature review on the use of clicker technology using the 3P model. Educ. Technol. Soc. **17**(4), 150–168 (2014)
14. Hwang, I., Wong, K., Lam, S.L., Lam, P.: Student response (clicker) systems: Preferences of Biomedical Physiology students in Asian classes. Electron. J. e-Learn. **13**(5), 347–356 (2015)
15. Kolb, A.Y., Kolb, D.: The Kolb learning style inventory – version 3.1 (2005) Technical Specifications. http://learningfromexperience.com/media/2010/08/tech_spec_lsi.pdf
16. Kuh, G.D., Kinzie, J., Buckley, J.A., Bridges, B.K., Hayek, J.C.: Piecing Together the Student Success Puzzle. Wiley Subscription Services at Jossey-Bass, San Francisco (2007)
17. Lee, J.W., Shih, M.: Teaching practices for the student response system at National Taiwan University. Int. J. Autom. Smart Technol. **5**(3), 145–150 (2015)
18. Linnenbrink, E.A., Pintrich, P.R.: Role of affect in cognitive processing in academic contexts. In: Dai, D., Sternburg, R. (eds.) Motivation, Emotion, and Cognition, pp. 57–87. Lawrence Erlbaum Associates, Mahwah (2004)
19. LoPresto, M.C., Slater, T.F.: A new comparison of active learning strategies to traditional lectures for teaching college Astronomy. J. Astronom. Earth Sci. Educ. **3**(1), 59–76 (2016)
20. Morice, J., Michinov, N., Delaval, M., Sideridou, A., Ferrières, V.: Comparing the effectiveness of peer instruction to individual learning during a chromatography course. J. Comput. Assist. Learn. **31**(6), 722–733 (2015)
21. Stefani, L.: Engaging our students in the learning process: some points for consideration. Int. J. Scholarsh. Teach. Learn. **2**(1), 1–6 (2008)

22. Ulbig, S.: Engaging the unengaged: using visual images to enhance students' "Poli Sci 101" experience. Polit. Sci. Polit. **42**(2), 385–391 (2009)
23. Williams, M., Burden, R.L.: Psychology for Language Teachers. Cambridge University Press, Cambridge (1997)
24. Wodi, S.W.: The concept of educational technology: problems and prospects of information and communication technology (ICT) in Nigeria. Int. J. Afr. Stud. **2009**(1), 4–10 (2009)
25. Yin, R.: Case Study Research: Design and Methods. Sage Publishing, Beverly Hills (1994)

Teaching Operating Systems: Just Enough Abstraction

Philip Machanick(✉)

Department of Computer Science, Rhodes University, Grahamstown, South Africa
p.machanick@ru.ac.za

Abstract. There are two major approaches to teaching operating systems: conceptual and detailed. I explore the middle ground with an approach designed to equip students with the tools to explore detail later as the need arises, without requiring the time and grasp of detail needed to understand a full OS implementation. To meet those goals, I apply various strategies to different concepts, for example, faking the detail and using techniques from computer architecture simulation. The course aims to give students a better sense of how things work than a conceptual approach without the time required for a full implementation-based course.

Keywords: Computer science education · Action learning

1 Introduction

Operating systems (OS) courses divide roughly into a general survey of OS features and variations — a conceptual approach — and those that dive into detail. The latter category includes use of a real OS (usually these days one with free source such as the Linux kernel), or an OS designed specifically for teaching and research such as MINIX [23].

At Rhodes University (South Africa's smallest research-intensive university), the third year OS module in a Computer Science major takes 4 weeks each with 5 lectures and one practical (of 3 h), and students usually take two third-year subjects, allowing 20 hours per subject per week. Timetabled contact time of 8 hours leaves 12 hours a week for independent work. That is insufficient time to go into much detail of a full-scale or even cut-back OS such as MINIX.

Since most programming courses at Rhodes are taught using higher-level languages that manage memory and abstract away all the details of the machine, one of my goals in the OS module is to reinforce exposure to the machine layer and notions like machine addresses, only seen in a small part of our curriculum. Finally, learning really requires some exposure to how professionals in the real world work [11] — so some aspect of developing code typical of OS internals is necessary for a real understanding of the area.

The approach I describe here attempts to achieve some of the benefits of a full-scale implementation-oriented OS course without the time commitment required to do so. Strategies used include:

© Springer International Publishing AG 2016
S. Gruner (Ed.): SACLA 2016, CCIS 642, pp. 104–111, 2016.
DOI: 10.1007/978-3-319-47680-3_10

Faking part of the system: e.g., to illustrate file system variations like a file allocation table (FAT) [5] or inodes [13], I implement RAM-based structures illustrating how the disk-based pointers would be organized;

Architecture simulation techniques: trace-driven simulation [24] allows a small part of a system to be simulated provided a trace of memory accesses is available to drive the simulation.

In the remainder of this paper, I provide background to relevant educational theory and other approaches to teaching operating systems. I go on to explain the design of my course followed by more detail. I share experience from running the course this way and wrap up with conclusions.

2   Background

Earlier theories of learning focused on cognition. The constructivist model, for example, inspired by the work of Piaget [18], was based on different levels of sophistication of building mental models [3], similarly to Bloom's Taxonomy, which ranks different levels of problem solving in terms of sophistication [10]. Social constructivism adds to constructivism the notion that there is a social aspect in learning — that construction of knowledge, while a cognitive process, is influenced by interactions with others [7]. The social construction model goes a step further and divorces learning from cognitive models, focusing instead on how knowledge is created by social interaction [4,11].

Whether we accept a cognitive view of learning or change our focus to a purely social model, the consensus is that learning requires *doing* — a strong argument against a pure survey approach. Understanding an OS requires overcoming a number of misconceptions [16]; it is hard to see how such misconceptions can be overcome without a strongly practical component to an OS course.

In the early 2000s, *instructional operating systems* such as Nachos, Topsy and Yalnix were designed to abstract key concepts to simplify teaching [2]; Pintos is more recent [17]. Some teach the Linux kernel [6,8,15] and others Windows internals [21]. All these whole-system approaches require significant time to learn the basics before getting into detail.

3   Course Design

For the Rhodes OS course, the approach I take is to cover major ideas in lectures and drill down to implementation in practicals. I provide detailed notes [12] and work through examples and concepts in class, interspersed with C programming techniques with the aim of preparing the class for the next practical exercise.

Main headings follow a typical OS course outline:

The Kernel
- system calls and interprocess communication (IPC)
- what goes in kernel *vs.* user space

- microkernels *vs.* monolithic kernels
- what the kernel does

Schedulers
- theoretical approaches
- practical approaches
- examples: Windows and Linux schedulers

IO and Files (including inodes and FAT file organiation)
- device interface
- files and devices
- performance (including speed as well as reliability and fault tolerance)
- protection and security
- other device types

Memory (mostly virtual memory (VM) using pages)
- history and rationale for memory management
- key concepts of VM
- more advanced concepts
- examples including real machines and translation lookaside buffers (TLBs)

Parallel Programming (including Pthreads, UNIX-style processes and IPC)
- concepts
- launching
- sharing and communication
- synchronization
- distributed systems and the cloud
- parallel programming hazards

All of this can relatively easily be covered with a survey approach; there are good OS texts that do just that [22, 23]. The challenge is how to approach these topics in more depth without a full implementation of an OS — or more specifically, in a relatively short time.

The approach I take is to implement small fragments of an OS that can be designed, implemented and tested independently so that a whole OS does not need to exist or be understood to do practical work. I describe here two major approaches: implementing a small, simplified subset of functionality in a way that can be tested in isolation and using trace-driven simulation to implement functionality that would normally be driven by execution of user-level code.

I also illustrate user-level functionality by showing how to use system calls and standard libraries that implement functionality that illustrates core concepts like synchronization and parallel programming.

3.1   Small Subset

File system concepts can be implemented at least to some extent without the whole OS. The key concepts I want to illustrate in the course are the way the file system can be layered (as in a UNIX-style file system with a virtual file system on top of which the actual file system is implemented) and the pointer structure of an inode or FAT file system.

3.2   Trace-Driven Simulation

To implement trace-driven simulation, I generate traces using Pin [9], which I use to generate a trace file out of a user-level executable containing a record of instructions fetched (as their address) and addresses read and written. To approximate the effect of interrupts, I add into the trace files artificially-generated records of interrupts, each with the latency of handling the interrupt.

3.3   User-Level Examples

Synchronization, process launching and threads, while good to understand at the kernel level, are hard enough at the user level that I consider it adequate to use user-level coding for these examples. Areas covered include Pthreads [14], UNIX-style `fork` and various modes of IPC (shared memory, memory maps and pipes). I also review various synchronization primitives including mutexes, spinlocks and barriers — including efficiency and implementation issues. The class does practical work to implement examples that are designed to illuminate principles.

4   Course Detail

To illustrate how all this works in practice, I provide examples of practical problems set, covering the various techniques. For a simplified subset that can be tested in isolation, I use the example of implementation of a file system. For trace-driven simulation, I use two examples: scheduling and VM. Finally, I illustrate the use of user-level examples with parallel programming.

4.1   Small Subset: File System

To illustrate how a file system is implemented, I provide code that crudely approximates to the split between a virtual and actual file system. A virtual file system (VFS) was originally designed to hide implementation details such as whether the file system is local or remote [20]; in my approximation to this, a low-level file system implements block operations on a device simulated in RAM that can be used without needing to know where blocks are stored, capturing the essence of a VFS without the complexity. This simplified VFS (Fig. 1) allows implementing operations on an inode-based system to create, remove or extend a file — or doing the same using FAT. A bitmap representing free or allocated blocks provides exercises in bitwise operations. Conceptual challenges students must deal with include understanding that file system pointers are not the same as memory pointers (they refer to device blocks, not bytes in main memory) and that data structures used to represent files can be complex to navigate.

Figure 2 illustrates my minimalist inode structure. It contains a pointer to a data structure defining the VFS in which it is contained; all other "pointers" are disk block numbers, as determined by the VFS. The VFS knows that a file system contains certain overheads — directories, top-level file pointers — and the actual file system initializes it with sizes of these overheads.

```
typedef struct FS_attributes {
 char fstype[FSTYPEN]; // type of FS
 blocksize_t blocksize;
 blockpointer_t numblocks;
 blockpointer_t maxfiles;
 blockpointer_t bitmapSize; // in blocks
 blockpointer_t directory; // must be followed by first_fileptr
 blockpointer_t first_fileptr; // must be followed by freespacelist
 blockpointer_t freespacelist; // must be followed by first_data_block
 blockpointer_t first_data_block;
 blockpointer_t mappedblocks; // minus attributes, directories, etc.
} FS_attributes;
```

Fig. 1. Highly simplified VFS structure. It includes just enough detail to find blocks that are either system overheads such as directories or file blocks.

```
struct Inode {
 // attributes: permissions and path
 char path[NAMELENGTH]; // byte 0 nonzero if a valid inode
 unsigned int permissions;
 unsigned int size;
 FS_t *filesystem;
 blocksize_t blocksize; // property of file system but fixed once set
 blockpointer_t direct_pointers[NUMBERDIRECT]; // size must be constant
 blockpointer_t single_indirect_pointers; // points to FS pointer block
};
```

Fig. 2. Simplified inode. I omit many details (e.g., timestamps, link count).

4.2   Trace-Driven Simulation: Scheduling and Virtual Memory

Pin allows me to produce trace files that mark memory addresses as one of read ("R"), write ("W") or instruction fetch ("I"). I add in fake interrupts at regular intervals, each of fixed latency ("X"; the number in the file in this case is the latency, not an address). Here is an example of an extract from a trace file:

```
I 0xb78882a0
W 0xbfd913d4
X 0x3E8
R 0xbfd91564
```

In this example, there is an interrupt with latency (in clock ticks) $0x3E8$ $= 1000_{10}$. Each instruction fetch is assumed to add 1 clock tick. If I am not simulating memory hierarchy, reads and writes are fully pipelined (add no latency).

To create a workload, my simulator reads in a list of trace file names that represent a process per trace file.

Scheduling To keep things simple I assume that all interrupts are only processed once a waiting process reaches the head of a single wait queue. To simulate scheduling, it is only necessary to process instruction fetches and interrupts from the trace file; memory reads and writes are ignored. If a process is interrupted, it goes to the wait queue until it reaches the head of the wait queue and after than becomes ready only after its latency has expired. This framework allows comparison of variations, e.g., round-robin scheduling and multilevel feedback queues (as in Windows [19] and some versions of Linux [1]). While avoiding the true complexity of a scheduler, in the spirit of "just enough abstraction", students see the main issues.

Virtual Memory VM is even harder to code at the true hardware level than scheduling, since implementation has to match hardware functionality closely. Trace-driven simulation simplifies exploring variations like alternative page table structures and the functioning of a TLB. By including reasonable numbers for latency of operations, even if the detail is not fully simulated, it is possible to illustrate the performance impact of design choices. In addition, giving the students an example and asking them to implement a variation makes it possible for them to get a sense of how a real system is implemented. Given a single-level page table, implementing a two-level page table provides a reasonably challenging programming example. Another example of similar levels of difficulty and insights is evaluating the effect of a TLB.

4.3   User-Level: Parallel Programming

Finally, to illustrate concepts related to processes, threads and IPC, user-level programming can provide good insights. Examples I use include:

- *Threads vs. processes*: given an example of one, recode using the other;
- *Shared memory vs. memory maps*: again, recode in the other type;
- *Synchronization*: focus on a subset of types of options (barrier, mutex, etc.);
- *IPC primitives*: coding using pipes adds another dimension.

To fit the limited time, I vary what is covered in lectures *vs.* in practicals.

5   Experience

My experience of explaining concepts like multilevel page tables and TLBs in lectures is that they are very difficult concepts to grasp in the abstract. Parallel programming is another area where doing is really required to learn. Some areas like scheduling are easier to learn conceptually, though conceptual texts present scheduling in a theoretical way unrelated to real OS design [22]. A case study of Linux scheduler evolution is more interesting and also exposes students to the debate about free versus proprietary software (why did Linux evolve so fast, while the Windows scheduler has not changed much in overall design since Windows NT?). It is difficult to make this sort of debate come to life without the students having a feel for how things are actually implemented.

That students battle with low-level concepts like pointers is not a reason to avoid them. If they must learn them somewhere, an OS course — at the interface between hardware and software — is a logical place to introduce them. An OS course also illustrates how pointers can differ in different layers of the system (file system pointers refer to disk blocks not bytes in memory).

6   Conclusion

The real test of any course is whether it helps the students grow — and that can be hard to measure in the short term particularly with a final-year course. The class generally finds the course challenging, as we move rapidly to new concepts and they are drawing on a very limited prior exposure to low-level coding in C (one 3-week module in second year). However it would be a lot more challenging were the course to be based on a real fully-implemented OS.

Students who have taken the course and return after a few years with reports on its usefulness will be the real test of the value of the approach; the course has not been running long enough in its current form for such an evaluation. My own experience is that students taught using this just enough abstraction approach have a better appreciation of implementation and design issues than those taught using a purely theoretical approach.

As the course evolves, I plan on varying the detail — changing for example where I use the three strategies (small subset, trace-driven simulations) and user-level coding — to find the right mix. In the meantime I invite others grappling with finding the right balance between abstraction and detail to share ideas.

References

1. Aas, J.: Understanding the Linux 2.6. 8.1 CPU scheduler. Technical report, Silicon Graphics Inc. (2005). https://github.com/bdaehlie/linux-cpu-scheduler-docs/blob/master/linux_cpu_scheduler.pdf
2. Anderson, C.L., Nguyen, M.: A survey of contemporary instructional operating systems for use in undergraduate courses. J. Comput. Sci. Coll. **21**(1), 183–190 (2005). http://dl.acm.org/citation.cfm?id=1088791.1088822
3. Ben-Ari, M.: Constructivism in computer science education. In: Proceedings 29th SIGCSE Technical Symposium on Computer Science Education, pp. 257–261. SIGCSE 1998. ACM, New York (1998)
4. Bijker, W.E., Hughes, T.P., Pinch, T., Douglas, D.G.: The Social Construction of Technological Systems: New Directions in the Sociology and History of Technology. MIT Press, Cambridge (2012)
5. Chen, J.B., Endo, Y., Chan, K., Mazières, D., Dias, A., Seltzer, M., Smith, M.D.: The measured performance of personal computer operating systems. ACM Trans. Comput. Syst. **14**(1), 3–40 (1996)
6. Dall, C., Nieh, J.: Teaching operating systems using code review. In: Proceeding 45th ACM Technical Symposium on Computer Science Education, pp. 549–554. SIGCSE 2014, ACM (2014)
7. Kim, B.: Social constructivism. Emerg. Perspect. Learn. Teach. Technol. **1**(1), 16 (2001)

8. Laadan, O., Nieh, J., Viennot, N.: Structured Linux kernel projects for teaching operating systems concepts. In: Proceedings of the 42nd ACM Technical Symposium on Computer Science Education, pp. 287–292. SIGCSE 2011 (2011)
9. Luk, C.K., Cohn, R., Muth, R., Patil, H., Klauser, A., Lowney, G., Wallace, S., Reddi, V.J., Hazelwood, K.: Pin: Building customized program analysis tools with dynamic instrumentation. In: Proceedings 2005 ACM SIGPLAN Conference on Programming Language Design and Implementation, pp. 190–200. PLDI 2005 (2005)
10. Machanick, P.: Experience of applying Blooms Taxonomy in three courses. In: Proceedings Southern African Computer Lecturers Association Conference, pp. 135–144 (2000)
11. Machanick, P.: A social construction approach to computer science education. Comput. Sci. Educ. **17**(1), 1–20 (2007)
12. Machanick, P.: 2OS: more programming from the machine up. Rhodes University, Grahamstown (2016). http://homes.cs.ru.ac.za/philip/Courses/CS3-OS/Cs3ToOS.pdf
13. McKusick, M.K., Joy, W.N., Leffler, S.J., Fabry, R.S.: A fast file system for UNIX. ACM Trans. Comput. Syst. **2**(3), 181–197 (1984)
14. Nichols, B., Buttlar, D., Farrell, J.: Pthreads programming: A POSIX standard for better multiprocessing. OReilly, Sebastopol (1996)
15. Nieh, J., Vaill, C.: Experiences teaching operating systems using virtual platforms and Linux. In: Proceedings 36th SIGCSE Technical Symposium on Computer Science Education, pp. 520–524. SIGCSE 2005 (2005)
16. Pamplona, S., Medinilla, N., Flores, P.: Exploring misconceptions of operating systems in an online course. In: Proceedings 13th Koli Calling International Conference on Computing Education Research, pp. 77–86. Koli Calling 2013 (2013)
17. Pfaff, B., Romano, A., Back, G.: The Pintos instructional operating system kernel. In: Proceedings 40th ACM Technical Symposium on Computer Science Education, pp. 453–457. SIGCSE 2009 (2009)
18. Piaget, J.: The Construction of Reality in the Child. Routledge, Milton Park (1954)
19. Pietrek, M.: Inside the windows scheduler. Dr. Dobbs J. **17**(8), 64–71 (1992). http://dl.acm.org/citation.cfm?id=134643.134652
20. Sandberg, R., Goldberg, D., Kleiman, S., Walsh, D., Lyon, B.: Design and implementation of the Sun network filesystem. In: Proceedings Summer USENIX Conference, pp. 119–130 (1985)
21. Schmidt, A., Polze, A., Probert, D.: Teaching operating systems: Windows kernel projects. In: Proceedings of the 41st ACM Technical Symposium on Computer Science Education, pp. 490–494. SIGCSE 2010 (2010)
22. Silberschatz, A., Galvin, P.B., Gagne, G.: Operating System Concepts, 9th edn. Wiley, Harlow (2012)
23. Tanenbaum, A.: Modern Operating Systems, 4th edn. Pearson, Harlow (2014)
24. Uhlig, R.A., Mudge, T.N.: Trace-driven memory simulation: A survey. ACM Comput. Surv. **29**(2), 128–170 (1997)

New Curricula

CS and IS Alumni Post-Graduate Course and Supervision Perceptions

André P. Calitz[(⊠)], Jean Greyling, and Arthur Glaum

Department of Computing Sciences, Nelson Mandela Metropolitan University,
Port Elizabeth, South Africa
{andre.calitz,jean.greyling,arthur.glaum}@nmmu.ac.za

Abstract. Stakeholders in academic departments at higher education institutions include faculty, alumni, advisory board members, current students and employers. Stakeholder analysis provides information that academic departments can utilise to evaluate their programme offerings, post-graduate supervision quality and programme relevance. This exploratory study focuses on CS&IS post-graduates' (alumni) perceptions of their education experience in a CS&IS department. The study further focuses on post-graduate courses they studied, their relevance in industry and if the academic programme adequately prepared them for a career in the ICT industry. The supervision of their post-graduate research was further investigated as well as their overall university experience. The results of the study indicate that the Department of CS&IS provided the relevant courses for employment in the ICT industry at the specific time they completed their studies. This research could assist academic departments in acquiring alumni feedback on their academic experience at an institution and improve post-graduate supervision practices.

Keywords: Post-graduate courses · Post-graduate supervision · Alumni study experience

1 Introduction

Academic departments at Higher Education Institutions (HEIs) are increasingly engaging with various stakeholders. The external stakeholders include alumni, employers, advisory board members and professional accreditation bodies. Stakeholder engagement ensures closer university and alumni/industry collaboration and liaison and is required for academic programme quality assurance. Stakeholder analysis refers to feedback obtained in various forms from stakeholders, specifically for programme quality evaluation and improvement.

A number of ICT related departments, such as Computer Science, Informatics, Information Systems (etc.) at academic institutions have established closer collaboration with industry. Industry advisory boards have been established at the academic institutions in order to address the industry ICT graduate skills requirements and establish closer collaboration [5]. The stakeholder engagement

S. Gruner (Ed.): SACLA 2016, CCIS 642, pp. 115–122, 2016.
DOI: 10.1007/978-3-319-47680-3_11

has further influenced computing curricula and the introduction of specific new courses, specifically at the post-graduate level.

Academic departments have used surveys, mailing lists, web-sites and social media, such as Facebook and LinkedIn, to maintain contact and acquire information specifically from graduates (alumni) working in industry [6,7,15]. Alumni tracking for programme quality assurance using web-based systems have become an important activity at HEIs [11]. Studies have also utilised alumni to meaningfully connect alumni to currently registered students [17]. Alumni further provide an important perspective and valuable contribution for the assessment of a department's academic programmes. Academic programmes have been restructured in response to international curricula [2,3] as well as recommendations by professional advisory boards and alumni [11,14].

Academic departments perform research, specifically at the post-graduate level and research supervision is an important academic process and practice. Successful and quality post-graduate research supervision is linked to study completion times and pass rates [9]. Post-graduate alumni feedback on their research supervision experiences are further important for academic departments and supervisors. Studies investigating the satisfaction ratings by alumni of research supervision emphasise the importance of continuous training and education of supervisors [9].

2   The Research Problem and Research Design

South Africa (SA) presently has 26 universities which have departments offering Information Technology (IT) related study programmes. Departments of Computer Science (CS) and Information Systems (IS) should utilise the information provided by stakeholders, such as advisory boards, employers and alumni, to evaluate their programme offerings. The research problem investigated in this study is based on the realisation that CS&IS departments in SA generally do not regularly survey post-graduate alumni to determine their post-graduate experience during their studies at the academic institution. Additionally the content of the CS&IS programme may not satisfy the requirements of industry and post-graduates (alumni) could identify additional courses and knowledge required by industry [6,12]. Further, CS&IS departments do not regularly ascertain the effectiveness of their post-graduate supervision by faculty.

The Nelson Mandela Metropolitan University (NMMU)'s Department of Computing Sciences offers CS and IS programmes. Post-graduate alumni are graduates who have completed either a BCom Honours, BSc Honours, MCom, MSc or PhD in Computer Science and Information Systems at NMMU. Post-graduate alumni would have had a supervisor(s) for their Honours treatise, Master's dissertation or PhD thesis. This exploratory study focused only on post-graduate alumni in the Department of Computing Sciences at NMMU.

The research question addressed in this study is:

– *What are the CS/IS alumni perceptions of their post-graduate studies?*

An alumni post-graduate questionnaire was compiled using a number of existing alumni questionnaires utilised in similar studies [4,12,16]. The NMMU post-graduate questionnaire consists of the following sections.

1. Degree details: Highest CS or IS degree, starting position, current position, years in industry;
2. Departmental post-graduate courses: Relevance of courses, suggested new courses;
3. Post-graduate experience: Positive and negative experiences, preparation for a career in ICT, supervision experience, suggestions for improvement; and
4. University experience: Positive and negative experiences, suggestions for improvement.

Sections 1 to 4 were all open-ended questions and qualitative in nature. A number of faculty in the Department of Computing Sciences and NMMU Business School evaluated the questionnaire and suggested changes and improvements. A pilot study was conducted among three alumni working at NMMU to validate the questionnaire initially.

The questionnaire was captured using the NMMU on-line survey tool. The next step in the research process was contacting post-graduate alumni who graduated and worked in industry. Social networks are increasingly being used and a large number of graduates are on social networks such as Facebook and LinkedIn. The Department of Computing Sciences created a profile on Facebook. The first call for participation was distributed via Facebook ($n = 1800$), LinkedIn and a departmental alumni e-mail address list ($n = 600$). The *snowball sampling technique* was utilised, requesting participants, through a referral network, to forward the survey request to other possible respondents. A total of 39 alumni completed the survey over a three week period and two requests for participation. The qualitative results were thematically analysed.

3 Alumni Surveys

Alumni surveys assess whether graduates feel that the academic programme adequately prepared them for their IT careers. McGourty et al. [12] conducted two surveys to establish alumni perceptions on the quality of their education. The surveys focused on undergraduate experience and employment. The results indicated surveying alumni is an effective method for gathering information regarding their perceptions of job preparation, employment, skills development and programme effectiveness.

Academic departments must continuously monitor the employability of their graduates in order to evaluate the effectiveness of their academic programme offerings. Lending and Mathieu [11] conducted a web survey amongst IS graduates ($n = 173$) and found that the programme prepared them well for software implementation, business process modelling and database solutions. The gaps identified in the programme were IT project management, analysis of technical solutions and non-technical writing skills. The value of the academic programmes to graduates, career placement (employability) and continued educational needs are areas departments must continuously investigate [19].

It is important that departments manage the information of their alumni, gathering information on alumni perceptions of programme offerings and employability of the graduates. Responses to alumni surveys have varied and researchers are increasingly investigating additional methods of acquiring the relevant information, utilising social media platforms such as Facebook and LinkedIn. Researchers have further implemented web-crawling algorithms, specifically focused crawlers to search for alumni information on the web [7]. Mijic [13] implemented a web-based system that was used as an efficient tool for communication between a HEI and its alumni. The system collected and analysed alumni related data that were used for different purposes, including improvement of academic programmes.

On-line surveys however still remain the most popular method of obtaining relevant information from alumni [4]. The surveys focus on obtaining information regarding programme quality and relevance, employability of the graduates and alumni departmental and university experiences. Generally alumni addresses are obtained from the university's Alumni Office, departmental Facebook pages and LinkedIn. Bulk e-mails are sent to the alumni requesting them to complete the surveys [4,12]. Various departments have established alumni groups on Facebook and LinkedIn to maintain contact with ICT graduates, track graduate destinations and engage with graduates in industry [18].

Limited studies focused on post-graduate surveys specifically. The majority focused on general alumni surveys [4,7,12,14]. Post-graduate course offerings and research topics are important factors influencing the employability of the post-graduates. Research supervision is specific to research projects conducted in post-graduate studies. Supervision research is an extensive specialised research area and will be discussed in more detail.

4   CS&IS Post-Graduate Courses and Supervision

Universities nationally and internationally generally follow the ACM and IEEE international CS&IS curricula — Computer Science departments follow the ACM CS2013 [2] and Information Systems departments the ACM IS2010 [3]. The curriculum guidelines suggest core and elective courses, credit values and possible career opportunities linked with specific subject combinations [3]. The CS2013 and IS2010 curricula guidelines specify specific core and elective courses. Departments of CS&IS in SA offer a variety of post-graduate (Honours/4th year) courses depending on the institution. A detailed comparison of individual departmental course offerings in comparison to the recommended curricula guidelines of the CS2013 [2] and IS2010 [3] is beyond the scope of this paper.

Good supervisory practices assist students to complete their research successfully and obtain their qualifications timeously [1]. The quality of research supervision is linked to study completion times and rates [9]. Supervisors and students must both have a clear understanding of their roles, expectations and responsibilities. Supervision is an established practice and research area and numerous studies have identified best practices in research student supervision, describing the responsibilities of both supervisor and student [1,9]. The responsibilities of an effective supervisor include providing advice on the research topic, the methodology, progress and timeous and constructive feedback on written work [1].

Kiley [9] reported on studies investigating the satisfaction ratings by students of research supervision and emphasized the importance of continuous training and education of supervisors. Research studies conducted on alumni's supervision experience have further indicated that students who completed their studies timeously generally felt satisfied with their supervision and that they appreciated regular meetings [8,12]. Keeping a *graduate student log* [1] or an e-Portfolio [10] has also been identified as a practice that contributes to successful supervision.

5   Alumni Post-Graduate Survey Results

The *Alumni Post-graduate* survey ($n = 39$) was completed by NMMU CS and IS post-graduates working in the ICT industry. Open-ended questions were used and thematically analysed. Standard biographical data such as gender and race were not included in the survey and the provision of names and personal information were optional in order to encourage reliable and honest feedback. The survey was completed by Honours ($n = 28$), Masters ($n = 9$) and Doctoral ($n = 2$) students.

Generally the respondents experienced their post-graduate studies in a very positive light, with some describing it as the highlight of their study careers. The most important themes that were identified are the following.

Challenging: As expected, most graduates remember the big effort they had to put in and acknowledge that this was an important part of their preparation for industry. Only one graduate said that the challenge was not big enough.

Beneficial: The general feedback is positive towards the content of what was taught, preparing graduates well for industry.

Enjoyable and interesting: It is interesting to note how often the fun aspect of the learning experience was highlighted. This could be attributed to the fact that the students have their own laboratory, a positive working environment as well as the fact that many tasks are done with peers. The aspect of interaction with fellow students is definitely a contributory factor to the enjoyment of postgraduate studies.

Team spirit: Amongst students as well as with academics. This includes a positive energetic atmosphere in the post-graduate laboratory that encourages learning; new friendships being formed during the year; the value of team work, whether formal or informal; and a more 'mature' interaction with academics in the department, including regular social interaction.

Supportive academic staff: A very strong thread throughout the responses is the positive impact academic, technical and administrative staff had on their experience as post-graduate students. Respondents specifically appreciate the high level of interaction with staff as well as the quality inputs they were getting from staff during their studies; and

Research activities: For specifically Masters and PhD students, the aspects linked to research such as travelling and presenting papers at conferences is highlighted as an important preparation for industry.

Although the negative feedback was limited, one student described post-graduate studies as *"the worst experience of my life"*, however no explanation is provided. One respondent indicated that a more flexible inter-discipline choice of honours modules would have been appreciated and a few respondents mentioned that they did not enjoy the 'free' hours they had to work in the department (3–5 h per week) mainly as student assistants. However others saw this as a positive aspect.

An interesting recommendation regarding the improvement of the postgraduate programme is related to interaction with industry. This includes more industry guest lectures, industry related research projects and internships. An interesting issue was raised by one respondent regarding the research topics available to students. A tension was identified between topics that are beneficial to the careers of a students versus topics related to areas that were driven by research funding.

This emphasis on industry interaction highlights the fact that students are aware that their ultimate goal would be employment after their studies. In a question related to how postgraduate studies prepared them for their career, a very important aspect of postgraduate studies is highlighted. In addition to positive feedback regarding the academic foundation provided by certain modules and the training in technical skills, a big emphasis was put on the soft skills acquired.

The following findings relate to post-graduate modules. The module that clearly stand out as generally valuable is *Project Management* $(n = 15)$, with others including *Human Computer Interaction* $(n = 7)$, *Research Methodology and Project* $(n = 6)$, *Data Warehousing* $(n = 5)$, *Databases* $(n = 5)$ and *Advanced Programming* $(n = 7)$. Four respondents were positive about all their modules. The two modules that were highlighted by most respondents as not valuable are *Computer Graphics* $(n = 8)$ and *Machine Learning* $(n = 7)$.

The supervision process is a complex task and requires substantial commitment from both the supervisor and student. The supervision process is open to negotiation and change depending on the supervisor and student involved, ensuring that the student makes good progress towards completion.

In this study, the alumni were generally positive and indicated that they were satisfied with the supervision process and the commitment of their supervisors. An aspect of supervision that was highlighted by many respondents was the 'personality match' between student and supervisor. It was stated that a healthy working relationship made a big contribution towards a successful outcome.

Although limited, the problems highlighted were that supervisors being too busy and therefore not involved enough with the research and one respondent felt that the pressure from the supervisor could have been more for better preparation for industry. One respondent had a very traumatic experience which nearly resulted in a 'mental breakdown'. Students also valued supervisors who had an understanding for their personal challenges and showed a caring attitude while maintaining a professional relationship.

Limited feedback was received from respondents regarding their general experiences at the university. A few suggestions included more access to bursaries as well as interdisciplinary interaction on a formal and social level.

6   Conclusions

Alumni are a rich source of information about programme quality and industry trends [4]. Departments should gather information from all key stakeholders regarding the effectiveness and quality of their academic programme and services [5,6]. Alumni surveys can provide information relating to academic programme quality and relevance, experiences, participation in institutional activities and specifically employment success, i.e. finding work [12]. Maintaining contact with alumni is essential for obtaining information on course relevance, graduate destinations and industry requirements [18]. Departments are utilising social media platforms such as Facebook to establish alumni groups, maintaining contact with graduates and position of employment [18].

This exploratory study provides additional supporting evidence regarding post-graduate perceptions and experiences. The results highlight the importance of relevant post-graduate courses and quality supervision. An important finding is that most alumni participating in this survey indicated that they were satisfied with the course offerings and the quality of supervision. Future research will include extending this exploratory study to include more recently graduated alumni, investigating continuous supervisor training and education and researching future ICT skills requirements.

References

1. Abiddin, N.Z., Hassan, A., Ahmad, A.R.: Research student supervision: an approach to good supervisory practice. Open Educ. J. **2**, 11–16 (2009)
2. ACM: CS2013 Computer Science Curriculum 2013: Final Report. Tech. rep. (2013)
3. ACM: IS2010 curriculum guidelines for undergraduate degree programs in information systems. Tech. rep. (2010)
4. Beidler, J.: Assessment: an alumni survey. In: Proceedings ASEE/IEEE Frontiers in Education Conference, Boston, USA, November 2002
5. Calitz, A.P., Greyling, J.H., Cullen, M.D.M.: S.A. industry ICT graduate skills requirements. In: Proceedings SACLA 2014, Port Elizabeth, SA (2014)
6. Calitz, A.P., Greyling, J.H., Cullen, M.D.M.: S.A. ICT graduate skills requirements. In: Proceedings SACLA 2015, Johannesburg, SA (2015)
7. Gonçalves, G.R., Ferreira, A.A., Tavares de Assis, G.T., Tavares, A.I.: Gathering alumni information from a web social network. In: IEEE 9th Latin American Web Congress (LA-WEB), pp. 100–108 (2014)

8. Guppy, N., Trew, M.: Graduate student experience at UBC – an assessment: Final report. Tech. rep. University of British Columbia (1995)

9. Kiley, M.: Developments in research supervisor training: causes and responses. Stud. High. Educ. **36**(5), 585–599 (2011)

10. Le, Q.: E-portfolio for enhancing graduate research supervision. Qual. Assur. Educ. **20**(1), 54–65 (2012)

11. Lending, D., Mathieu, R.G.: Workforce preparation and ABET assessment. In: Proceedings 2010 ACM Special Interest Group on Management Information Systems, Vancouver, Canada, May 2010

12. McGourty, J., Besterfield, M., Shuman, L., Wolfe, H.: Improving academic programs by capitalizing on alumni's perceptions and experiences. In: Proceedings 29th ASEE/IEEE Frontiers in Education Conference, San Juan, Puerto Rico, November 1999

13. Mijic, D.: Design, implementation, and evaluation of a web-based system for alumni data collection. E Soc. J. Res. Appl. **3**(2), 25–32 (2012)

14. Mijic, D., Jankovic, D.: Towards improvement of the study programme quality: alumni tracking information system. In: Kocarev, L. (ed.) ICT Innovations 2011. Advances in Intelligent and Soft Computing, vol. 150, pp. 291–300. Springer, Heidelberg (2012)

15. Schlesinger, W., Cervera, A., Pérez-Cabañero, C.: Sticking with your university: the importance of satisfaction, trust, image and shared values. Stud. High. Educ. 1–17 (2016)

16. Schneider, S.C., Niederjohn, R.J.: Assessing student learning outcomes using graduating senior exit surveys and alumni surveys. In: Proceedings IEEE Frontiers of Education Conference, vol. 1 (1995)

17. Shannon, C.A., Kiper, J., Rebelsky, S.A., Davis, J.: Engaging CS alumni from afar. In: Proceedings 47th ACM Technical Symposium on Computing Science Education, pp. 78–79 (2016)

18. Steele, A., Cleland, S.: Staying LinkedIn with ICT graduates and industry. In: Proceedings ITX 2014, pp. 8-10, Auckland, New Zealand (2014)

19. Thompson, C.A., Senseney, M., Baker, K.S., Varvel, V.E., Palmer, C.L.: Specialization in data curation: preliminary results from an alumni survey, 2008–2012. Proc. Am. Soc. Inf. Sci. Technol. **50**(1), 1–4 (2013)

Introducing Health Informatics as an Elective Module in an Information Systems Honours Degree: Experiences from Rhodes University

Greg Foster$^{(\boxtimes)}$ and Jane Nash

Department of Information Systems, Rhodes University, Grahamstown, South Africa
{g.foster,j.nash}@ru.ac.za

Abstract. A priority within South Africa's eHealth strategy is the development of skills needed to implement and support health information systems. In view of the time frames involved in creating and delivering new undergraduate curricula, a feasible short-term approach to capacity building is to equip Information Systems (IS) graduates with relevant knowledge of healthcare systems and eHealth technologies. The IS Department at Rhodes University introduced an elective module in Health Informatics within their one-year Honours program, aimed at preparing IS students for careers in eHealth. This paper outlines the module content and in-sights gained from student feedback.

Keywords: Health informatics · Education · Information systems · Student experience · Curriculum development

1 Introduction

In 2012, South Africa released its eHealth strategy, which aims to improve the country's health information system [5]. The strategy articulates ten key priorities, one of which is the need to build *"a workforce that can innovate, develop, deploy, maintain and support all eHealth interventions, especially health information systems and health management information systems"* [5]. While the establishment of this national eHealth strategy is a significant milestone for national health system reform, its successful implementation will depend on the existence of a highly skilled work-force that can design, build, implement and maintain effective eHealth systems [6,17].

Health Informatics (HI) can be defined as *"a science that defines how health information is technically captured, transmitted, and utilized"* [1]. HI thus focuses on how the principles of informatics, information technology and information systems can be applied within the continuum of healthcare delivery, placing HI firmly at the core of eHealth systems. Graduates qualified in Information Systems (IS) and who have an understanding of the healthcare domain and the vital role that technology can play in eHealth will be uniquely positioned to contribute to the design and development of high-quality and efficient healthcare solutions intended to improve patient outcomes and reduce costs [7].

© Springer International Publishing AG 2016
S. Gruner (Ed.): SACLA 2016, CCIS 642, pp. 123–130, 2016.
DOI: 10.1007/978-3-319-47680-3_12

In response to the need for eHealth capacity building, an elective module in HI was introduced into the IS Honours degree program at Rhodes University. It was hoped that the module would appeal to IS students with an interest in healthcare who wanted to explore technology-related aspects of health informatics, in order to prepare them for potential careers in eHealth. In this paper we report on the initiative by first outlining the module content and then presenting students' feedback regarding their experience of the module.

2   Health Informatics Education

Global demand for HI professionals is expected to increase substantially in the foreseeable future [9]. A variety of educational programs have been established in an attempt to meet this demand, ranging from specialist postgraduate degree programs [18] and HI streams within existing academic programs [11] to short HI courses [13] and professional certification programs [10]. However, such initiatives tend to focus either on developing the ICT knowledge and skills of students who are already familiar with the healthcare domain; or else on providing existing ICT practitioners with the do-main-specific knowledge needed for working in healthcare [16]. The well-rounded graduate with comprehensive knowledge of healthcare, information systems and health informatics remains an elusive ideal [3].

The International Medical Informatics Association (IMIA) encourages and develops HI education globally [12] and has provided guidelines to assist institutions in defining the content of their HI curricula. Dedicated HI bachelor's degrees are currently being created [3,19] in some cases by replacing the programming modules in existing IS degrees with HI modules and changing the business focus to a clinical focus [15]. These new HI degree programs adhere to the IS 2010 curriculum guidelines [20] and support the IS requirements of the IMIA guidelines [15]. However, they are not yet producing HI graduates in sufficient numbers to meet the demand for practitioners with both technical and clinical skills [3].

The HI module described in this paper represents the first step towards developing an integrated Health Informatics program at Rhodes University, which would combine knowledge of health systems, health data and health technologies with content from our existing information systems courses.

3   Curriculum Development

In designing our Honours HI module we considered the recommendations of IMIA's undergraduate bachelor's program [12] and included the three core knowledge do-mains as recommended by IMIA for HI professionals with an Informatics/Computer Science background, i.e. HI core knowledge and skills; health system organization; and technologies relevant to HI. These knowledge domains were in turn mapped to COACH's core competencies for health informatics professionals [4]. Since our IS graduates are already familiar with Information

Management, Information Technology, Organizational Management and Project Management, we extended this prior knowledge to include aspects of information, technology and information systems that are specific to the health domain. Other topics which were covered in some detail include clinical processes and terminology; health data formats, structures and standards; determinants of health and the role of technology in improving healthcare including the use of data analytics; and challenges faced in developing and adopting IT-based healthcare systems. We also sought expert practical advice from a well-established academic working in the HI domain.

Table 1. Health Informatics module: Lesson topics and content

Lesson topic	Content
Introduction to HI	Overview of South Africa's healthcare system; Introduction to Health Informatics; South Africa's eHealth strategy
Clinical Information Systems and EHRs	Clinical Information Systems; Electronic Health Records (EHRs); The role of EHRs in managing healthcare data; EHR implementation benefits; Meaningful use of EHRs
Health Data Fundamentals	The need for coding in eHealth systems; Overview of coding systems; Classification systems (ICD-10) versus terminologies (SNOMED-CT); How coding systems are used in practice
Clinical Decision Support Systems (CDSS)	Overview of CDSS and their role in clinical decision-making; Evidence-Based Medicine in clinical practice; CDSS acceptance and outcomes
Interoperability	Achieving interoperability in health systems; Messaging standards e.g. HL7, RIM, CDA, CCD, CCR, DICOM
Telehealth and mHealth	The value of telehealth in healthcare; Telehealth models and types of telehealth; Telehealth in South Africa; The role of mHealth and mobile health apps in healthcare
Developing and Implementing eHealth Systems	Success and failure of eHealth systems; Development approaches for eHealth systems; Potential barriers to successful eHealth implementation in South Africa
Population Health and Data Science	Epidemiology and surveillance; Determinants of health; Data analytics in healthcare and the impact of big data; The role of data science in healthcare
Guest Lecture	Insight into the role of Health Informatics in SA healthcare
Case Study Assignment	Student presentations and written reports on healthcare project management cases (successes and failures)

The HI module was delivered over a two-week period and comprised 20 seminar-style contact hours with accompanying readings, as well as a case study assignment (10 h) for which students were required to prepare a class presentation and submit a written report. A final guest lecture was given by a representative of the South African healthcare industry. Table 1 outlines the structure of the curriculum and the topics that were covered.

At Rhodes University, IS Honours students are required to select two elective modules from three possible choices. Of the 35 students enrolled in the Honours program, 26 (74 %) opted to take HI as an elective. Their final module result was based on the case study project (20 %) and a three-hour written examination (80 %), with the module as a whole contributing 10 % to the students' overall Honours result. All 26 students passed the module, with marks ranging from 52 % to 81 % and a class average of 66 %.

4   Course Evaluation

To assess student opinions of the new HI module, students were asked to provide feedback via an anonymous evaluation at the end of the course. Fourteen completed questionnaires were returned.

Table 2. Student rating of HI lesson topics (1 = disliked, 10 = enjoyed)

Rank	Lesson topic	Mean ± S.D
1	Introduction to HI	8.43 ± 1.09
2	Guest Lecture	8.21 ± 1.85
3	Telehealth and mHealth	8.18 ± 1.75
4	Health Data Fundamentals	7.92 ± 1.41
5	Clinical Information Systems and EHRs	7.89 ± 1.47
6	Developing and Implementing eHealth Systems	7.64 ± 1.86
7	Clinical Decision Support Systems	7.57 ± 1.50
8	Case Study Assignment	7.50 ± 2.38
9	Population Health and Data Science	7.39 ± 1.52
10	Interoperability	7.21 ± 1.58

The module evaluation questionnaire was divided into two parts. The first part of the questionnaire assessed students' enjoyment of each lesson topic covered, the guest lecture presentation, and the self-study assignment. The results for this section of the questionnaire are summarised in Table 2.

The first part of the questionnaire also assessed students rating of the difficulty, level of detail, and pace of the module. The results for this section of the questionnaire are summarised in Table 3.

The second part of the questionnaire consisted of open-ended questions intended to elicit feedback about students' personal experience and suggested improvements for the module. In addition, students were asked if they would choose this module again as an elective. A selection of representative comments is given in Table 4.

Table 3. Student rating of HI module delivery

Module aspect		Mean ± S.D
Difficulty	(1 = too simplistic, 5 = too complicated)	3.14 ± 0.36
Level of detail	(1 = too general, 5 = too specific)	3.29 ± 0.83
Pace of delivery	(1 = too slow, 5 = too fast)	3.29 ± 0.91

Table 4. Student remarks about the HI module

What was your experience of the HI module?
- *"Very eye-opening and gave me insight into an emerging industry"*
- *"Interesting, gives insight into the complexity of systems"*
- *"Very enjoyable. Nice change from the things we normally learn"*
- *"Interesting course, good variation from typical IS business-type modules"*
- *"The Health Informatics module was interesting and a well put together look into an industry I never knew existed"*
- *"It was a very informative module, had a good experience learning it"*

What aspects would you suggest need improvement?
- *"Seems like there may be a bit of parrot learning which isn't ideal"*
- *"Decrease the scope"*
- *"More in-class exercises to keep us engaged"*
- *"A visit to Settlers Hospital and actually see how the health sector operates"*
- *"Practical use of some eHealth systems could be useful"*
- *"Perhaps touch on cloud computing in mHealth and eHealth"*
- *"Could relate the content to more South African specific examples and the challenges SA health systems face"*

If you were able to go back in time and choose your electives again, would you still want to do Health Informatics?
- *"Yes"* from all students

5 Discussion

The results indicate that students responded positively to the introductory HI module and were happy that they had chosen it as one of their electives.

Table 2 shows the mean rating awarded for each lesson topic. All lesson topics received favourable ratings (above 7 out of 10) with the highest rated topics being the introductory lesson; telehealth and mhealth; and health data fundamentals. Lesson topics that included a greater level of complexity (interoperability; population health and data science; and clinical decision support systems) received lower enjoyment ratings. This is in line with Jaspers et al. [13] who also found that students experienced difficulty with decision support and image processing. The guest lecture was particularly well received, while the assignment case studies were regarded less favourably.

Table 3 provides the mean rating for various aspects of the module delivery, all of which scored about 3 out of 5. It is encouraging to see that the module was not deemed too difficult and that the level of detail was appropriately set for this module. In addition, students were comfortable with the pace at which these topics needed to be presented in order to be accommodated within the scheduled two-week time-frame.

Table 4 presents a selection of typical responses given by student to the open questions. These indicate that students enjoyed the module and found it informative. A clear recommendation was made to include more practical aspects, particularly around setting up and using eHealth systems. Practical skills have been highlighted as an essential skill set in HI programs [8]. It was pleasing to see that all students indicated they would do the module again if they could, and again confirmed that the students found the module worthwhile.

6   Concluding Remarks

In light of the positive reception that the Health Informatics module received from the initial student cohort, we expect to retain it as an elective in future Honours curricula. Before doing so, we intend to carefully review and revise the module objectives, content and structure, and teaching and assessment methods, based on relevant literature together with our own experience reported here. This review process and its outcomes will be the subject of a future paper.

In future iterations of the module we will also increase the practical skills component to support and reinforce the theory taught in the various lesson topics; for example, using a tool such as Tableau (www.tableau.com) to perform analytics on population health data. Given recent increases in health data breaches [14], it would also be pertinent going forward to introduce a topic on security and privacy of health information. The ability to apply knowledge of health information security and privacy to eHealth systems is regarded as crucial [2].

Many higher education institutions offering HI programmes are constrained by a lack of specialised resources and limited access to real-world settings [21]. Strategic partnerships between academic institutions and relevant government departments (in particular Health and Education) would be invaluable in facilitating the skills development needed to support South Africa's eHealth strategy. Without such alignment it is probably unrealistic to expect individual tertiary institutions to build HI capacity across all dimensions of the eHealth strategy; however, closer collaboration between institutions, each building on their own strengths, could go a long way towards ad-dressing South Africa's HI training needs.

Until such time as dedicated HI degrees are offered in South Africa, it is highly recommended that IS Departments at South African universities consider including Health Informatics modules within their curricula to help create awareness of the role ICTs plays in modern healthcare. In so doing, IS students will be better prepared for an exciting career in healthcare and will be able to contribute to the country's eHealth strategy.

Acknowledgement. The authors wish to thank Prof Anthony Maeder (University of Western Sydney) for his many hours of valuable discussion on health informatics curricula.

References

1. AHIMA: What is health information? (2016). http://www.ahima.org/careers/healthinfo
2. Blumenthal, D., McGraw, D.: Keeping personal health information safe: the importance of good data hygiene. JAMA **313**(14), 1424–1424 (2015)
3. Campbell, M., Pardue, J.H., Longenecker, B., Barnett, L., Landry, J.: Treating the healthcare workforce crisis: a prescription for a health informatics curriculum. Inf. Syst. Educ. J. **10**(3), 35 (2012)
4. COACH: Health Informatics Professional: Core Competencies v3.0 (2012). https://www.coachorg.com/en/resourcecentre/resources/Health-Informatics-Core-Competencies.pdf
5. DoH: eHealth Strategy South Africa 2012–2017 (2016). https://www.health-e.org.za/wp-content/uploads/2014/08/South-Africa-eHealth-Strategy-2012-2017.pdf
6. Franzke, L., Tolentino, H.: Strengthening health systems through interprofessional education. In: 2015 CSTE Annual Conference (2015)
7. Haluza, D., Jungwirth, D.: ICT and the future of health care: aspects of health-promotion. Int. J. Med. Inform. **84**(1), 48-57 (2015)
8. Haux, R.: Biomedical and health informatics education at UMIT: approaches and strategies at a newly founded university. Int. J. Med. Inform. **73**(2), 127–138 (2004)
9. Hersh, W.: The health information technology workforce: estimations of demands and a framework for requirements. Appl. Clin. Inform. **1**(2), 197–212 (2010)
10. HISA: Certified Health Informatician Australasia (2016). http://www.healthinformaticscertification.com/
11. Hovenga, E.J.: Globalisation of health and medical informatics education: what are the issues? Int. J. Med. Inform. **73**(2), 101–109 (2004)
12. IMIA: International Medical Informatics Association (2016). http://www.imia-medinfo.org/
13. Jaspers, M.W., Gardner, R.M., Gatewood, L.C., Haux, R., Evans, R.S.: An international summer school on health informatics: a collaborative effort of the Amsterdam Medical Informatics Program and IϕE: the international partnership for health informatics education. Int. J. Med. Inform. **76**(7), 538–546 (2007)
14. Liu, V., Musen, M.A., Chou, T.: Data breaches of protected health information in the United States. JAMA **313**(14), 1471–1473 (2015)
15. Longenecker, H., Campbell, S.M., Landry, J.P., Pardue, J., Daigle, R.J.: A health informatics curriculum compatible with IS 2010 and IMIA recommendations for an undergraduate degree. In: Information Systems Education Conference, ISECON 2011 (2011)
16. Mantas, J., Ammenwerth, E., Demiris, G., Hasman, A., Haux, R., Hersh, W., Hovenga, E., Lun, K., Marin, H., Martin-Sanchez, F., Wright, G.: Recommendations of the International Medical Informatics Association (IMIA) on education in biomedical and health informatics: first revision. Acta Informatica Medica **18**(1), 4 (2010)
17. Mars, M.: Building the capacity to build capacity in e-health in sub-Saharan Africa: the KwaZulu-Natal experience. Telemedicine e-Health **18**(1), 32–37 (2012)

18. Murray, P., Betts, H., Wright, G., Tshayingca-Mashiya, N.: Health informatics education and capacity building in Eastern Cape Province, South Africa. Yearbook of Medical Informatics, pp. 158–163 (2008)
19. Tilahun, B., Zeleke, A., Fritz, F., Zegeye, D.: New bachelors degree program in health informatics in Ethiopia: curriculum content and development approaches. Stud. Health Technol. Inform. **205**, 798–802 (2014)
20. Topi, H., Valacich, J.S., Wright, R.T., Kaiser, K., Nunamaker Jr., J.F., Sipior, J.C., de Vreede, G.J.: IS 2010: Curriculum guidelines for undergraduate degree programs in information systems. Commun. Assoc. Inf. Syst. **26**(18), 359–428 (2010)
21. Were, M.C., Siika, A., Ayuo, P.O., Atwoli, L., Esamai, F.: Building comprehensive and sustainable health informatics institutions in developing countries: Moi university experience. Stud. Health Technol. Inform. **216**, 520–524 (2015)

Towards an Interdisciplinary Master's Degree Programme in Big Data and Data Science: A South African Perspective

Linda Marshall$^{(\boxtimes)}$ and Jan H.P. Eloff

Department of Computer Science, University of Pretoria, Pretoria, South Africa
{lmarshall,eloff}@cs.up.ac.za

Abstract. Many businesses see Big Data and Data Science as a catalyst for innovation. The problem is that many of these businesses are hesitant to embrace these new technologies mainly because of a shortage in skilled manpower. On a global level, higher education institutions are in the process of developing curricula for graduate degree programs relating to Big Data and Data Science. Developing such curriculum has its own challenges. For example: What level of knowledge is required from disciplines such as Computing and Statistics? What underlying foundations in Mathematics are required? This paper presents a framework for the design of an interdisciplinary Big Data and Data Science curriculum on the Master's level.

Keywords: Big Data · Data Science · Interdisciplinary · Curriculum design

1 Introduction

Big data has emerged from the growth in data volumes and the fact that data nowadays is available in multiple formats. Many businesses in South Africa see Big Data and Data Science as catalysts for innovation enabling them to, amongst others, improve product delivery and customer experience. However, many of these businesses are hesitant to embrace these new technologies mainly because of a shortage in skilled manpower.

A recent Data Science salary survey [10] conducted with respondents from 53 countries reported on two important aspects. Firstly, employees with graduate degrees such as a Master's or a Doctorate in Data Science earn significantly more than their counterparts. Secondly, a high premium is placed on tool usage indicating that employees need to embrace new technologies such as Hadoop and cloud based services. This indicates that there is not only a need for Data Science education on the graduate level but also that the graduates should have the correct skills to manipulate Big Data sets in an intelligent manner.

It is for the above mentioned reasons that many higher education institutions are in the process of developing curricula [15] for graduate degree programs in

© Springer International Publishing AG 2016
S. Gruner (Ed.): SACLA 2016, CCIS 642, pp. 131–139, 2016.
DOI: 10.1007/978-3-319-47680-3_13

Big Data and Data Science. Developing such curricula have their own challenges, such as depth versus breadth of content, which need to be overcome. For example: What level of detailed knowledge is required from disciplines such as Computing (to which Computer Science and Information Systems belong), Statistics and Mathematics? To distinguish between the extent to which a graduate curriculum in Big Data and Data Science should be of multidisciplinary [14], interdisciplinary or transdisciplinary nature is a complex task [11].

The goal of this paper is to address the challenges discussed above. It presents a conceptual framework that can be employed for the design of a Data Science curriculum with the focus on managing and manipulating Big Data on the Master's level.

As a starting point, a combination of industry expectations from a Data Scientist and interdisciplinary curriculum design principles are used to identify skills and knowledge domains that will be needed by successful Data Scientists with the focus on the manipulation of Big Data sets. Concluding from the existing literature, previously referenced, it is suggested that an interdisciplinary approach towards the design of a curriculum shows potential. In short, multiple disciplines are providing resources and expertise. Furthermore, within a module of such a degree programme, where multiple departments take ownership of the content and the presentation thereof, the research at hand will refer to such a module as being of transdisciplinary nature. The resulting framework presented in this paper can serve as an input to the design of a Master's Big Data and Data Science curriculum.

2   What Is Big Data and Data Science?

The concept of data has been around for a very long time. The well-known Oxford Dictionary defines data as *"facts or statistics collected together for reference or analysis"*. Data was mostly of a singular type and therefore homogeneous in nature. The search for new and novel ways in managing data gave rise to the concept of Data Science as *"the extraction of knowledge from data that are structured or unstructured"* [4].

The term 'Big Data' has emerged from the growth in data volumes and the fact that data nowadays is available in multiple formats. Data Science requires sorting and filtering through big volumes of data. Conventional ways of data processing have been shown to be ineffective, especially with regard to the extraction of knowledge from Big Data. Furthermore, over the past few years it also became clear that the world could benefit from the behavioural aspects of data, which, in most cases, is hidden and therefore requires complex and intelligent algorithms to be discovered.

2.1   Requirements for a Data Scientist

To call oneself a Data Scientist requires specific knowledge and skills. In this paper, knowledge is defined as information acquired by visual, auditory, reading and kinesthetic (learning by doing) means. Graduates are required to be able to transfer the knowledge, for example: the Data Scientist should know about the various machine learning algorithms available for detecting hidden features in a Big Data set. Skills on the other hand relate to the ability to apply knowledge and can be developed through practice [2]. With reference to machine learning algorithms it will be expected of the Data Scientist to choose for example the Apriori algorithm [18], as an appropriate algorithm for building association rules between the attributes of a Big Data set and then apply a genetic algorithm to cluster these associations.

Table 1. Knowledge and Skills required by Data Scientists

Reference	Knowledge									Skills						
	Computer science	Data munging and cleaning	Data visualisation	Domain expert in application area	Machine learning	Mathematics	Probability	Statistics	Software Engineering	Business acumen	Coding	Communication	Data visualisation	Experiment design	Problem solving	Tools
[14]	×		×	×	×	×	×	×			×	×				
[8]		×			×	×	.	×	×			×	×		×	×
[7]								×		×	×	×	×		×	×
[12]	×	×						×			×	×	×	×		×
[17]	×		×	×	×			×	×			×			×	

Table 1 summarises literature on the knowledge and skill requirements for Data Scientists.[1] Statistical knowledge is high on the list of knowledge requirements. Furthermore, [12] points out that traditional statistics taught to students does not cover the knowledge required by a Data Scientist. Knowledge of machine learning is only specifically mentioned in [8,14,17], however [7,12] do mention knowledge of computational techniques to manipulate Big Data as being important. Furthermore, it is important that the Data Scientist is an excellent communicator and more specifically in terms of the technical aspects of the field [14]. It is interesting that [14,17] see data visualisation in terms of knowledge while [7,8] refer to it in terms of a skill, whilst [12] views data visualisation as a component of tool usage. Embracing new technologies is mentioned by [10] as a requirement for the Data Scientist.

Some authors value coding as a skill, others see the Data Scientist as a user of software rather than a builder thereof [6]. Nonetheless, the authors of this paper refer to programming as it encapsulates coding as well as problem solving to some extent. This may explain the fact that not all authors agree on the extent

---

[1] 'Data munging' refers to mapping data from one form to another.

to which Computer Science knowledge should be a requirement for the Data Scientist. Last-mentioned can also be explained by thinking of Data Science as the new discipline which is emerging from a foundation in Mathematics and Computer Science as was mentioned by [17].

2.2   The Data Science Lifecycle

[5] states that data should only be collected and processed if there is a need for it and went on to define a so-called USGS (United States Geological Survey) Science Data Life Cycle Model. This model consists of 9 phases, namely: Plan, Acquire, Process, Analyse, Preserve, Publish, Describe, Manage and Backup. It is argued that the data component of Data Science also contains these 9 data life cycle phases and furthermore that the Acquire phase is of special importance. This is because of the fact that getting access to Big Data (terabytes) is one of the most difficult and time consuming tasks in any Data Science exercise.

Data scientists need to be skilled in all the above mentioned aspects of data handling and it is suggested that curricula are designed to ensure a detailed practical knowledge of all data life cycle phases but with special emphasis on data streaming.

3   Interdisciplinary Curriculum Design

The term interdisciplinary is defined in the Oxford Dictionary as *"Relating to more than one branch of knowledge"*. Designing a curriculum which crosses disciplinary boundaries fosters interdisciplinary thinking skills. Graduates are required to bring knowledge from multiple disciplines together, thereby advancing the combined learning in a direction which the individual disciplines would not do [16]. An interdisciplinary curriculum therefore needs to be designed to facilitate this combined learning and research experience for Data Science. The work presented in [9] proposes a continuum of options for interdisciplinary curriculum design, beginning with independent modules focussing on a single discipline to a fully integrated programme. It has been shown that by combining these options, a curriculum with an increased success rate can be developed.

Designing a Big Data and Data Science curriculum can benefit from focussing the design of *Complementary Discipline* and *Interdisciplinary* modules [9]. For example, a module which introduces machine learning and statistical learning requires machine learning knowledge from Computer Science discipline and statistical learning knowledge from Statistics. By bringing these two aspects together, the module no longer presents the knowledge independently, but synergistically. This synergy may lead to new developments in regression and intelligent classification. Defining a curriculum and saying it is interdisciplinary, does not guarantee that the programme will be successful. Specific problems must be designed which highlight the interdisciplinary nature of the learning material. The challenge is to provide both breadth and depth within the program [15].

For example, machine learning relates to Artificial Intelligence (AI) within Computer Science. It is not necessary for the curriculum to provide a foundation in all aspects of AI, it is however important for the curriculum to provide sufficient underpinnings in AI to be able to understand and apply machine learning within the Data Science and Big Data context.

3.1   Considerations for Developing an Interdisciplinary Curriculum

When developing a curriculum in Big Data and Data Science, consideration should be given to, the knowledge and skills (summarised in Table 1) within and between the dominant disciplines (Computing, Mathematics and Statistics) and the life cycle described in Sect. 2.2. Additionally, consideration should be given to outcomes, stakeholders from the respective disciplines and the regulatory requirements placed on the curriculum. Once the curriculum has been developed, an in-depth assessment of the curriculum should be conducted to determine the coverage of the curriculum and the level of prior knowledge required.

Outcomes of a Big Data and Data Science Curriculum. The outcomes of the Data Science degree programme are linked to the core disciplines. Students can either focus on a broad education or focus their studies on one of the multiple tracks, e.g. business analytics or computational intelligence, as was explained in the work reported on in [1]. Outcomes for the Master's qualification in Data Science should be viewed on both the macro as well as the micro level.

Considering the outcomes on a macro level it is expected that such a degree program delivers individuals who embrace fast changing environments, both technological as well as organisational. This can be achieved through a combination of interdisciplinary knowledge, extensive exposure to different tool usage and a fundamental understanding of the various phases in the life cycle.

On the micro level, the expected outcomes of a graduate are well documented in existing literature. Consider for example the work done by [14] where the focus is on 'data intensive computing' with outcomes categorised amongst others as: *Data analytics* (machine learning as well as predictive modelling), and *Data visualisation.*

Stakeholders. Stakeholders fall into two categories, those who provide the technical expertise needed for the application of the life cycle; and those who provide the expertise of the domain to which the life cycle is to be applied. It is not necessary for these two groupings to be mutually exclusive, it is however required that the former category of stakeholders provide a solid technical foundation in Computing, Mathematics and Statistics, onto which the application domain stakeholders build [1]. Consultation with the stakeholders is of utmost importance. Stakeholders providing technical expertise need to agree on how the interdisciplinary aspects of their respective disciplines are to be designed so the content of modules are both *Complementary* and *Interdisciplinary.*

Regulatory Requirements. Curricula are not the only concern when developing degree programmes. Both governmental and institutional requirements are placed on curricula particularly for accreditation purposes. Governments define frameworks for primary, secondary and tertiary education to ensure seamless progression through the education system. In South Africa, the National Qualifications Framework (NQF) defines three categories of certificates in education and training, beginning in primary school and ending with Doctoral studies. NQF exit levels 5, 6 and 7 are considered undergraduate study. Graduate study occupies levels 8 (Honours), 9 (Master's) and 10 (Doctorate). The minimum credit requirements for a level 9 qualification is 180 over 1 or 2 years. One credit equates to 10 hours of study, referred to as notional hours. At least 90 credits must be dedicated to a research project [13]. Institutions, other than needing to comply to the governmental frameworks, may add additional requirements which differentiate them from other institutions. These requirements need to be taken into account during the development of the curriculum.

Prior Knowledge. Following on from regulatory requirements, it is assumed that qualifications within qualification frameworks build on knowledge gained after successful completion of previous levels within the framework. It is therefore important to consider what the expected prior knowledge should be in terms of the qualifications framework when designing a degree programme. For the Master's programme in Big Data and Data Science, foundational prior knowledge in the disciplines of Computing, Mathematics and Statistics would be required. For example, undergraduate knowledge of databases, programming, calculus, linear algebra and probability.

3.2   Existing Curricula in Big Data and/or Data Science

The international trend is to introduce Data Science focussed degree programmes on the graduate level and modules with a data-centric focus on the undergraduate level. According to [1], in 2013 there were 61 Knowledge Discovery and Data Mining related degree programmes on offer in the US and Canada, of which only 4 were undergraduate degree programmes. In April of 2016, 513 programmes were listed on the Data Science community website [3] from countries across the world. Of these, 124 were certificate programmes — the majority of which are online, 43 Bachelor programmes, 323 Master's programmes with most being solely course-driven and 23 Doctoral programmes. Currently none of the programmes listed are from South Africa.

4   Recommendations for a Big Data and Data Science Master's Curriculum

The main contribution of this paper is a framework, given in Fig. 1, that can be employed for the design of a Master's level Big Data and Data Science curriculum. Aspects already discussed are: *Disciplines* (branch of knowledge), *Knowl-*

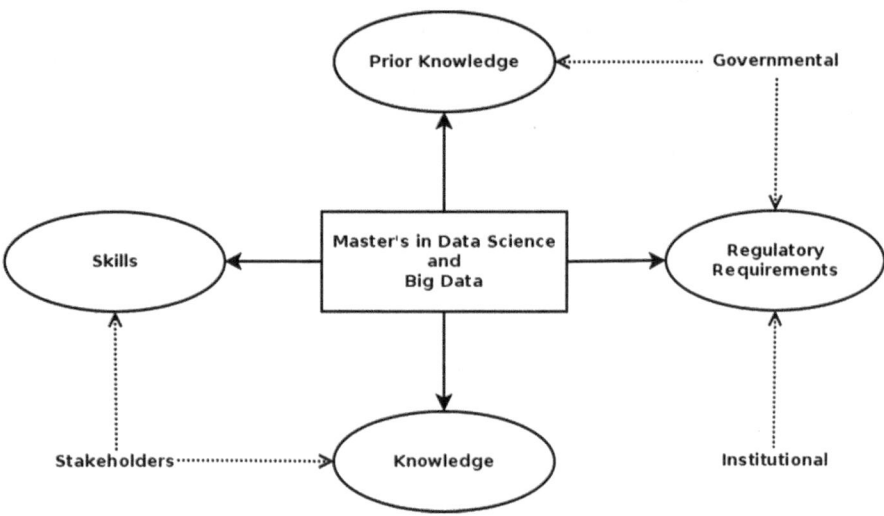

Fig. 1. A Framework for an interdisciplinary Big Data and Data Science Master's

edge (acquired information that can be transferred), and *Skills* (ability to apply knowledge and can be practiced).

Interdisciplinary collaboration is the most important aspect for such a degree programme. The disciplines identified in Sect. 3.1 all relate in their own way to different and in some cases the same knowledge domains. It is argued that the following knowledge domains are relevant for this Big Data and Data Science curriculum: machine learning, data visualisation, modelling, statistical learning, large distributed data sets and application domains. Knowledge and skills are interrelated. Skills development of the curriculum should focus on: tool usage, communication, research, programming and problem solving.

5 Conclusion

An overview of a framework that can be employed for the design of a Master's curriculum on Big Data and Data Science, was presented in this paper. A combination of industry requirements and interdisciplinary curriculum design principles were employed to identify skills and knowledge domains that serve as building blocks for becoming a successful Data Scientist working with Big Data.

6 Future Work

An in-depth study of the Master's degree programme curricula listed on the Data Science community website [3] is to be conducted. This study will consider whether the degree programmes listed on the website cover all aspects considered to be necessary for a Master's in Big Data and Data Science. A comparison between the listed programmes and the recommendations as defined by the framework presented in Fig. 1 will need to be completed. Immediate future work will present modules and the topics related to the modules highlighting the interdisciplinary nature of the modules.

References

1. Anderson, P., Bowring, J., McCauley, R., Pothering, G., Starr, C.: An undergraduate degree in data science: curriculum and a decade of implementation experience. In: Proceedings 45th ACM Technical Symposium on Computer Science Education (SIGCSE 2014), pp. 145–150 (2014)
2. Bollet, G.: Identifying the difference between knowledge and skills (2015). http://elearningindustry.com/difference-between-knowledge-and-skills-knowing-not-make-skilled
3. Data Science Community. http://datascience.community/colleges
4. Dhar, V.: Data science and prediction. Commun. ACM **56**(12), 64–73 (2013)
5. Faundeen, J., Burley, T., Carlino, J., Govoni, D., Henkel, H., Holl, S., Hutchison, V.B., Martn, E., Montgomery, E., Ladino, C., Tessler, S., Zolly, L.: The United States geological survey science data lifecycle model: U.S. geological survey open-file Report 2013–1265, Techn. rep., U.S. Geological Survey, (2013). doi:10.3133/ofr20131265
6. Hall-Holt, O.A., Sanft, K.R.: Statistics-infused introduction to computer science. In: Proceedings 46th ACM Technical Symposium on Computer Science Education (SIGCSE 2015), pp. 138–143 (2015)
7. Harris, J.G., Shetterley, N., Alter, A.E., Schnell, K.: The team solution to the data scientist shortage. Techn. rep, Accenture Institute for High Performance (2013)
8. Holtz, D.: 8 skills you need to be a data scientist (2014). http://blog.udacity.com/2014/11/data-science-job-skills.html
9. Jacobs, R., Hayes, H. (eds.): Interdisciplinary Curriculum: Design and Implementation. Association for Supervision and Curriculum Development (1989)
10. King, J., Magoulas, R.: 2014 Data Science Salary Survey. O'Reilly, San Diego (2015)
11. Kroeze, J.H.: Transdisciplinarity in IS: The Next Frontier in Computing Disciplines. All Sprouts Content. Paper 489 (2012). http://aisel.aisnet.org/sprouts_all/489
12. McAfee, A., Brynjolfsson, E.: Big data: the management revolution. Harv. Bus. Rev. **90**(10), 60–66, 68, 128 (2012)
13. Pandor, G.N.M.: The Higher Education Qualifications Framework. Government Gazette, South Africa, October 2007
14. Ramamurthy, B.: A practical and sustainable model for learning and teaching data science. In: Proceedings 47th ACM Technical Symposium on Computing Science Education (SIGCSE 2016), pp. 169–174 (2016)
15. Sosa, R., Connor, A.M.: !orthodoxies in multidisciplinary design-oriented degree programmes. In: Proceedings of 2015 IASDR Conference: Interplay, November 2015
16. Spelt, E.J.H., Biemans, H.J.A., Tobi, H., Luning, P.A., Mulder, M.: Teaching and learning in interdisciplinary higher education: a systematic review. Educ. Psychol. Rev. **21**(4), 365–378 (2009)

17. van der Aalst, W.M.P.: Data scientist: the engineer of the future. In: Mertins, K., Bénaben, F., Poler, R., Bourriéres, J.P. (eds.) Enterprise Interoperability VI: Interoperability for Agility, Resilience and Plasticity of Collaborations. Proceedings of the I-ESA Conferences, vol. 7, pp. 13–26. Springer, Heidelberg (2014)
18. Wu, X., Kumar, V., Ross-Quinlan, J., Ghosh, J., Yang, Q., Motoda, H., McLachlan, G.J., Ng, A., Liu, B., Yu, P.S., Zhou, Z.H., Steinbach, M., Hand, D.J., Steinberg, D.: Top 10 algorithms in data mining. Knowl. Inf. Syst. **14**(1), 1–37 (2007)

Social Skills

Reflections on a Community-Based Service Learning Approach in a Geoinformatics Project Module

Serena Coetzee and Victoria Rautenbach[✉]

Department of Geography, Geoinformatics and Meteorology, University of Pretoria, Pretoria, South Africa
{serena.coetzee,victoria.rautenbach}@up.ac.za

Abstract. Geoinformatics (also known as geographic information science) is the science and technology that underpins the collection, representation, processing, analysis, visualisation and dissemination of geographic information. Such information is hugely valuable in solving environmental and social problems in society. In this paper we reflect on a community-based service learning approach in a third year geoinformatics module. Students mapped an informal settlement, captured information about dwellings and conducted a number of studies in support of environmental and social problem solving. The aim was to raise awareness of social issues, to understand students' sense of social responsibility and their understanding of the role of geoinformatics in solving community problems. After completion of the module, we conducted in-depth interviews with ten students. The results confirm the value of community-based service learning in enhancing understanding of theoretical concepts and contributing to local communities. Further work is needed to better understand how South African geoinformatics students can be made aware of the role of geoinformatics in solving problems in society.

Keywords: Social responsibility · Community-based service learning · Geoinformatics · Geographic information science · Informatics · Education

1 Introduction

Humanity is currently facing many global challenges, such as climate change, global health problems, extreme poverty and rising wealth inequality [18]. Many of these challenges can be linked to egoism, i.e. acting in the interest of one's self without consideration for others. For example, by not considering the carbon footprint when buying imported fruits. Geoinformatics professionals, through the use of geographic information, have enormous potential to contribute towards addressing these challenges. However, one needs to have a sense of social responsibility to want to contribute to solving such challenges that are not of direct interest to oneself.

© Springer International Publishing AG 2016
S. Gruner (Ed.): SACLA 2016, CCIS 642, pp. 143–159, 2016.
DOI: 10.1007/978-3-319-47680-3_14

Social responsibility is the obligation that an individual or organisation feels to society and specifically the disadvantaged [1,4,8]. Social responsibility combines the values and actions rooted in the obligation to contribute to society [2], i.e. one should act in accordance with care, objectivity, and considering others' perspectives and the impact of one's actions [3]. Canney and Bielefeldt [4] argue that engineers need a well-developed sense of social responsibility in order to contribute to social and development problems of undeserved populations. The same can be said about many other professions, including geoinformatics professionals.

Social responsibility education is of interest in many disciplines, but we could not find any that focus on geoinformatics. Canney and Bielefeldt [3] suggested that an understanding of professional social responsibility would nurture the required skills and attitude in engineering students, and encourage them to use their skills to address global challenges. They developed an integrated model to help understand the development of personal and professional social responsibility in engineers. The model has been used to evaluate engineering students' views on social responsibility [1,3,16,17]. According to Leveson and Joiner [12], historically, business education has focused on the procedural, organization-centric, geared towards the ethics of personal advantage. In contrast, teaching social responsibility requires appreciation for the views and values of students [12]. Harvey [9] proposes that the education of GIScience and technology professionals should go beyond abstract scholarly ethics to applied approaches based on practical wisdom.

Service learning is an experiential pedagogy in which community service is integrated into academic activities [15]. The aim is to enhance understanding of theoretical concepts and to facilitate contributions to local communities [19]. Dorsey [5] highlights that community-based learning provides unique opportunities for students to implement theoretical knowledge and gain hands-on experience while trying to address a real-world issue. The focus of service learning is on the student: the student learns from and contributes to the community, while the community benefits and contributes to the student's learning [15]. Warren [19] reports that many studies have shown service learning to have positive effects on students' cultural awareness and social responsibility, and that it encourages students to act as responsible citizens. In the United States, the integration of service learning into academic curricula is increasing [15] and in some South African engineering and information technology faculties, a community-based project is compulsory [11]. Community-based service learning has been applied in various fields, including architecture, education, engineering, health science and geography [5–7,10,13,14], but to our knowledge, studies in geoinformatics, which combines geography with technology, have not been done.

In this paper we conducted qualitative research that reflects on a community-based service learning approach in a third year geoinformatics module. This was the students' first opportunity to apply geoinformatics knowledge and skills acquired through their undergraduate studies in a single project from conception to completion. Students mapped an informal settlement, captured information about dwellings and conducted a number of studies in support of environmental and social problem solving. The aim was to raise awareness of social issues. We also wanted to understand students' sense of social responsibility and their perception of the role of geoinformatics in solving community problems. After completion of the module, we conducted in-depth interviews with ten students. The remainder of the paper is structured as follows. Section 2 provides background about the community project. Section 3 explains how the interviews were conducted. In Sect. 4, the results of the interviews are presented and discussed, followed by a conclusion in Sect. 5.

2   Community-Based Service Learning: Mapping the Informal Settlement of 'Alaska' in Mamelodi (ZA)

The University of Pretoria has a long-standing partnership with the Viva Foundation, in the 'Alaska'[1] informal settlement in the City of Tshwane, to improve the safety of the informal settlement dwellers. The Viva Foundation aims to transform informal settlements and other high-priority poverty areas into stable and economically viable communities.[2] Amongst others, the Viva Foundation coordinates the South African People's Response Initiative (SAPRI) project, which provides the settlement dwellers with panic buttons that can be used to call for assistance in case of emergencies. In 2015, the final year geoinformatics students worked on improving the SAPRI project that is currently paper based, by mapping the most southern part of 'Alaska' immediately surrounding the Viva centre. Viva community care workers accompanied the students to introduce them to the community members and to provide them with additional information about the community and its history.

Over the course of three days, seventeen final year students captured the locations of 1350 dwellings in 'Alaska', as well as information about each dwelling, such as the address and the use of the dwelling (e.g. home, tuck shop or shebeen). This digital information was handed to the SAPRI project. In addition, the students investigated the following:

1. optimal distribution of the panic buttons;
2. identifying areas that are potentially at risk of damage during thunderstorms (based on terrain and slopes);
3. planning emergency response routes to dwellings during fires; and
4. identifying a suitable location for a health post in 'Alaska'.

Each of these investigations addresses a specific need in the community. A number of maps (hardcopy and interactive) of these investigations were given to the Viva Foundation.

This community project was integrated into the academic activities of the semester module, GMT320 (Geoinformatics project). The module provides a

---

[1] Locals have named this settlement 'Alaska' because of its remote location from the city centre.
[2] http://www.viva-sa.co.za.

unique first learning opportunity for the students to be involved in a real-life project with a client. Up until then, students work with hypothetical scenarios where 'perfect' data and a breakdown of the solution are provided to them. For GMT320, students have to implement the entire project management process, capture their own data, and then implement an innovative solution with the data they have captured. During GMT320 students get a first opportunity to work with handheld and differential global positioning system (GPS) devices, and to gain fieldwork experience. This experience is invaluable to the students who will plan projects and capture data in the field during their professional careers.

3   Methodology

The final year geoinformatics students completed the community project in the second semester of 2015. In March 2016, these students were invited to participate in an in-depth interview on their experience and thoughts on social responsibility. Due to the small number of participants and the type of interview, this research is of a qualitative nature.

Before the interview was conducted, the participants were asked to complete an adapted version of the Engineering Professional Responsibility Assessment (EPRA)[3] survey. The only adaptation was replacing engineering with 'GISc' in the text. We used the assessment from the engineering discipline because a questionnaire for geoinformatics does not exist. Similar to engineers, geoinformatics professionals are sometimes involved in solutions designed to solve problems of underserved populations. A social responsibility score (SR score) between 8 and 56 was calculated based on the description by Canney [2] as well as Rulifson and Bielefeldt [16] who designed the EPRA survey. The SR score provides an indication of a participant's degree of social responsibility; a higher SR score indicates a participant who is more aware of social responsibility.

The interviews were conducted in March 2016. They consisted of eighteen questions and were 30 to 60 min long. The questions covered a variety of topics, such as undergraduate experience, general opinion on social issues and how the community-based service learning module influenced their views. The interview questions are presented in Table 1. The questions are adapted from Rulifson and Bielefeldt [16,17]. The sessions were voice-recorded and the interviewers also took notes during the session.

4   Results and Discussion

4.1   Overview of Participants, SR Scores and EPRA Survey Results

Ten geoinformatics students accepted the invitation to participate in the interviews. All of them completed the GMT320 module with the community-based service learning approach in 2015. Table 2 provides an overview of the participants. The group consisted of six male and four female participants from various ethnicities (African, Indian and European). The ages ranged from 21 to 29 years.

---

[3] http://bit.ly/2al9F0u.

Table 1. Interview questions

1.	Why did you decide to study BSc Geoinformatics?
	a. Where did you hear about geoinformatics for the first time?
2.	Was BSc Geoinformatics your first qualification?
	b. If not, why did you decide to do another degree?
3.	Did you change from another degree to BSc Geoinformatics?
	c. If yes, for which degree were you registered before switching to BSc Geoinformatics?
	d. Why did you change to BSc Geoinformatics?
4.	Experience during your undergraduate geoinformatics degree:
	a. Positive experiences? What did you enjoy?
	b. Negative or frustrating experiences?
5.	What interests you the most about geoinformatics?
	a. Why do you like geoinformatics?
	b. What motivated you through the tough classes?
6.	What is your ideal future career path currently? Why?
7.	Are you looking for any specific qualities of a job and company? Why are these qualities important?
8.	Do you already know of companies where you'd like to work (not considering bursaries obligations)? If so, which ones?
9.	Do you do any volunteer or community work?
	a. If yes, at which scale: globally, locally, within your family/friends?
	b. How and why are you involved? What are the benefits you see for them and yourself?
10.	What social issues are important to you?
	a. Did anything influence you to see these issues as important?
	b. How do you see yourself involved in these social issues?
	c. Do you see geoinformatics playing a role in addressing these issues?
11.	How would you define social responsibility?

Provide definition of social responsibility:
Based on Rulifson and Bielefeldt [7] and Herkert [19], social responsibility and a GISc professional's social responsibility:
Social responsibility is the ethical duty one has to act in ways that benefit society.
A GISc professional's social responsibility encompasses protecting public welfare, and extends to concerns around environmental protection and sustainability, the social context of GISc work, empathy and caring, striving for social justice and peace, and pro bono work.

12.	Did GMT320 influence the social issues you consider important?
13.	Did GMT320 affect your understanding of social responsibility?
14.	After completing GMT320, do you expect social responsibility to be part of your future geoinformatics career?
	a. How?
	b. How strongly?
	c. In what ways?
15.	After completing GMT320, does your sense of social responsibility move you towards or away from a geoinformatics career?
	a. Are there certain kinds of geoinformatics work that you will avoid?
	b. Are there certain kinds of geoinformatics work that you will prefer or go for?
16.	Is there one social issue that you feel particularly passionate about trying to address?
	a. Why?
	b. Can your geoinformatics abilities help with this issue?
	c. Can other majors in geoinformatics better help you to address this issue?
17.	Thinking about your experience during the GMT320 field work and community engagement:
	a. Positive experiences? What did you enjoy?
	b. Negative or frustrating experiences?
	c. What did you like about the fieldwork? What not?
	d. What motivated you through the tough times?
18.	Is there anything else you would like to share, or questions you have?

Table 2. Overview of the participants

Participant	P1	P2	P3	P4	P5	P6	P7	P8	P9	P10
SR score	45.35	50.67	38.92	42.43	43.55	43.16	43.75	53.77	42.35	42.24
Age	≤22	≤22	>22	≤22	≤22	>22	≤22	≤22	>22	≤22
Have you been in an informal settlement prior to GMT320 in 2015?	No	Yes	Yes	No	Yes	Yes	Yes	No	No	Yes
Have you been in a township prior to GMT320 in 2015?	No	Yes	Yes	Yes	Yes	Yes	Yes	Yes	Yes	Yes
Previous GISc work experience	None	None	None	None	None	Part-time/internship	None	Part-time/internship	Part-time/internship	None

Six participants indicated that they are religious (i.e. affiliated with an orga-nized religion), and two participants specified that they are spiritual. Six par-ticipants indicated that they have been in an informal settlement prior to the community project, and nine have been in a township. Only three participants had previous work experience in the form of a part-time job or internship. An SR score was calculated for each participant. Two male participants had the highest SR score (above 50), followed by most of the remaining participants with a SR score between 42 and 45. The lowest score was ≈39.

In the EPRA survey, participants were asked to indicate which job qualities are important to them in a future job. Figure 1 shows how participants rated these job qualities. Community development is rated as important by all partic-ipants, but only three participants rated it above 10 % (at 20 %). Helping people is rated above 10 % by all participants, except two who rated it 10 % and one did not consider it as important at all. Most participants (except one) rate salary as an important job quality (20 % or above). This can probably be explained by the fact that most participants are in their fourth year of study and will have accumulated some study debt.

The EPRA survey also covered the reasons for volunteering currently or in the past (see Fig. 2). 60 % of the participants indicated that the main motivation for volunteering is/was to gain a new skill or that it was required for class. 40 % indicated that helping others is or was the motivation. Religious participants typically participated in volunteering activities organised by their religious com-munities. No participant indicated that international travel was a motivation for volunteering.

Figure 3 shows the breakdown of factors that currently or previously inhibited participation in volunteer activities. The largest factor is lack of time due to

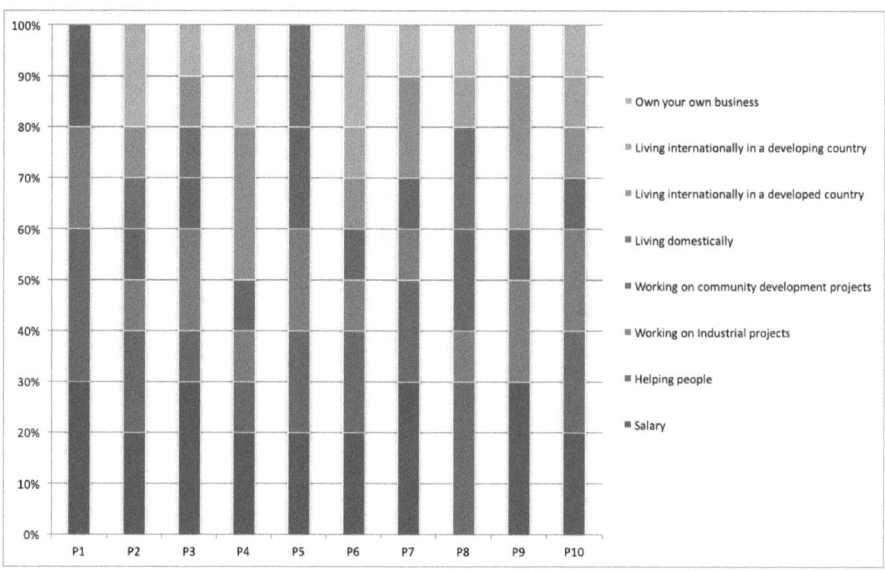

Fig. 1. Important job qualities as indicated per participant

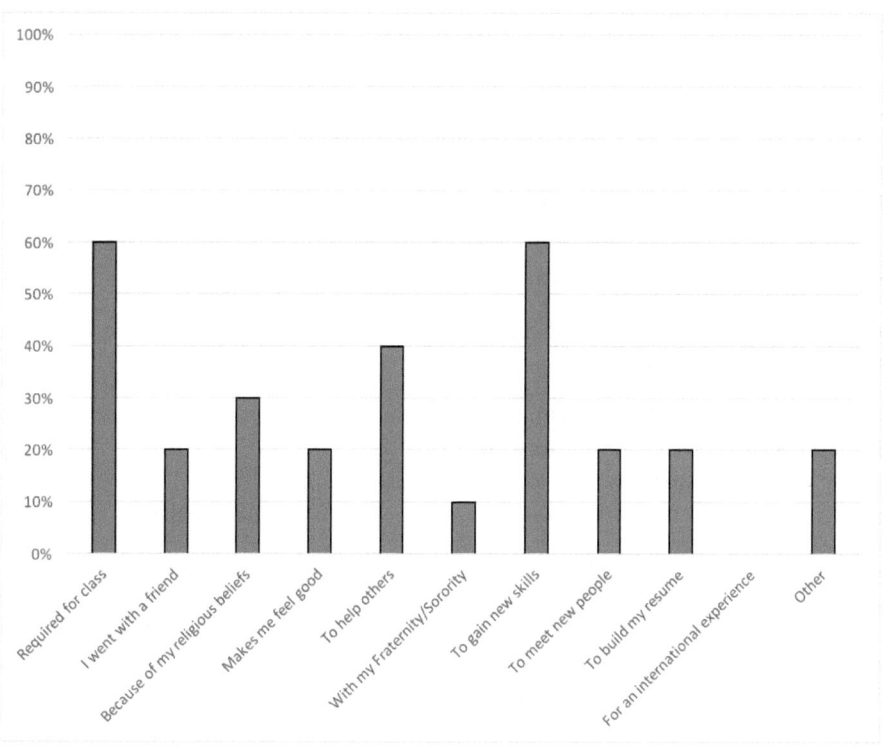

Fig. 2. Reasons provided by participants for volunteering currently or in the past

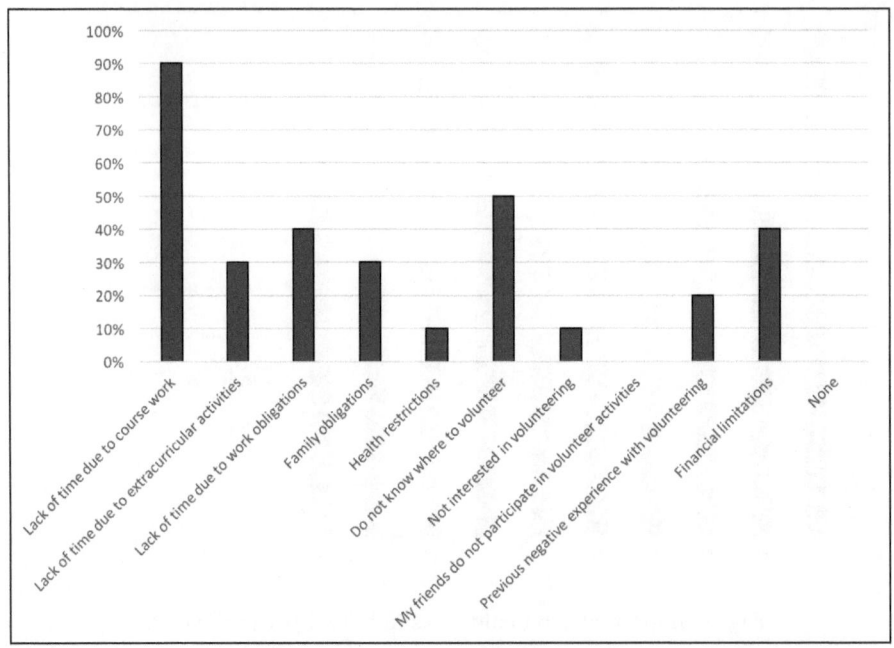

Fig. 3. Factors currently or previously inhibiting participation in volunteer activities

course work (28 %). 16 % of participants indicated that they did not know how to get involved in volunteering. Financial limitations (13 %) and lack of time due to work obligations (13 %) were also significant factors.

4.2   Results and Discussion of Interviews

In this section, we present and discuss the interview results under the following topics:

– perception of social responsibility;
– social issues considered important;
– role of geoinformatics;
– future career in geoinformatics in solving community problems;
– reasons for studying geoinformatics; and
– experience during community-based service learning module.

These topics serve to reflect on the objective to raise awareness of social issues, and to contribute to understanding students' sense of social responsibility and their perception of the role of geoinformatics in solving community problems.

Perception of Social Responsibility. Each participant completed the EPRA survey before starting his/her interview. The survey includes definitions for 'community service', 'social responsibility', 'social justice' and 'pro bono'. Social responsibility is defined as *"an obligation that an individual (or company) has to act with concern and sensitivity, aware of the impacts of their actions on others, particularly the disadvantaged"* [2]. Participants would have read this definition in the survey, but were asked again halfway through the interview to define social responsibility. The participants' definition of social responsibility helps to understand their attitude towards social responsibility and how they exploit volunteerism.

All participants were able to identify aspects of social responsibility in their definition. The focus was on community or society, followed by a focus on benefits. This focus encapsulates two key points of social responsibility. However, the concept of ethical duty was only mentioned, as 'obligation', by one participant. The following four distinct definitions illustrate participants' diverse perceptions of social responsibility:

- One participant defined social responsibility as *"your obligation to act in such a way that you positively affect the greater community"*.
- One participant spoke about assisting a community to the extent of one's abilities. This idea of "to the extent of one's abilities" aligns with the "proportional to the opportunities and skills which one has been afforded" in the definition by Rulifson and Bielefeldt [16].
- One participant had a very different view on social responsibility and focused more on not being involved in unethical practices and using one's skills to benefit society. Social responsibility is strongly connected to ethics and ethical duty, and it was interesting that this participant focused on unethical practices.
- One participant had a more passive approach to social responsibility and stated that one should *"not make things worse"*.

Participants with a high SR scores provided more accurate definitions of social responsibility and reported previous involvement in volunteerism. For example, one participant provided a near accurate definition of social responsibility. This participant has a strong sense of social responsibility (highest SR score), indicated a religious preference, indicated five reasons for volunteering (highest number of reasons), and also detailed involvement in weekly volunteer activities relating to church, tutoring, and everyday activities. On the other end of the spectrum, a participant with a low SR score reported lack of time and interest in volunteering as major factors inhibiting volunteering. This participant indicated a focus on environmental issues in the interview, while the EPRA survey was focused on volunteering related to humans. These results suggest that the EPRA survey can determine whether a participant has a sense of social responsibility towards humans. However, it is not suitable to identify social responsibility towards the environment.

Social Issues Considered Important. During the interview, the participants were asked twice which social issues are important to them; before (question

10) and after (question 16) discussion of the community-based service learning module (GMT320). From the discussion, it was evident that participants' background greatly influenced the social issues that they consider important. Below three specific motivations for social issues are discussed:

- One participant considers gender equality as important, and mentioned that ethnicity and family background were the main influences for considering these issues as important. In many communities in South Africa and across the world, women are still fighting against gender discrimination.
- Three participants are in the ethnic group that was previously disadvantaged in South Africa. All three participants consider education as the one social issue that they are passionate about. The three participants are from various (urban and rural) areas in South Africa and from different age groups, but all of them believe that education is important for people to improve themselves and their living circumstances.
- Three participants indicated that environmental issues are important to them. One of them was a 'Junior Honorary Ranger'[4] while at school. The participant volunteered in the South African National Parks (SANParks), amongst others, by removing alien invasive plants and identifying snares. Similarly, another participant had a botanist family member and grew up helping with 'Environmental Day' interventions (e.g. litter clean-up or alien invasive plant projects in local nature reserves).

Figure 4 provides an indication of how the participants changed their consideration of important social issues after discussing their experience of the community project. The graph shows the number of participants who indicated a specific issue in their responses to questions 10 and 12. After the discussion, participants were asked to single out one social issue that they are most passionate about. It is interesting to note that lack of service delivery was mentioned as a social issue for the first time after the discussion. This can be attributed to the lack of service delivery infrastructure in 'Alaska', Mamelodi. Other issues that received more attention afterwards are education, poverty and environmental issues. This shows that the experience in the community-based service learning module has raised their awareness of important social issues in the community.

Role of Geoinformatics in Solving Community Problems. The participants were asked how geoinformatics could be used to address social issues. This question focuses on the practical application of geoinformatics. All participants stated that geoinformatics could assist with mapping the issues, thus making them more visible. However, geoinformatics is generally also used to understand a social issue, aid in decision making, and sometimes also in identifying possible solutions. Only four participants focused on using geoinformatics to solve a social issue, and three on visualizing an issue to understand it better. Two participants stated they could be role models as geoinformatics professionals and

---

[4] http://www.sanparksvolunteers.org/.

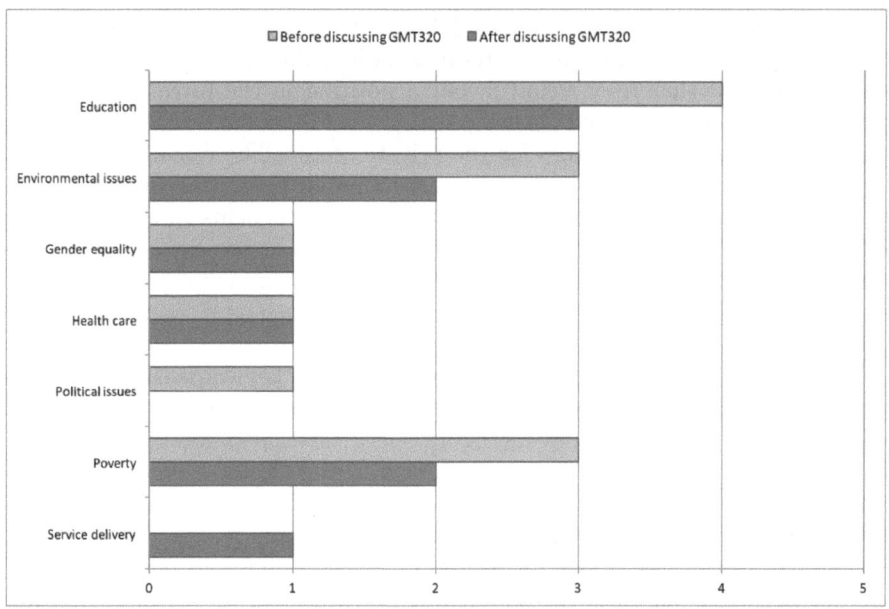

Fig. 4. Social issues mentioned by participants during the interview

that this could inspire others to overcome social issues, such as gender equality and poverty through education. One participant focused on using their education to educate others in less fortunate communities. These results suggest that the role of geoinformatics in understanding social problems and in solving them needs to receive more attention in the undergraduate curricula.

Future Career in Geoinformatics. Figure 1 provides an overview of the job qualities that participants indicated as important to them in the EPRA survey. To supplement this question, the participants were asked in the interview:

– to describe their ideal future career;
– which sector they would prefer to work for;
– possible companies that they have identified for future employment; and
– the qualities of a job or company that they consider important.

The participants are all in their 4th year of study, and most of them are likely to enter the job market at the end of this year. Five participants indicated that they would prefer an opportunity to work as a geoinformatics analyst, and one participant as a geoinformatics project manager. Geoinformatics analyst is the most common career path for a geoinformatics graduate, and the result is thus as expected. Four participants would prefer to start their own businesses; three of them in geoinformatics. Lastly, one participant indicated a research position in interdisciplinary research in mining and agriculture.

When asked if they would prefer a job opportunity in the public sector, private sector or at a non-governmental organization, the majority of participants (eight) indicated that they would favour a position in the private sector. The variety of projects, perceived challenges they would face, and making a greater impact was cited as motivators for the private sector. The remaining two participants indicated that they would prefer the public sector, because it offers a comfort zone and because of the additional employee benefits in the public sector. Currently, most participants (seven) do not have a preference for a future employer. Google and Esri were identified as ideal future employers in the private sector, and local municipalities or parastatals, such as Eskom (electricity), in the public sector.

The 'wordle'[5] in Fig. 5 provides an overview of the keywords that the participants used when describing the qualities that are important to them in a job opportunity or company. From the figure it is clear that a good work environment is most important to the participants, followed closely by opportunity for progress, variety of projects and a good salary. Two participants mentioned that community work would be important qualities for them.

The participants were asked which opportunity they would pursue if offered two positions of equal pay, one opportunity with a focus on social responsibility projects (i.e. community projects) and the other one not. All participants, except one, selected the job opportunity with social responsibility projects. The participant who did not select the social responsibility opportunity, motivated this choice by stating that such an opportunity would be emotionally draining and that it would be difficult to separate work from personal life. The participant would prefer to be involved in community projects or volunteering in a personal or private capacity.

Fig. 5. Key qualities mentioned by the participants (produced with 'wordle')

---

[5] http://www.wordle.net.

Reasons for Studying Geoinformatics. To get a better understanding of the participants reasons for studying geoinformatics, they were asked:

- why did they study geoinformatics?
- what in geoinformatics interests them?
- what do they like about geoinformatics?
- and, lastly, about positive and negative experiences during their undergraduate geoinformatics studies.

Seven participants were motivated by their geography school teacher to study geoinformatics. This started commonly as a love for geography and maps, and the job opportunities available in geoinformatics. Many participants also mentioned a love of technology. Two participants have previous qualifications, in architecture and surveying respectively. They indicated that they started studying geoinformatics because the previous degree was not a good fit for them or did not allow personal growth. After graduation, one participant is now perusing a degree in civil engineering, as he discovered a love for engineering through his undergraduate studies.

The range of possibilities and versatility of the application of geoinformatics interests participants about the field. They also mentioned that geoinformatics is new and still evolving and could thus provide them with numerous challenges. The use of software and tools to perform analyses, and the more practical use of geoinformatics were the aspects that the participants liked the most about geoinformatics.

The community-based service learning module was mentioned by five participants as a positive experience during their undergraduate studies. Their experience during this module will be presented in the next sub-section. Other positive experiences include learning new skills and the wide range of modules in different subjects in their first year of study (these include human geography, geomorphology, environmental sciences, meteorology, programming, systems theory, and information systems theory). However, some participants considered the large number of subjects and their relevance as frustrating. Programming modules were regarded as both positive and negative experiences, depending on whether participants found them challenging or not. Participants agreed that once they grasped the concept of programming, it turned into a positive experience. Nevertheless, most participants would not pursue a career in geoinformatics software development, and prefer analysis work. Interacting with industry representatives and guest lectures were positive experiences for five participants. Financial problems were negative experiences for some participants, and also motivated them through tough times (to avoid payment for repeating modules). One participant was motivated to "make the family proud".

Experience During the Community-Based Service Learning Module. GMT320 is the first module during their undergraduate degree for which only geoinformatics students can enrol. Positive experiences during the module included the opportunity to do field work, getting hands-on experience using a

GPS, completing a project from start to finish, and engaging with the community. All participants mentioned community interaction as a positive experience. They enjoyed learning about the community and sharing their knowledge about aerial photographs and GPSs with the community. The community was an inspiration to the participants because its members have so little, but are nevertheless full of pride.

The terrain, heat and the language barrier were challenges during the field-work, but provide the students with a true reflection of fieldwork in the 'real world'. The participants cited the need for the data to complete their project as their main motivation when fieldwork got tough. A frustrating, but positive experience, that most participants mentioned was the challenge of integrating the data captured by the four groups. As a result of poor planning, the integra-tion was not optimal and had to be repeated more than once. This was definitely an obstacle for the participants, but all participants noted that this mistake had taught them the importance of proper planning when starting a project.

The participants were very grateful for the opportunity to work with the Viva Foundation, but due to their many other priorities and commitments, the participants experienced Viva as having a lack of interest in the community project. This led them to question the usefulness of the project. One participant also had a bad previous experience with a community project (everything that the students contributed with their community project was destroyed after a few months) and that had influenced the participant's perspective on commu-nity engagement. Such experiences may negatively influence the participants' willingness for future community engagement.

5   Conclusion

In this paper we presented students' experiences of a community-based service learning approach in a third year geoinformatics module. Students mapped an informal settlement, captured information about dwellings and conducted a num-ber of studies in support of environmental and social problem solving. The aim was to raise awareness of social issues. We also wanted to understand students' sense of social responsibility and their perception of the role of geoinformatics in problem solving. After completion of the module, we conducted qualitative research through in-depth interviews with ten students.

After completion of the module in the second semester of 2015, in-depth interviews were conducted with ten students in March 2016. Before each inter-view, the participant completed a professional responsibility assessment (EPRA) from which a social responsibility score was calculated. The EPRA survey was developed to better understand students' attitude towards social responsibility and the effectiveness of educational interventions. An SR score for each partic-ipant was calculated from the EPRA survey, and showed that all participants, except one, scored in the upper quarter, meaning that most of them have a high sense of social responsibility.

Results of the in-depth interviews show that the participants have diverse perceptions of social responsibility; some can even be regarded as misperceptions.

A strong social responsibility score correlates with a participant's involvement in volunteering. The participants' experience in the community-based service learning module has raised their awareness of important social issues in the community, such as education, poverty, environmental issues and the lack of service delivery infrastructure. If given the choice, participants would prefer to work for an organisation that is involved in social responsibility projects.

Participants mentioned visualization and mapping as a means of raising awareness of social challenges through geoinformatics. The participants' responses to questions about the role of geoinformatics in addressing challenges, suggest that the role of geoinformatics in understanding social problems and in solving them needs to receive more attention in the undergraduate curricula. The real world experience of the community project provided the participants with valuable lessons for their future careers. It taught them about the numerous challenges one may face in fieldwork, such as terrain, weather and data integration. Additionally, students learned the importance of planning. They needed to plan how four groups would go about capturing data and how the data would be integrate into a single harmonised dataset.

The results of the in-depth interviews confirm the value of community-based service learning in enhancing understanding of theoretical concepts [5,19] and facilitating contributions to local communities [19]. In addition, the experience prepared students for their future career, as also reported by Helzer [10].

Generally, interview participants reported a love of geography, maps and technology as the reason for choosing geoinformatics as a career. The range of possibilities and versatility of the application of geoinformatics interests participants about the field, there was no mention of contributing to society as a reason for becoming a geoinformatics professional. These results are significantly different to EPRA survey results with engineering students in the US who generally linked engineering to social responsibility in some manner [17]. However, more studies need to be done to make any general conclusion.

This was a first experience with a community-based service learning approach in a geoinformatics module and it raises many questions for further work. For example, in future, we will ask students about their perceptions of social responsibility before and after completion of the module. This will provide a clearer indication of how the module influenced their perceptions. The professional responsibility assessment needs to be revised to consider both human and environmental issues, as both are relevant to geoinformatics work. The assessment questions also need to be adapted to be more suitable for geoinformatics students (as opposed to engineering) and they should consider South African circumstances. For example, international travel as a motivation for volunteering seems to be irrelevant to South African students.

South Africa has a highly diverse population with a Gini coefficient of 59.3,[6] indicating very high wealth inequalities in the population. There are also many environmental and social challenges to be addressed and it is important to

---

[6] http://data.worldbank.org/indicator/SI.POV.GINI?locations=ZA.

understand how geoinformatics students can be made aware of the role of geoinformatics in addressing these challenges.

Acknowledgments. We would like to thank the Viva Foundation for the productive collaboration on the GMT320 project in 'Alaska'. We appreciate the financial support for transportation of the students to the informal settlement provided by Community Engagement at the University of Pretoria. Finally, we would like to acknowledge the contribution by the ten students who participated in the interviews.

References

1. Bielefeldt, A., Canney, N.E.: Social responsibility attitudes of first year engineering students and the impact of courses. In: Proceedings 121st ASEE Annual Conference and Exposition, paper #9569, Indianapolis (2014)
2. Canney, N.E.: Assessing engineering students' understanding of personal and professional social responsibility. Ph.D. thesis, University of Colorado (2013)
3. Canney, N.E., Bielefeldt, A.: A framework for the development of social responsibility in engineers. Int. J. Eng. Educ. **31**, 414–424 (2015)
4. Canney, N.E., Bielefeldt, A.: A model for the development of personal and professional social responsibility for engineers. In: Proceedings 199th ASEE Annual Conference and Exposition, San Antonio (2012)
5. Dorsey, B.: Linking theories of service-learning and undergraduate geography education. J. Geogr. **100**, 124–132 (2001)
6. Duffy, J., Barry, C., Barrington, L., Heredia, M.: Service-learning in engineering science courses: does it work? In: Proceedings ASEE Annual Conference and Exposition, Austin (2009)
7. Giles, D.E., Eyler, J.S.: The impact of a college community service laboratory on students' personal, social, and cognitive outcomes. J. Adolesc. **17**(4), 327–339 (1994)
8. Hamilton, C., Flanagan, C.: Reframing social responsibility within a technology-based youth activist program. Am. Behav. Sci. **51**(3), 444–465 (2007)
9. Harvey, F.: Values, choices, responsibilities: thinking beyond the scholarly place of ethics for the GIScience and technology profession and GIScience. J. Geogr. High. Educ. **38**, 500–510 (2014)
10. Helzer, J.: Elearning by doing: a geographic approach to service learning and building community. Calif. Geogr. **50**, 75 (2010)
11. Jordaan, M.: Community project module. University of Pretoria (2016). http:// www.up.ac.za/en/community-project-module/article/1949838/jcp-module
12. Leveson, L., Joiner, T.A.: Exploring corporate social responsibility values of millennial job-seeking students. Educ. Training **56**, 21–34 (2014)
13. Mohan, J.: Thinking local: service-learning, education for citizenship and geography. J. Geogr. High. Educ. **19**, 129–142 (1995)
14. Neuman, M.: Teaching collaborative and interdisciplinary service-based urban design and planning studios. J. Urban Des. **21**(5), 596–615 (2016)
15. Pedersen, P.J., Meyer, J.M., Hargrave, M.: Learn global, serve local: student outcomes from a community-based learning pedagogy. J. Exp. Educ. **38**(2), 189–206 (2015)
16. Rulifson, G., Bielefeldt, A.: Engineering students' varied and changing views of social responsibility. In: Proceedings 122nd ASEE Annual Conference and Exposition, paper #13591, Seattle (2015)

17. Rulifson, G., Bielefeldt, A.: Understanding of social responsibility by first year engineering students: ethical foundations and courses. In: Proceedings 121st ASEE Annual Conference and Exposition, paper #9425, Indianapolis (2014)
18. United Nations: United Nations Sustainable Development Goals (2015). http://www.un.org/sustainabledevelopment/sustainable-development-goals/
19. Warren, J.L.: Does service-learning increase student learning? A meta-analysis. Mich. J. Community Serv. Learn. **18**(2), 56–61 (2012)

Which Are Harder? Soft Skills or Hard Skills?

Vreda Pieterse[1(✉)] and Marko van Eekelen[2,3]

[1] Department of Computer Science, University of Pretoria, Pretoria, South Africa
vreda.pieterse@up.ac.za
[2] Open University of the Netherlands, Heerlen, The Netherlands
marko.vanEekelen@ou.nl
[3] Radboud University Nijmegen, Nijmegen, The Netherlands

Abstract. This paper describes some technical and employability skills that are essential for our students to succeed in a career in software development. We conducted research aimed at understanding the students' problems when required to develop these skills. We explain our techniques for observing skills gaps. Knowledge about these gaps enables us to intervene and suggest remedial action. We discuss how we create opportunities for our students to enhance their skills, based on our experience and the findings of our research.

Keywords: Software development · Technical skills · Employability skills · Soft skills

1 Introduction

Apart from equipping our students with the technical knowledge and practical experience needed to enter the workforce, it is our educational responsibility to create opportunities for them to develop their employability skills.

Employment experts agree that technical skills may secure an interview, but that soft skills may well be a decisive factor in landing and keeping a job. Potential employees are expected not only to have the skills required in the job description of a vacancy, but also to convince their potential employer that they will be able to make progress in an enterprise and contribute successfully to its strategic directions.

Our teaching is aimed at providing a complete learning experience to cover the spectrum of skills required in a career in software development. These skills can roughly be classified in two categories, namely technical skills, often called hard skills and employability skills, commonly referred to as soft skills. Here we mention a broad selection of each of these types of skills relevant to our context and describe how we create opportunities for our students to develop these skills in our final-year software engineering module.

2 Technical Skills

A software engineering course should introduce students to common software engineering practices and tools from both a theoretical and a practical

© Springer International Publishing AG 2016
S. Gruner (Ed.): SACLA 2016, CCIS 642, pp. 160–167, 2016.
DOI: 10.1007/978-3-319-47680-3_15

perspective [10]. Every student should aquire the necessary technical fluency skills such as unit testing, pair programming, refactoring and continuous integration. Besides these general skills and those specified in the Computer Science Curricula 2013 report by ACM/IEEE [6], the following should receive attention:

Problem Solving. Higher cognitive skills such as inference, problem solving and product development are learned through life experiences similar to those for learning social skills. Stokes and Fisher [14] observe that working with constraints is critical to creative achievement. For this reason, we emphasise constraints when presenting the software development tasks in our course.

Configuration Management. It is common practice to use modern configuration management tools, such as `git`,[1] or subversion so that a team of people can be facilitated to work concurrently on the same artefacts, resolving conflicts as needed. We expect our students to use these tools.

Build Tools. Modern software systems are generally complex and building complex systems requires identifying and configuring the dependencies among a variety of components, which may themselves be developed in different technologies. Activities such as linking, compiling, testing, packaging, deployment and distribution of these systems are complex. It is standard practice in industry to use platform-independent build tools which automate these activities. Examples include `make`, `Apache`, `Ant`, `Maven`, `Gradle` and `npm`.

3   Employability Skills

The need for employability skills is emphasised in the Computer Science Curricula 2013 report by ACM/IEEE, where the knowledge areas explicitly include social issues and professional practice as well as project management with all its facets, as part of the software engineering knowledge area [6]. Liebenberg and Pieterse [7] observe that high-value computing skills and capabilities alone are not enough when one has to compete and succeed as a software developer in industry. The following skills are important in all careers:

Communication. The success or failure of a software engineering project can often be attributed to the effectiveness of communication among the various stakeholders of the system under development [1]. We monitor our students' communication skills by regularly evaluating all forms of communication, from the quality of their comments in code and git commit messages, the quality and coherence of the documentation of their projects to their presentation skills when demonstrating their projects.

---

[1] https://git-scm.com/.

Management and Planning. It is well known that software engineering management and planning involve balancing the scope, budget, time-to-market and quality of a software project. The consequences of bad planning may include the failure of the project as well as interpersonal disasters [4]. We encourage the use of software tools for project management, including the use of burn-down charts and Gantt charts.

Teamwork and Collaboration. Teamwork is not merely the ability to work well as a member of a team. It includes aspects such as getting along with people of different ages, genders, races, religions or political persuasions; defining one's role in a team; identifying the strengths of the other team members; and being able to lead a team effectively [8]. We aim to enhance the teamwork skills of our students by fostering the characteristics of high-performing collaborative teams identified by Cheruvelil et al. [3], namely the positive interdependence of team members, effective communication, and individual and group accountability.

Interpersonal Relations. Interpersonal skills have two components, namely social sensitivity and emotional engagement. Social sensitivity is the capacity to maintain healthy social relationships [16]. Emotional engagement is the level of empathy one has for the other team members and one's devotion to the project as a whole [11]. During the first six weeks of our course, we assigned students to short-lived teams to complete a task. This strategy provides a platform where students are exposed to situations where they could use interpersonal skills in cases where mistakes could be made without having to resolve the harm caused.

4   Relative Difficulty of Learning Hard and Soft Skills

We conducted a survey, asking our students to compare the difficulty of learning technical skills with the difficulty of acquiring social skills. There were three options: the Pretoria University Software Engineering class, the Radboud University Software Engineering class [2], or both. To avoid the influence of cultural differences, we chose a single university: Pretoria, since this university had the highest number of students. The students had to answer the multiple-choice question of Fig. 1, and then write a sentence or paragraph to explain the reasons for their answer.

   At the time, the participants were working in teams on their final capstone projects. Of the 160 students in the class, 107 completed the survey, giving us a response rate of 67 %. Five of the responses were incomplete and have not been included in our analysis. We used the explanation that the respondents who selected the middle option to classify them as being either *both are challenging* or *both are easy*.

   To visualise the relative ease with which the students mastered the two categories of skills, we classified each type separately in four classes, namely *very easy, easy, challenging,* and *very challenging*. When classifying each respondent in terms of their ease of acquiring social skills, students who indicated that both

COS301 is about learning skills in a variety of domains. The development of skills, whether technical or social, requires practice. Rate the level of difficulty for you to acquire social skills relevant to work in your team in relation to the difficulty you experience in acquiring technical skills relevant to your project.
— *Acquiring social skills is fun: it comes naturally to me*
— *Acquiring social skills is easier*
— *I find both equally challenging or easy*
— *Acquiring technical skills is easier*
— *Acquiring technical skills is fun: I like solving technical problems*

Fig. 1. The question students had to answer

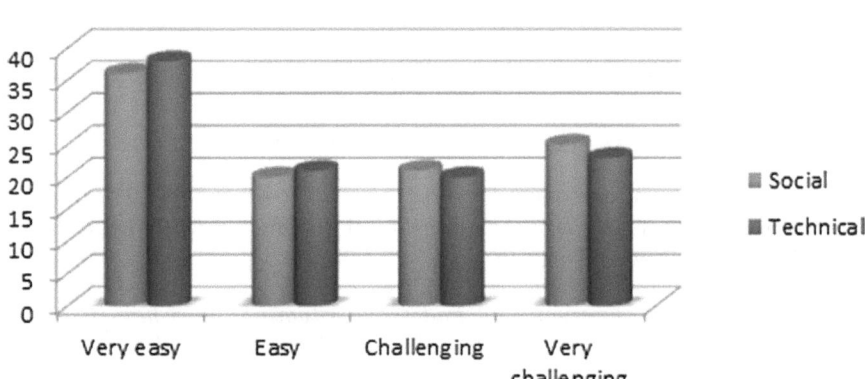

Fig. 2. Number of students in each category per type of skill (n = 102)

were easy as well as those who indicated that they found social skills much easier were counted as *very easy*; those who responded that social skills were easier were counted as *easy*; those who said technical skills were easier were counted as *challenging*; and the rest were counted as *very challenging*. Similarly the students were classified in terms of their comfort about learning technical skills. Figure 2 shows the results.

It is clear that the number of students in each of the classes is almost the same for both types of skills, though the number of students who found it very easy to overcome technical obstacles was marginally higher than the number of students who had issues with mastering social skills. Stated differently, those who struggle with social skills are only slightly higher in number than those who struggle with technical skills. The majority of the students stated that they found learning technical skills and acquiring social skills equally easy. A gifted student who claimed to breeze through the academic programme made the following claim:

I am already quite a social person and I really like to think I have a knack for understanding technology at the same time.

Many students who claimed that they did not have difficulties when social skills were needed, based their argument on the fact that they already had these skills or had the right personality to help them perform teamwork almost effortlessly. The following remark is representative of the comments of these students:

I'm a social person. I do well in social situations and am the most sociable guy in the group. So learning to interact with fellow group members wasn't challenging at all to me. I actually enjoyed it.

Another frequent reason the respondents gave for finding the acquisition of social skills very easy was simply that the other people with whom they had to work were pleasant and accommodating.

Since we are all friends I find the question above to be one sided since we have already established the social skills in the group to work together. Therefore I would find acquiring social skills to be easier.

Students who claimed that they found it easy to learn technical skills often admitted that they shied away from the need to interact with people, as is evident from the following remark:

I'm a more technical person and find social situations very hard to deal with, so I'd much rather solve technical problems than deal with social problems.

A number of students explained the aspects of social interaction that contributed to their finding it difficult to master social skills. In contrast to technical knowledge which is more likely to be exact, they pointed out that people were complex and might be inconsistent. Often there are many ways to deal with people and none of them is unconditionally wrong or guaranteed to have the required positive effect. These uncertainties might make it more challenging for these students to collaborate with people than to learn technical aspects, as explained in the following remark:

I am not the most social of people and dealing with technical aspects can be frustrating but not as much as dealing with people. People can be quite difficult at times.

A respondent found it difficult to trust other people and might be tempted to do work on their behalf so as to ensure that the project would not fail not realising that he was denying himself the opportunity to improve his management skills and also denying the other team members an opportunity to gain technical experience. The following comment by this respondent reveals this:

People tend to be unreliable and it is easier to finish a 1 hour bug fix than to wait days or weeks for others to get to it. Ensuring others do their jobs sometimes helps, however it also does put oneself behind on work and that is risky.

5   Recommendations

This pilot study revealed that, although many students are confident that they are capable of learning the required skills, some individuals may need assistance and encouragement to learn some of the skills. It is often the case that someone who has reached high technical competency may lack social skills, and vice versa. We recommend that a complete learning experience for all our students should be ensured. We describe how we attempt to identify the skills gaps of our students on an individual basis and how we provide opportunities for students to close these gaps. This should serve as inspiration for others to apply similar strategies, appropriate to their situation, to achieve the same goals.

5.1   Uncovering Skills Gaps

We subscribe to the learning theory of Gibbs [5], supported by Schank [13], that doing is an effective way of learning. We believe that students learn best by resolving their own issues because this increases their sense of accomplishment. It is possible, however, that problems which are not dealt with appropriately at an early stage may grow into bigger problems which may be difficult to resolve at a later stage. For this reason, we observe the team activities closely and are constantly on the alert to signs of underdeveloped skills that often manifest as turmoil in a team.

We instruct our students to complete peer reviews at regular intervals. The main purpose of these peer reviews is to provide a structured opportunity to reflect on teamwork experiences. Such self-reflection may lead an individual to discover personal skills gaps. Apart from serving as a reflection tool, we use these reviews as an instrument to gauge the skill levels of the students. The questions that the students have to answer are intended to guide them to reflect on their own contributions and also on the contributions of the other members. The questions used in our reviews are described by Marshall et al. [9].

We analyse the feedback the students provide in their peer ratings, using the procedure described by Pieterse and Thompson [12]. This analysis reveals whether or not there is conflict in a team, which may be an indication of a lack of social skills. Students may report the inability of one or more of their peers to complete certain tasks, in which case the lack of technical skills can be identified.

5.2   Closing Skills Gaps

Technical skills as well as social skills can be enhanced when students work in teams. When students with varying viewpoints are grouped together for a project, conflict is likely to arise. When a team deals constructively with this conflict and follows procedure, the act of resolving as well as the resolution itself will probably motivate the members. This in turn can contribute to improved team performance. If a team performs at its peak, the combined achievement could surpass the sum of the achievements of the individual members [15].

The downside of differences in opinion and misunderstanding among members, is that it may decrease motivation. We try to intervene swiftly and with a constructive agenda when we observe signs of destructive conflict. We call our unobtrusive intervention our *chat-walk-chat* strategy [10]. Ideally, from the student's point of view, these chats should seem coincidental, but from the staff member's point of view, they are an active means of seeking opportunities to create a "coincidental" meeting. The use of social media and knowledge of the lecture schedules of the courses for which the students are registered, make it possible to bump into a student on campus and start a conversation aimed at guiding the student to deal with the lurking problem.

When a student complains to staff members, we try to respond openly and as soon as possible. In such a case, we arrange a meeting with all the students involved. The meeting venue is the lecturer's office and the time is agreed individually with the students involved. We try to be as discreet and sympathetic as possible and are careful not to reveal the whistle-blower to the affected parties. We simply state that the issue came to our attention, describe the issue in general terms and then ask all parties, including the whistle-blower, to state their opinion about the truth of our summary of the problem. In most cases the discussion can be steered towards better mutual understanding. Often the whistle-blowers had a greater role in instigating the problem than they may care to admit.

6   Conclusion

Our research revealed that many of our students were confident that they could master the required skills. The students who stated that some of the skills might be difficult to acquire have also succeeded in identifying the reasons for finding it difficult and proposed actions they would take or had taken to overcome their difficulties. This is evidence that our teaching strategies have been successful and that the students are generally appreciative of our efforts.

In our presentation of the software engineering module, we aim to create optimal opportunities for students to learn by doing tasks on their own, and to develop the required skills through experiential learning, without smothering or policing them.

In future work, we also intend to use the available data to check whether there is a correlation between how students have participated and performed and how hard they found the acquisition of the skills (both soft and hard). Furthermore, it is the intention to enhance this study with a comparison between a Dutch university and a South-African university, including the possibility of cultural influences too.

References

1. Bostrom, R.P.: Successful application of communication techniques to improve the systems development process. Inf. Manage. **16**(5), 279–295 (1989)
2. Buisman, A.L.D., van Eekelen, M.: Gamification in educational software development. In: Proceedings of the Computer Science Education Research Conference, CSERC 2014, NY, USA, pp. 9–20 (2014). http://doi.acm.org/10.1145/2691352.2691353
3. Cheruvelil, K.S., Soranno, P.A., Weathers, K.C., Hanson, P.C., Goring, S.J., Filstrup, C.T., Read, E.K.: Creating and maintaining high-performing collaborative research teams: the importance of diversity and interpersonal skills. Front. Ecol. Env. **12**(1), 31–38 (2014). http://0-dx.doi.org.innopac.up.ac.za/10.1890/130001
4. Ferrucci, F., Harman, M., Ren, J., Sarro, F.: Not going to take this anymore: Multi-objective overtime planning for software engineering projects. In: Proceedings of the 2013 International Conference on Software Engineering, ICSE 2013, pp. 462–471. IEEE Press, Piscataway (2013). http://0-dl.acm.org.innopac.up.ac.za/citation.cfm?id=2486788.2486849
5. Gibbs, G.: Learning by Doing: A Guide to Teaching and Learning Methods. Far Eastern University Publications, Manila (1988)
6. Joint Task Force on Computing Curricula ACM/IEEE: Computer sciencecurricula 2013: Curriculum guidelines for undergraduate degreeprograms in computer science, January 2013. http://dl.acm.org/citation.cfm?id=2534860
7. Liebenberg, J., Pieterse, V.: Career goals of software development professionals and software development students. In: Proceedings of the Computer Science Education Research Conference, CSERC 2016. ACM, New York (2016)
8. Marock, C.: Grappling with youth employability in South Africa. Technical report, Human Sciences Research Council, Pretoria (2008)
9. Marshall, L., Pieterse, V., Thompson, L., Venter, D.M.: Exploration of participation in student software engineering teams. ACM Trans. Comput. Educ. (TOCE) **16**(2), 5:1–5:38 (2016). http://doi.acm.org/10.1145/2791396
10. Omeleze, S., Pieterse, V., Solms, F.: Teaching modular software development and integration. In: 6th Annual International Conference on Computer Science Education: Innovation & Technology, pp. 178–197. GSTF (2015)
11. Parker, J.N., Hackett, E.J.: Hot spots and hot moments in scientific collaborations and social movements. Am. Sociol. Rev. **77**(1), 21–44 (2012)
12. Pieterse, V., Thompson, L.: Investigating the applicability of Belbin Roles on participatory levels in IT student teams. In: Proceedings of the 44th Annual Conference of the Southern African Computer Lecturers' Association (SACLA), pp. 161–169. University of the Witwatersrand, Johannesburg (2015)
13. Schank, R.C.: What we learn when we learn by doing. Technical report, Technical Report No. 60, Institute for Learning Sciences, Northwestern University (1995)
14. Stokes, P.D., Fisher, D.: Selection, constraints, and creativity case studies: Max Beckmann and Philip Guston. Creativity Res. J. **17**, 283–291 (2005)
15. Tziner, A., Eden, D.: Effects of crew composition on crew performance: does the whole equal the sum of its parts? J. Appl. Psychol. **70**(1), 85–93 (1985)
16. Woolley, A.W., Chabris, C.F., Pentland, A., Hashmi, N., Malone, T.W.: Evidence for a collective intelligence factor in the performance of human groups. Science **330**(6004), 686–688 (2010)

Various Experiences

A Case Study in the Use of the Five Step Peer Evaluation Strategy to Improve a First Year Computer Literacy Course: An Exercise in Reflective Evaluation Practice

Mosiuoa Tsietsi[✉]

Department of Computer Science, Rhodes University, Grahamstown, South Africa
m.tsietsi@ru.ac.za

Abstract. In this paper, I recount my experiences in conducting a comprehensive five step evaluative exercise which was aimed at collecting feedback from various sources in order to help inform future teaching interventions for a first year computer literacy course in a South African university. The exercise centres on a focus group study that was conducted with a number of students who had completed the course between 2013 and 2015 and solicited their feedback on the basis of their own personal experiences. The five step process in which this study was executed included collecting feedback from a critical peer in addition to synthesising the author's own insights. The study was prompted by the author's realization that feedback is most often mistaken for evaluation, whereas evaluation is better conceived as the triangulation of various sources of information. The use of a focus group study instead of the common feedback method of the questionnaire also helped engage the students more robustly and was better suited as a tool to collect a richer set of qualitative data. The study yielded useful insights which have implications for teaching and learning activities, assessment of student learning and the curriculum at large.

Keywords: Computer literacy · Reflective evaluation

1 Introduction

The focus of this paper is a first year computer literacy course that is offered by the Department of Computer Science at my university. It is a single semester, non-continuing course for non-computer science majors. The purpose of the course is to provide students with the tools they need in order to be proficient enough with computers and technology to be able to use them appropriately within their departmental contexts. To facilitate this, the course is divided into four modules: Spreadsheets, Human Computing and Publishing, with a brief three week Introduction module at the beginning which I teach.

The literacy course is open to students from across the university, but is peculiar in that it is mandatory for all first year Pharmacy students. Figure 1 shows

© Springer International Publishing AG 2016
S. Gruner (Ed.): SACLA 2016, CCIS 642, pp. 171–178, 2016.
DOI: 10.1007/978-3-319-47680-3_16

enrolment figures from 2011 to 2016. It is evident from the bar chart that class sizes have remained moderately high throughout the years, no doubt in large part due to the steady stream of incoming Pharmacy students.

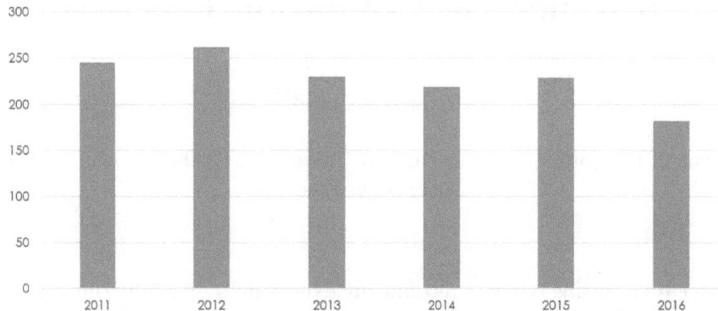

Fig. 1. Overall Enrolment Figures from 2011 to 2016

Not only is the class size typically large, but the student population is usually also very diverse. Diversity manifests itself in at least two different ways. Firstly, there is a considerable degree of racial diversity. This is evident from Fig. 2 which shows the same enrolment, only according to race. Figure 2 also shows that a significant proportion of the students come from the historically disadvantaged racial groups.

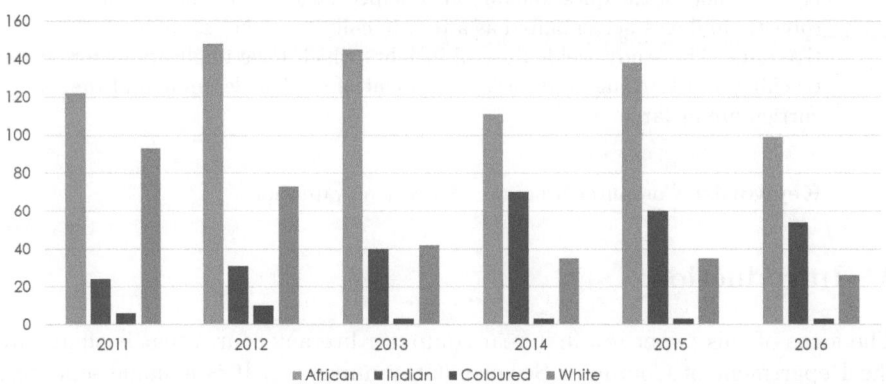

Fig. 2. Enrolment by Race from 2011 to 2016

Though it cannot be said for certain, but given the socio-political history of the country, it is likely that a significant number of them come from rural or township schools, and as such may not have had adequate exposure to computers and technology due to the financial cost of setting up and maintaining a computer lab. There is at least some anectodal evidence to support this whereby at the start of every academic year I usually ask the students who had not studied computers in high school to indicate this by raising their hands. About $\approx 75\%$ confirm this year after year, and the bulk of them are from the said racial groups.

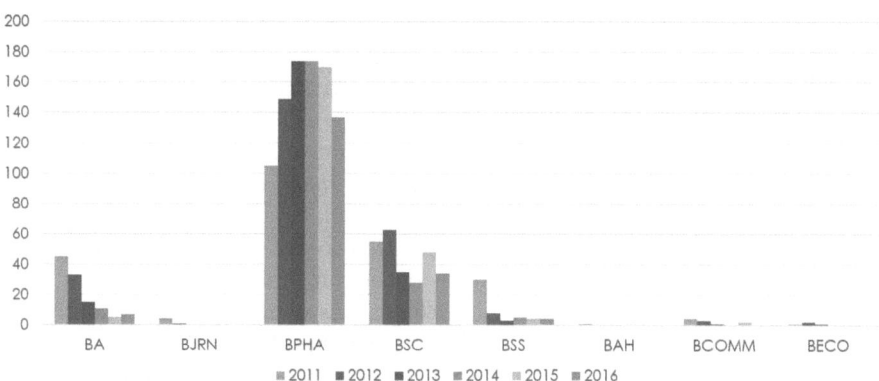

Fig. 3. Enrolment by Degree (Curriculum) from 2011 to 2016

Secondly, diversity also manifests itself in the range of disciplinary back-grounds from which the students come from. Figure 3 shows the degrees for which the students who participated in the course were enroled. The figure shows the dominance of the Pharmacy degrees, but also shows a signficant number of BSc and to a lesser extent, BA degrees. It is important to note that my university is informed to a large extent by a strong liberal arts tradition, and therefore per-mits students to incorporate different specialisations from different faculties into their degrees. So even where BSc or BA degrees appear, there is further diversity if one drills down and explores how those individual degrees are composed.

2   Motivation

In light of these realities, I was interested in collecting data that could help assess the extent to which the course was being taught in a manner that helped address the challenges of massification and diversity. This is part of what is referred to as reflective practice, where a teacher reflects on her experiences, and tries to assess the efficacy of their approach in light of factors that impinge on their practice.

Over the years, I have conducted various feedback exercises, exclusively through the medium of a questionnaire. My use of the questionnaire format was a knee-jerk reaction that I executed without much critical engagement since it was just standard practice in my department. However it is shown in [8] that while questionnaires are quite common, there is little evidence to show that they are well suited to help improve teaching practice. Furthermore, Morley [5] and

Murray [6] argue that feedback taken only from students cannot be used to reliably interrogate all aspects of teaching. They propose that additional sources be incorporated into feedback exercises in order to triangulate data and derive a more accurate assessment. As such, over the years, it became apparent to me that evaluation is best conducted in a more comprehensive way that considers feedback from various sources and not just the student.

3   Theoretical Underpinnings of Evaluation

In order for the teacher to know that she has taught in a good way, that teaching must be evaluated. Evaluation is a contentious space for many reasons. Some of the ways in which this is so are discussed in [9]; it shows that the process of evaluation should not be considered in isolation from teaching activities, which are often informed by the teacher's attitudes about teaching.

He shows that there is a continuum that spans qualitative and quantitative dimensions of teaching, which inform how teaching is then evaluated. The quantitative dimension of teaching is mostly teacher-focused, and is therefore associated with methods of evaluation that are geared toward measurability, scientific rigor and precision. On the other hand, the qualitative method of teaching is typically student-focused, and is geared toward reflection (examining one's practices to reform what one does) and reflexivity (examining one's attitudes/beliefs to reform what one does).

While the author's goal is not to denigrate the quantitative dimension, he does show that, by itself, it lacks the capacity to realise the full potential that evaluation exercises can deliver within critically reflective spaces in academia. For instance, the two strategies could be mixed in ways that can facilitate a better learning environment for the student.

The quantitative-qualitative paradigm is strikingly reminiscent of Pratt's work [7] on teaching perspectives. According to Pratt [7], all teachers adopt particular perspectives when teaching, and those perspectives can be categorised neatly into a finite number of qualitatively different perspectives. Those perspectives are transmission, apprenticeship, developmental, nurturing and social reform. They can be conceived as different expressions of teaching that are either teacher-focused, student-focused, or a mixture of both, with transmission (strong teacher-focus) and social reform (strong student-focus) at opposite ends of the continuum. The author's own teaching perspectives profile consists of a mixture of a strong transmission and apprenticeship perspective.

Trigwell [9] admits that perspectives often straddle the line between the two extremes. What does emerge, even for teachers with a strong teaching focus, is that there is value in the adoption of a student-focus that considers what the student is doing [1]. The teacher is encouraged to be reflexive and scholarly in their approach to teaching, and to use evaluation as a internally-inspired exercise that seeks to improve the quality of teaching for the benefit of the student, as opposed to merely using it as an instrument to provide a set of results for academic managers.

4   Exploring My Concerns

It is evident that class size and diversity are factors that require careful consideration when conducting teaching and learning activities in such a course. In line with this, as I reflected on my practice, I had a number of concerns related to the way in which my teaching spoke to these realities. Therefore, I decided that in line with creating a more enabling learning atmosphere that is more student-focused, I would conduct a feedback exercise to solicit feedback that could better help me respond to these special circumstances. Those concerns were as follows.

Suitability of the Lecture Venue: Due to class size, lectures are conducted in large teaching venues, but I have always thought that the best environment to teach in would be a computer laboratory. This would allow students to engage better with the practical skills they need to be able to demonstrate in mid-week practical sessions. Furthermore, my suspicion is that students who have been exposed to computers and technology before would be able to navigate this gap between lecture and laboratory, but those will less preparation would be hampered the most in their learning.

Relevance of the Curriculum to Student's Context: As a literacy course, none of the students who complete the course will continue to pursue a qualification in computer science. As such, it follows that students will be using what they are taught to enhance their learning in their own departmental contexts. As such, I was interested in finding out the extent to which what we teach them is able to translate into proficiency in the student's own contexts.

5   The Evaluation Instrument

5.1   Choosing an Instrument

One of the main objectives I had was to develop feedback for a specific purpose, and to choose a suitable instrument for doing so. Much has been written about the ineffectiveness of questionnaires as tools to transform teaching [3]. As such, I began exploring alternative methods of addressing the concerns I had. In [4] it is argued that quantitative feedback rarely helps to improve teaching practice. The authors go on to suggest alternative mechanisms for conducting evaluation including portfolios and interviews. Another example is a focus group where a small number of participants are invited to collectively provide feedback on the basis of a set of questions that an interviewer has prepared. The benefit of this format is that the group can feed off each other and develop each others' ideas as each contributes their opinion. I felt that would be a good way to proceed.

To conduct my focus group, I involved former students who had completed the course. Because I wanted to keep the session small and interactive, I reasoned that a good sub-group would be the class representatives, so I invited six representatives from previous years. With the help of the course-coordinator from the Pharmacy faculty, the students were contacted and requested to participate.

5.2   Choosing a Format

The five step strategy for peer review is a framework that identifies steps that a teacher and a critical peer can use to develop a well-managed peer interaction. The strategy is supported by the Centre for Higher Education Research Teaching and Learning at my university [2]. While it is not a widely known strategy, it is based on well known concepts such as self and peer assessment. It consists of the following steps:

1. *Pre-observational Meeting:* This is meant to achieve a number of objectives such as to develop rapport between the lecturer and the critical peer, communicate the purpose of the evaluation exercise and outline the aspects of teaching that are to be evaluated.
2. *The Observation:* This refers to the actual session that informs the evaluation. The peer is invited to attend the session where he or she must take into consideration the objectives of the teacher and the specific aspects of the session that the teacher wishes the peer to provide feedback on.
3. *Period of Analysis:* Once the session is over, the peers go away and consider what they have observed. This process is meant to occur as soon as possible after the session while the peers' observations are still fresh in their minds.
4. *Post-observational Meeting:* Later, the peers report on their findings. The lecturer can then speak back to this feedback and the two can discuss strategies to manage any matters arising.
5. *The Report:* Finally, a written report is given to the lecturer with a summary of their findings.

6   Results and Discussion

The process was highly valuable and helped to shape and inform the focus group study that I executed. In this section, I give a broad overview of the main points that I gathered from the study, and the issues the students raised that I feel are pertinent to my practice as a teacher.

6.1   The Unsuitability of the Lecture Venue

One of my main concerns had to do with the lecture venue being poorly suited for teaching a practical course like computer literacy. One of the participants explained that she had been intent on taking detailed notes in class. However, when some of the more practical parts of the course began to be taught she began to doubt whether there was any value in what she was doing:

> *"Honestly, I started off writing notes, then I just stopped. It felt like I wasn't learning anything"* (Participant 4).

Another participant suggested that the lecturer could find some way of integrating the lectures and the practicals in some way:

"Maybe you can find a way, to like, integrate the lectures and the tuts, like make it one thing almost ... something to that effect ... lectures should be done in the computer labs on the screen and then you follow what the lecturer is doing" (Participant 3).

As a result of these contributions some useful interventions could be employed. For instance detailed notes with screenshots and steps could be provided which the students could follow in-lieu of an actual computer in front of them. Also, since students do their practicals in the middle of the week, a small amount of time (i.e. 15 min) could be allocated at the start of the practical to do some drill-and-practice exercises involving the repetition of actions in order to teach or develop a skill. The benefit of such exercises is that they can be utilised as foundational blocks for more meaningful learning.

6.2   Teaching in the Departmental Context

The participants showed that as part of their externship in a pharmacy, they have to use a computer program known as 'Unisolv':

"They have a computer system called Unisolv so we were thrown into the deep end because we had never seen this program before we have never used it before ... and it's hard for the pharmacists and assistants who are working to teach you because they have their own work to do" (Participant 3).

Hearing this from the students was interesting because it identified a gap in our curriculum. While I do not advocate that domain specific programs be taught in the course, I do believe that it is possible to expose students on some level to different kinds of interfaces and how those interfaces compare with standard Microsoft packages. To help ease the students into packages like Unisolv, the mastery of shortcuts needs to be re-informed, since there are no buttons and less of an emphasis on menu items. The abstraction of a number of interface layers that cannot be seen (unlike in Windows where multiple windows can be opened) could be better emphasised so that students are able to understand that systems can manage windows or multiple interfaces in different ways.

7   Conclusion

This paper has detailed work in progress related to the development of teaching interventions that were inspired by robust, qualitative evidence derived from student and peer interaction. It has shown how lecturers should be aware of the contexts in which they teach and attempt to respond to factors that impinge on their practice, such as massification and diversity. Notably, it was shown in [10] that closing the feedback loop, which is a term for providing feedback to participants, is an important yet neglected aspect of evaluation exercises. As such, after this study was executed, a summary of the findings and list of intended interventions was sent to the students. It is hoped this democratic gesture will have implications on how students respond to feedback exercises in future and demonstrate that they can be active participants in curriculum development.

References

1. Biggs, J.: What the student does: teaching for enhanced learning. High. Educ. Res. Dev. **18**(1), 57–75 (1999)
2. Centre for Higher Education Research Teaching and Learning: Evaluation of teaching and courses. Rhodes University, Grahamstown (2013)
3. Kember, D., Leung, D., Kwan, K.: Does the use of student feedback questionnaires improve the overall quality of teaching? Assess. Eval. High. Educ. **27**(5), 411–425 (2002)
4. McKeachie, W., Kaplan, M.: Persistent problems in evaluating college teaching (2007). http://cedar.olemiss.edu/depts/vc_academic_affairs/problems.html
5. Morley, D.: Claims about the reliability of student evaluations of instruction: the ecological fallacy rides again. Stud. Educ. Eval. **38**, 15–20 (2012)
6. Murray, H.: Does evaluation of teaching lead to improvement of teaching? Int. J. Acad. Dev. **2**(1), 20–41 (1997)
7. Pratt, D.: Good teaching: one size fits all?. In: Ross-Gordon, J. (ed.) An Update on Teaching Theory, pp. 5–16. Jossey-Bass, San Franciso (2002)
8. Saroyan, A., Amundsen, C.: Evaluating university teaching: time to take stock. Assess. Eval. Highjer Educ. **26**(4), 341–353 (2010)
9. Trigwell, K.: Judging university teaching. Int. J. Acad. Dev. **6**(1), 65–73 (2001)
10. Watson, S.: Closing the feedback loop: ensuring effective action from student feedback. Tert. Educ. Manag. **9**(2), 145–157 (2003)

Enterprise Resource Planning Teaching Challenges Faced by Lecturers in African Higher Education Institutions

Khadija M. Mahanga and Lisa F. Seymour$^{(\boxtimes)}$

Department of Information Systems,
University of Cape Town, Cape Town, South Africa
mhnkha002@myuct.ac.za, lisa.seymour@uct.ac.za

Abstract. Enterprise Resource Planning (ERP) is considered a scarce graduate competence due to ERP pervasiveness in industry. In response the international Information Systems 2010 curricula includes ERP courses. Yet most African HEIs struggle to integrate and teach technology due to challenges such as poor technology infrastructure. Hence developing ERP courses comes with major challenges. Therefore this research aimed to identify challenges of teaching ERP in African HEIs. The study in a case from Namibia and Tanzania confirmed literature challenges such as financial constraints and insufficient technological infrastructure, and new challenges emerged such as course scheduling challenges and dealing with diverse students such as part-time and distance learning students. The study proposes strategies to deal with these challenges.

Keywords: Enterprise resource planning · ERP education · ERP challenges · African ICT education · Tertiary education · Teaching challenges

1 Introduction

African Higher Education Institution (HEIs) have been striving to integrate Information Communication Technologies (ICTs) in their curricula [16], in response to pressure and demand by industries for ICT graduates. Yet ICT integration in African HEIs a complex process [4,12]. An Enterprise Resource Planning (ERP) system is an enterprise-wide software system that provides comprehensive functionality and allows integration of core business processes in organizations [14]. ERP systems offer benefits to ERP adopters [6,13] which has driven adoption and the demand for ERP specialists to implement, maintain and support these systems in organizations [5,19]. In response to this demand, the international information systems (IS) model curriculum (IS2010) recommends that most IS career tracks include enterprise systems [17]. Several HEIs globally and in Africa have integrated ERP knowledge into curricula [14]. Yet, introducing new ICT in teaching introduces challenges for HEIs and these are more pronounced in Africa [10]. Hence motivating this study to identify and describe challenges faced by HEIs while teaching ERP in African HEIs and

© Springer International Publishing AG 2016
S. Gruner (Ed.): SACLA 2016, CCIS 642, pp. 179–186, 2016.
DOI: 10.1007/978-3-319-47680-3_17

suggest solutions to dominant challenges. Also answering a call for more ERP education research as the area has been described as under-researched [8].

2   Challenges in Teaching Technology in Africa

Many studies have identified barriers to ICT teaching in Africa. Firstly, implementing new courses in HEIs is protracted due to its long process [4]. Some administrators fear the expense of starting new courses while others keep away from new tracks as they are rooted to their traditional tracks [1]. The lack of a systematic approach to ICT implementation is also reported as a challenge [16]. Many HEIs in developing countries embrace the ICT integration process without clear plans and strategies to guide the process of integration [10]. Furthermore, most HEIs in Sub Saharan Africa (SSA) have limited infrastructure such as internet access, bandwidth, hardware and software provision and unreliable access to electricity [3]. Lack of technical and structural support is another barrier [16]. Other challenges are teachers' lack of expertise and confidence in ICT, lack of appreciation and negative attitude towards ICT integration, lack of top management involvement and lack of funds [18]. As with ICT integration, ERP integration is challenging. Firstly, developing ERP curricula demands detailed planning, high ICT support, and is time consuming [4]. ERP Curricula development includes organizing course materials, qualified trainers, ERP systems, case studies, and examinations [14,15]. Developing ERP case studies that can adequately capture the range of complexities and decision points of the dynamic nature of process implementation in organizations is challenging [4]. Moreover, HEIs cannot afford to adopt ERP equipment at the same rate as ERP implementers, making it difficult to offer ERP courses that are relevant and up-to date [7]. On the other hand, it is mentioned that ERP systems provided by vendors to institutions are not designed for instructional purpose, making the whole learning process challenging to students [4]. These potential ERP teaching challenges were used as a framework for this research.

3   Research Method

This paper aimed to answer the main research question: *What are the challenges faced while teaching ERP education in African HEIs?* As ERP education is new to African HEIs, the research adopted an exploratory and qualitative approach to seek insights on the challenges faced. A case study strategy was used using both observations and interviews. Two HEIs (coded as NT and UD) were purposively selected. Both had joined the Enterprise Systems Education for Africa (ESEFA) project [9], a HEI public-private funded project collaborating on curriculum and training. Data was collected through semi structured interviews with ERP lecturers (Table 1), and through observations during the first ERP course which included hands-on ERP exercises and theory through class lectures.

Table 1. Profile of participants

Interviewee	Job Title	ERP Theory Teaching Experience	ERP Practical Teaching Experience
I1	Senior Lecturer	10 years	4 years
I2	Lecturer	6 years	3 years
I3	Lecturer	1 years	1 years
I4	Lecturer	4 years	2 years
I5	Senior Lecturer	8 years	4 years
I6	Senior Lecturer	6 years	0 years
I7	Lecturer	2 years	0 years

Table 2. Table of findings and source of data

Challenges		Literature	Interview NT	UD	Observe NT	UD
Admin-istration	Lack of management commitment and support	[16, 10, 3]	7	3	√	√
	Resistance to change	[3]				√
	Lack of appreciation of the technology	[18]				
Techno-logy	Poor technological infrastructure	[16, 3]	9	7	√	√
	Poor or no access to ERP systems	[7]				
	Lack of technical support	[16, 7]				
Re-sources	Lack of financial resources	[16, 3]	6	3		
	Insufficient expertise and confidence	[11]	4	3	√	√
Students	Cannot afford the course	[4, 3]	3			
	Student background and enrolment status		5			
	Not motivated, and unable to understand	[2]				
Teaching	Difficulties in course planning	[4]	2	2		
	Insufficient course content	[4, 3]				
	Scheduling		4	1		

4   Data Analysis and Findings

Table 2 shows the challenges identified by the two sources of data (interviews and observation) from each case study. The conversational density (how many times each challenge was mentioned) of themes is provided for interviews per case and a mark is given for challenges observed. Italicised themes were not found in the literature.

4.1   Administration Challenges

Two administration challenges that emerged were insufficient support and commitment from senior administration and resistance to change. Lack of appreciation of ICT was found in the literature but was not evident in this research. Senior administration assist in operational strategies for teaching ICT which may include promoting and advertising the course to students and staff, managing ICT and other resources and managing the effectiveness of the teaching process [3]. Lack of management involvement and administrative support is one of the barriers of teaching ICT in most African HEIs [16]. Interviews confirmed this: *"So for now, the support is there but it is not really enough. We need more assistance from them. We lack enough resources, the labs are not sufficient"* (I5). *"We truly do not have the support from the administration. Lecturers need to put more effort to make sure the course succeeds"* (I7). Resistance to change by administrators and policymakers of HEIs in recognizing, accepting, and responding to the significant change in ICT innovation and industrial demands has been noted [3]. We observed some reluctance to adopt ERP. In contrast with the literature which notes little knowledge and appreciation of integrated ICTs [18], it was evident that despite poor involvement in ERP teaching at HEIs, top management had appreciation of ERP systems: *"A senior administrator of the school gave a speech to the class which introduced the ERP ESEFA short course, and highlighted the importance and demand of ERP systems in the country and encouraged students to put effort on the course"* (I6).

4.2   Technology Challenges

Technology related challenges to achieving ERP learning objectives identified in the literature were poor infrastructure, poor or no access to ERP systems and lack of technical support. Lack of technical support did not emerge in the interviews, however one author observed that technical administrators solved technical problems that arose and the HEI project helpdesk also provided technical support. Consistent with the literature [3] poor technology infrastructure was a dominant challenge: *"We face technology problem like slow internet connection, insufficient number of computers in the labs to accommodate students"* (I7). Students have better understanding and satisfaction of ERP courses when incorporating hands-on ERP systems [14]. Yet HEIs cannot afford to adopt ERP systems at the same rate as ERP implementers [7]. The HEI project reduced this challenge: *"The challenge we had was to find a real live system to train students"* (I1).

4.3   Resource Challenges

Two dominant themes were identified under the resource challenge category: lack of financial resources and lack of expertise. ERP teaching in HEIs demands financial resources to support it [7]. The lack of funds was related to lack of administration support. Top management fail to commit themselves to ERP teaching because of insufficient funds. This resulted in poor or no access to ERP systems for instructional purpose. *"So I think they would want to support us, but however money is a problem"* (I7). *"Before the ESEFA project, we had access to SAP ERP systems for practice but the initiative failed because the university did not have money to pay for the license"* (I5). Studies indicated that HEIs lack teachers with expertise and confidence in ICT hindering the teaching of technology in most developing countries [11]. Specific expertise is needed for the planning and delivery of ERP courses to students. Academics with these skills also play a role in motivating faculty who are not convinced or do not appreciate the ERP technology. HEIs lack enough expertise, quoting participants: *"The plan is having more student intake next time we run the course, which definitely points to the need of having more lecturers as they won't be enough"* (I4).

4.4   Student Challenges

Student related challenges that were identified in literature included: lack of motivation, student understanding, and cost issues where students could not afford the course. These, however, did not emerge from the interview. Lecturers commented that students were fully motivated and could afford the course. Affordability, however, was mentioned in that it would be a concern once the HEI project funding ends. *"Students could not afford earlier ERP programme, TERP10, which we tried. With ESEFA, at least some can afford. So they are overcoming the finance challenge"* (I2). Interview analysis identified student background and enrolment status as challenges under this category. This theme was a new theme not found in the literature. ERP courses are often taught in multiple disciplines and to a variety of students, and this was a challenge as some students do not have the business background needed. *"When it comes to theoretical part, some students have difficulty to relate to the content because they don't have the business background"* (I4). Challenges were faced in one case with regards to students' enrolment status. The HEI model appears to be moving from the more traditional full-time student and NT students were either full time, part-time, or distance learning. This raised concerns on student attendance in terms of time and other responsibilities. *"Most part-time students are familiar and motivated to ERP especially having the hands-on experience with system. But the challenge they have is getting enough time to accommodate this course"* (I2).

4.5   Teaching Challenges

Literature teaching challenges were difficulty in planning and structuring courses and insufficient course content. Scheduling was a new theme that emerged. While literature had identified insufficient ERP course content in HEIs (i.e. learning manuals, ERP case studies that capture the range of complexities in industries, and examinations) as a barrier towards ERP teaching [4], the HEI project provided course content to HEIs lessening this challenge although academics are keen to expand the number of modules covered and develop more ERP case studies: *"ESEFA ERP course is more detailed than our previous course. But I think the system itself covers a lot of things (modules) that we can also cover in the course. And there is a need to have more industry case studies"* (I5). Planning ERP courses involves detailed preparation and structuring of content such as case studies and setting up of theory classes and practical classes. ERP courses need qualified trainers, sufficient infrastructure and sufficient content [5,14,15]. Interview analysis did not point out substantial challenges in the preparation of the course content, which could be as a result of the HEI project curriculum used. Courses that have both theory and practical need a well-planned schedule. Scheduling was a theme that was evident in both cases. NT ran an ERP course during a short vacation period when computer laboratories are easily accessible and there is a fast internet connection. Academics raised a concern that scheduling the ERP course in their traditional schedule is an enormous challenge considering part-time and distance students. At UD the course needed to repeat practical sessions because of insufficient computers. This was resolved by installing the ERP user interface on some students' personal computers. The scheduling challenge is seen to be linked to the lack of technical resources (i.e. hardware, network bandwidth) in HEIs, insufficient expertise, and student enrolment status which affects their course management. As quoted: *"The only challenge we faced planning the course, is getting labs. So we end up booking in this short vac. However, this has limit the distance learning students as they mostly use vacation period to meet their lecturers and catch up"* (I2). *"As you can notice now, practical sessions are hard to conduct with students in 4 different labs and few number of lecturers that we have"* (I5).

4.6 Discussion of Findings

When contrasting literature challenges with those HEIs experience the HEI project was able to reduce some. Firstly HEIs were able to get affordable access to ERP systems hosted elsewhere. Secondly ERP courses were more affordable due to less cost being incurred in course preparation and system access. Thirdly the project curriculum resolved difficulties with insufficient course content and finally training of lecturers by the project improved the expertise and confidence of academics. The concern is that many challenges might re-emerge after the funding ends and while the project grapples with ensuring sustainability post funding. Yet on the positive side the project has shown the benefits of HEIs partnering and sharing teaching content to improve learning outcomes and decrease teaching challenges.

Figure 1 shows the dominant ERP teaching challenges experienced by the two HEIs in this case study. Most challenges were initially caused by a lack of financial resources. This results in poor technological infrastructure and insufficient expertise (in the form of lecturers and technical support staff). A further challenge was catering for part-time and distance students. The main resultant challenge appeared to be scheduling ERP courses considering the combination of insufficient infrastructure, insufficient lecturers and part-time and distance students. Already the HEIs studied were trying to overcome these challenges by allowing students to install the ERP software on their own personal computers and by duplicating classes. This would suggest that there is a need for a more flexible teaching model which allows students remote access to ERP systems and on-line lecture recordings. These are strategies HEIs could adopt to assist in overcoming these challenges.

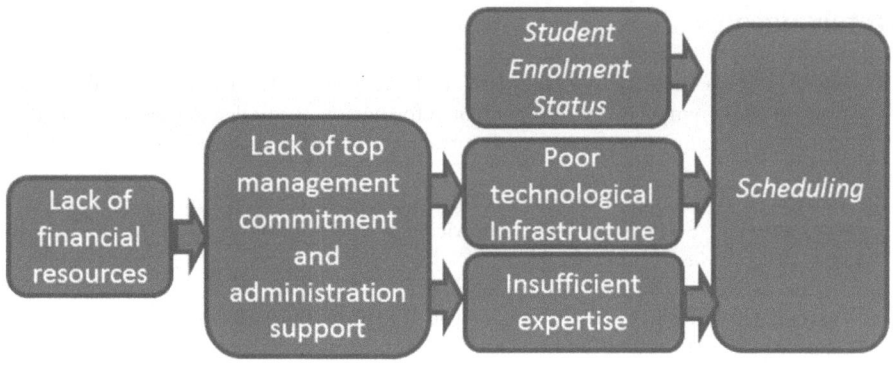

Fig. 1. Model of dominant ERP teaching challenges

5   Conclusion

This research aimed to identify ERP teaching challenges faced in SSA HEIs. Potential challenges were identified from the literature by merging challenges of teaching technology in Africa and challenges of teaching ERP. The study then analyzed two cases. A limitation is that only lecturers were interviewed. Teaching ICT requires computer technicians, teaching assistants and tutors and a richer understanding of ICT education challenges would emerge from a broader range of interviewees. Four categories of challenges emerged. Firstly some challenges relevant to other technologies such as lack of student motivation did not emerge. Secondly it was noted that a HEI collaborative project was able to overcome some challenges such as expertise and confidence of educators and insufficient course content. It seems African ICT education can benefit from such public-private ICT projects and more research on these projects, their benefits and sustainability is needed. Thirdly challenges which were consistent with the literature included lack of financial resources, poor technological infrastructure, insufficient expertise and lack of top management commitment and administrative support. Finally new challenges emerged inductively such as challenges in scheduling and dealing with students with different enrolment statuses. These new challenges seem to be challenges emerging as the nature of HEIs evolves and needs more research. The final resultant model of dominant challenges that HEIs experienced as they started teaching ERP points to the need for strategies that can deal with technological constraints at HEIs and part-time and distance students. Strategies suggested include the recording of lectures and making software more accessible to students off campus. However the unintended consequences of these strategies needs research.

References

1. Alford, K.L., Carter, C.A., Ragsdale, D.J., Ressler, E.K., Reynolds, C.W.: Specification and managed development of information technology curricula. In: Proceedings of the 5th Conference on Information Technology Education, pp. 261–266 (2004)
2. Alshare, K.A., Lane, P.L.: Predicting student-perceived learning outcomes and satisfaction in ERP courses: An empirical investigation. Commun. Assoc. Inform. Syst. **28**, 571–584 (2011)
3. Bingimlas, K.A.: Barriers to the successful integration of ICT in teaching and learning environments: A review of the literature. Eurasia J. Math. Sci. Tech. Educ. **5**, 235–245 (2009)
4. Cameron, B.H.: Enterprise systems education: New directions and challenges for the future. In: Proceedings of the 2008 ACM SIGMIS CPR Conference on Computer Personnel Doctoral Consortium and Research, pp. 119–126 (2008)
5. Chen, K., Razi, M., Rienzo, T.: Intrinsic factors for continued ERP learning: A precursor to interdisciplinary ERP curriculum design. Decis. Sci. J. Innovat. Educ. **9**, 149–176 (2011)
6. Cronan, T.P., Douglas, D.E.: Assessing ERP learning (management, business process, and skills)and attitudes. J. Organ. End. User. Comput. **25**, 59–74 (2013)
7. Davis, C.H., Comeau, J.: Enterprise integration in business education: Design and outcomes of a capstone ERP-based undergraduate e-business management course. J. Inform. Syst. Educ. **15**, 287–300 (2004)
8. Eden, R., Sedera, D.D., Tan, F.: Archival analysis of enterprise resource planning systems: The current state and future directions. In: Proceedings ICIS 2012 (2012)
9. ESEFA: http://www.esefa.ac.za
10. Furuholt, B., Ørvik, T.U.: Implementation of information technology in Africa: Understanding and explaining the results of ten years of implementation effort in a Tanzanian organization. Inform. Tech. Dev. **12**, 45–62 (2006)
11. Hennessy, S., Harrison, D., Wamakote, L.: Teacher factors influencing classroom use of ICT in sub-Saharan Africa. Itupale Onl. J. of Afri. Stud. **2**, 39–54 (2010)
12. Lotriet, H.H., Matthee, M.C., Alexander, P.M.: Challenges in ascertaining ICT skills requirements in South Africa. S. Afr. Comput. J. **46**, 38–48 (2010)
13. O'Leary, D.E.: Enterprise resource planning (ERP) systems: An empirical analysis of benefits. J. Emerg. Tech. Account. **1**, 63–72 (2004)
14. Scholtz, B., Cilliers, C., Calitz, A.: A comprehensive, competency-based education framework using medium-sized ERP systems. J. Inform. Syst. Educ. **23**, 345 (2012)
15. Shtub, A.: A framework for teaching and training in the enterprise resource planning (ERP) era. Int. J. Prod. Res. **39**, 567–576 (2001)
16. Sife, A., Lwoga, E., Sanga, C.: New technologies for teaching and learning: Challenges. Int. J. Educ. Dev. ICT. **3**, 57–67 (2007)
17. Topi, H., Valacich, J.S., Wright, R.T., Kaiser, K., Nunamaker Jr., J.F., Sipior, J.C., de Vreede, G.J.: IS 2010: Curriculum guidelines for undergraduate degree programs in information systems. Commun. Assoc. Inform. Syst. **26**, 18 (2010)
18. Tusubira, F., Mulira, N.: Integration of ICT in organizations: Challenges and best practice recommendations based on the experience of Makerere University and other organizations. In: International ICT Conference held at Hotel Africana, Kampala, Uganda, September 2004
19. Winkelmann, A., Leyh, C.: Teaching ERP systems: A multi-perspective view on the ERP system market. J. Inform. Syst. Educ. **21**, 233 (2010)

Grit and Growth Mindset Among High School Students in a Computer Programming Project: A Mixed Methods Study

Delia Kench[1]([✉]), Scott Hazelhurst[2], and Femi Otulaja[3]

[1] School of Computer Science,
University of Witwatersrand, Johannesburg, South Africa
kenchd@stbenedicts.co.za
[2] School of Electrical and Information Engineering,
University of the Witwatersrand, Johannesburg, South Africa
scott.hazelhurst@wits.ac.za
[3] Science Teaching and Learning Centre, Faculty of Science,
University of the Witwatersrand, Johannesburg, South Africa
femi.otulaja@wits.ac.za

Abstract. This paper investigates the effects of grit ("passion and perseverance for a long-term goal") and growth mindset in grade 11 high school students (**Terminological clarification:** Throughout this paper the term 'students' refers to the pupils in secondary education *before* university. In the South African discourse they are typically refered to as 'learners'.), as they code a non-trivial programming project in Java. Students are guided through the stages of the development of a programming project by the teacher and are given a rubric describing the criteria for assessment. The project is scaffolded by the teacher. Assessments are frequent with detailed feedback provided to the students. The students' grit and mindset are measured using questionnaires to form part of the quantitative data, together with the number of times each student submitted his project. Six students were interviewed to provide detailed qualitative data to interrogate the qualitative data. Although the correlation between the grit and mindset was weak, a stronger correlation was determined between the number of submissions and the project scores..

Keywords: Grit · Growth mindset · Teaching programming · Secondary education (highschool)

1 Introduction

Computer programming is difficult for students to master because of its complexity. This includes learning the syntax of the language, the use of the Integrated Development Environment (IDE), problem-solving strategies, testing strategies and coping with errors. This paper focuses on how students cope with errors and their resulting problem-solving strategies. In order to master the skills of programming, a student needs to persevere to fix the many different errors and

© Springer International Publishing AG 2016
S. Gruner (Ed.): SACLA 2016, CCIS 642, pp. 187–194, 2016.
DOI: 10.1007/978-3-319-47680-3_18

mistakes. The logic in programming is like mathematics where the skills accumulate over time with each concept building on previous concepts [1].

Students developing programming projects are often frustrated when they encounter errors and find difficulty in completing complex programming tasks. Programming, in itself, is difficult and requires discipline with constant practice. Students need to seek out alternate strategies [10] and be prepared to fail without reacting negatively. This trait is known as grit, i.e. passion and perseverance for a long-term goal, which can predict success over and above intelligent quotient (IQ) [6].

Linked to the lack of grit is the students' perception of their intellectual ability as being fixed and their failure to achieve as something they cannot control [1]. Students with a growth mindset who believe that their intelligence can be changed with perseverance and effort will, more likely, succeed. Learning to program can easily produce a fixed mindset [5] since there are so many ways a student can get stuck which can induce a student to give up. Students with a growth mindset are more likely to employ alternate strategies to address their problems as the problems arise.

An important factor in this process is the use of praise and feedback. Students who are praised for their efforts as opposed to their intelligence and ability are more likely to focus on developing their skills by mastering new materials [11]. The use of constructive and formative feedback to increase motivation [9] and guide the student to the solution has been proven to produce positive outcomes.

Little research has been done that combines grit and growth mindset in high school students whilst they develop a significant programming project in South Africa. This paper explores how grit and growth mindset influence/shape the learning of high school students in a programming project (PAT). We measured academic performance, grit and mindset, number of submissions and conducted interviews with a subset of the students participating in the project. A mixed methods approach [4] is used to analyse the data.

2 Literature Review

2.1 What Is Growth Mindset?

In a study of junior high school students in a mathematics course, Blackwell et al. [1] showed that adolescents' beliefs about their intelligence inform their motivation for achievement. Some students believe that intelligence is fixed or unchangeable, (fixed 'entity'), which is termed an entity theory. Others believed that intelligence can change and be developed, which they termed an incremental theory. Blackwell discovered that students who had a more incremental theory of intelligence had a distinct advantage over those with a more entity theory of intelligence stance; and had achieved better results in their first year of junior high [1]. The adolescents who endorse an incremental theory of intelligence held stronger learning goals and held a positive belief about efforts, made more positive statements about their ability and created strategies based on efforts in relation to failure which as a result boosted their achievement in mathematics.

Cutts et al. [5] used a growth mindset approach to teaching programming with first year university students in an introductory programming course over a six-week period with test scores being used as a measure of effectiveness. They discovered that when students struggle with programming problems, they can develop a fixed mindset unless they are encouraged with alternative strategies. After six weeks, there was a positive effect for those who received growth mindset training. On the average, people who were taught about mindset showed a shift toward a growth mindset and those who were not taught about mindset showed a shift toward a more fixed mindset during the course [5].

2.2 What Is Grit?

Grit overlaps with but is different to mindset. According to Duckworth et al. [6], grit is a non-cognitive quality that emphasises the long-term stamina of an individual who will finish tasks and pursue an aim over a period of years. Grit is not a single entity; it is made up of efforts and continued interest despite failure or adversary. The study of grit as predictor of success has been developed to include a grit scale which is a tool to measure grit in individuals [7].

While there is a vast amount of research relating IQ to academic achievement, there is far less on the non-intellectual strengths of an individual compared to his/her academic achievement. Little is known about other factors that could predict academic performance. In studying why some individuals accomplish more than others with similar intelligence, there is need to consider other attributes of an individual [6]. Research has indicated that individuals identified as possessing grit often seem to demonstrate sustained efforts and interests over many years regardless of failures and setbacks. As examples, they found that IQ was less of a predictor for academic performance than self-discipline in a longitudinal study involving the 2005 Scripps National Spelling Bee and freshman candidates who entered the United States Military Academy, West Point, in July 2004.

2.3 Scaffolding Combined with Feedback

Feedback is significant when a student is developing a project as it forms part of formative assessment. The student is able to answer questions like [2]:

- What knowledge or skills do I aim to develop?
- How close am I now?
- What do I need to do next?

With the use of the adapted rubric provided by the Independent Examination Board (IEB), a grade 12 assessment body, which clearly denotes the skills and level of competency required at each stage, students can determine their success in the project they are programming. Feedback needs to address cognitive and motivation factors. This leads to the feeling of having control over their progress, which could be the motivational factor [2].

Contemporary learning theories support two ideas, namely [12]: that knowledge is constructed, and that learning and development are processes that are embedded in our culture and supported socially.

Scaffolding and formative assessment help move a student through a zone of proximal development (ZPD) [13]. Scaffolding is the support given by teachers to students in the form of hints, encouragement, and reminders to ensure the successful completion of a task.

In a study conducted on teaching software engineering to 16-to-18-years old high school students, the importance of positive feedback in increasing motivation was emphasized [9]. The researchers recognised that motivated students can outperform a more talented student with less motivation. They linked motivation to interests in the topic with the teacher assessing whether the choice was feasible and the additional skills required for students to be able to develop their project [9]. The gap in their knowledge was bridged by scaffolding in the form of tutorials and articles.

In programming, students will frequently experience problems with their coding; either in syntax, run time or logical errors. Successful students will employ a repertoire of strategies to get 'unstuck' when programming [10] linked to this success is the ability to persevere when coding problems occur. A student may need to use a variety of strategies, such as [10]:

1. getting help from other sources (peers, the Internet, and books);
2. working on similar examples;
3. trying to understand the problem by representing it using diagrams or breaking it down into smaller parts; and lastly
4. by 'using the force', which is described as the student telling him/herself to remember, think and persevere.

3   Study Design

3.1   Study Setting

This study was performed in a private Catholic school which highly values academic achievement. The school is located in a wealthy area of a large South African city and most, if not all, participants come from affluent families. Most students are white with a few Asian, Indian and Black students. By the start of this project the boys were familiar with the programming concepts taught previously and were able to code objects, arrays of objects, a basic GUI in Java and create a database in Microsoft Access. The students had basic programming skills to debug code, fix run time and logical errors for small programs.

Whilst debugging a program is important, this skill was not measured, only the grit and perseverance when debugging a program will be measured. Students may improve their debugging skills during the study, but this result will not form part of the study.

3.2 Mixed Methods Methodology

Mixed methods design is a research design for collecting, analysing and reporting research by integrating both quantitative and qualitative data [4]. Mixed methods gather both quantitative and qualitative data, integrates both types of data and then draws interpretations on the combined results to understand the research problem. By combining both quantitative and qualitative data the assumption is that combined strength of both data will provide a better understanding of the problem [3].

In January 2015, there were a total of twenty-nine students studying programming divided into two classes. The one class was taught by the researcher (14 students) and the other by a colleague (15 students). The students were in their second year of their three-year course and were taught programming structures such a simple data types, sequencing, selection and iteration statements in Java.

In the third term of 2015 the students had to code their own projects using a topic of their own choosing and this was assessed by the adapted IEB rubric. After the requirements had been established, students developed their projects in sections. Students designed, coded and tested each section (Graphical User Interface, classes, database) before moving on. The project was developed over a six-week period with students attending seven periods of thirty-five minutes long per week. The project was assessed at the end of their grade 11 which formed the foundation of their grade 12 project. The PAT has a significant weighting of 25 % of the year mark. The mark for the PAT depended on the specification, design and the functionality of the code.

3.3 Quantitative Data

The students were assessed using the grit short-scale questionnaire [7] and an adaptation of the growth mindset questionnaire [8]. They were assessed at the beginning of the project, after they had completed their design and at the end once their project was completed. The three scores for grit and the three scores for mindset produced by each student were averaged to produce a single grit score and a single mindset score. In addition, the number of submissions of each student was also recorded. Each time their project was assessed, the score was updated on the mark sheet by the teacher. In most cases the teacher assessed the project in the presence of the student ensuring the student had immediate feedback detailing where they went wrong and what they could do to improve. The students' average grit score, average mindset score, their number of submissions and their final PAT result were recorded in a spreadsheet.

3.4 Qualitative Data

Using the quantitative data, 6 students were identified to be interviewed. The purpose of the interviews was to understand the lack of correlation between the grit, mindset and PAT results. The students were asked questions to identify their process when they found errors and whether they gave up or persevered when they encounter errors.

4   Results

Students did very well; only 2 students achieved below 80 % (most scored 100 % for the project). This narrow range of scores makes it difficult to differentiate between the students' scores. Table 1 summarises the quantitative data in terms of grit, mindset, number of submissions and the PAT scores while Table 2 examines the correlation coefficients.

The strongest correlation was between the number of submissions and PAT score with a correlation of 0.52. The correlation between PAT, mindset and grit was weak at 0.13 and 0.48, respectively. The correlation between grit and the number of submissions was even weaker at -0.06. The strongest relationship was determined between number of submissions and the PAT results with $r(29) = 0.52$ and the significance of this relationship is determined by a p value of 0.002. The correlation between grit and the PAT was $r(29) = 0.48$ with a significance of $p = 0.004$. These results imply that both grit and the number of submission are related to the PAT scores. To investigate these findings six students were interviewed — their results are shown in Table 3.

All the students interviewed faced problems during the coding phase. All students displayed perseverance by devising problem-solving strategies to correct their code. The problem-solving strategy chosen was personal to each student. Student A and Student E both achieved 100 % with 6 to 8 submissions. Both students did not ask their classmates during class or use the WhatsApp group but instead traced through their programs to find their errors. Student A was an extremely shy student who did not like asking for help in class. Student E did not want his classmates to think he could not solve the problems; so, he persevered by himself. Student E is a high-achieving student who has academic, sporting and cultural colours and was selected to be a leader in the school. He enjoyed the

Table 1. Results of quantitative data

Stud.	Average	Highest	Lowest	Std.Dev.
Grit out of 5	3.4	4.3	2.3	0.56
Mindset	50.9 %	72.2 %	38.9 %	8.52 %
#Submissions	7.3	11	4	1.75
Final PAT Score	96 %	100 %	67 %	7.28 %

Table 2. Correlation coefficients (CC)

CC for	Grit	Mindset	#Submissions	PAT
Grit	1.00			
Mindset	0.62	1.00		
#Submissions	0.24	−0.06	1.00	
PAT	0.48	0.13	0.52	1.00

Table 3. Results of students interviewed

Pseudonym	Grit	Mindset	#Drafts	Overall
Student A	2.6	43	6	100 %
Student B	3.1	42	7	93 %
Student C	4.2	72	5	89 %
Student D	2.9	50	8	97 %
Student E	4.3	58	8	100 %
Student F	4.0	51	7	97 %

challenge of the project and used the teacher's advice, the internet as a resource when he was experiencing problems with his coding. He also traced his program to locate the errors. Both boys found the deadlines motivational in terms of submitting on time and encouraging to keep their project on track.

Student D persevered by tracing his program on paper and asked friends and family for help when he was stuck while Student F researched the internet. Student F also asked classmates and the teacher for help whenever he was stuck. Both of them found the deadlines motivational and used the multiple submissions to improve their marks.

Student C devised a system of coding multiple solutions to each problem. Using these solutions, he chose what he considered to be the best solution and then moved on from there. He found difficulties in keeping track of the versions of his solutions. His method was time consuming; however, he was still able to submit his PAT five times.

Student B alternated coding his solution with a computer game. Each time he was stuck on either project, he switched to the other. Student B was not able to successfully separate the working code from the front end. Most of his logic was in the front end; and once on this path, he could not move the code and still have a working solution. He did, however, persevere in getting the code to work by tracing his program and explaining his logic to his father. He admitted to frequently procrastinating; although, he submitted his PAT seven times.

The qualitative data revealed that each student persevered when problems were encountered although this is not reflected in their grit and mindset scores.

5   Conclusion and Future Work

Upon initial investigation, there appears to be little relationship between grit, mindset and the PAT scores. However, upon further investigation into the qualitative data, grit can be seen by the perseverance displayed by the students. Students did not give up when they encountered errors and went on to develop problem-solving strategies to fix their errors. The deadlines served to motivate the students and kept them on track with their projects. A possible reason for the lack of correlation between the grit, mindset and PAT scores could be the students' immaturity in completing the questionnaire or their fixed mindset in that they considered themselves to already be very intelligent, which is supported by their PAT results. The sampled population was skewed toward a more affluent demographic together with an existing motivation to achieve good results.

This study could be enhanced by investigations into the problem-solving strategies developed by the students. Since no problem-solving strategy was taught, there is clear evidence that the problem-solving strategies were developed independently by the students and each were varied. Studies could be conducted to determine whether teaching a particular problem-solving strategy would be beneficial as opposed to students developing their own. Since the sampled population was skewed towards the more affluent demographic, further studies could be performed in government schools, among female students in single-gender female schools with a more diverse race groups; and in schools where the class average is lower and with a wider range.

References

1. Blackwell, L.S., Trzesniewski, K.H., Dweck, C.S.: Implicit theories of intelligence predict achievement across an adolescent transition: a longitudinal study and an intervention. Child Dev. **78**(1), 246–263 (2007)
2. Brookhart, S.M.: How to Give Effective Feedback to Your Students. ASCD, Alexandra (2008)
3. Creswell, J.W.L., Clark, V.L.P.: Designing and Conducting Mixed Methods Research, vol. 2. Sage, Thousand Oaks (2011)
4. Creswell, J.W.L., Plano-Clark, V.L.P., Gutmann, M.L., Hanson, W.E.: Advanced mixed methods research designs. In: Tashakkori, A., Teddlie, C. (eds.) Handbook of Mixed Methods in Social and Behavioral Research, pp. 209–240. Sage, Thousand Oaks (2003)
5. Cutts, Q., Cutts, E., Draper, S., O'Donnell, P., Saffrey, P.: Manipulating mindset to positively influence introductory programming performance. In: Proceedings 41st ACM Technical Symposium on Computer Science Education (SIGCSE 2010), p. 431 (2010)
6. Duckworth, A.L., Peterson, C., Matthews, M.D., Kelly, D.R.: Grit: perseverance and passion for long-term goals. J. Pers. Soc. Psychol. **92**(6), 1087–1101 (2007)
7. Duckworth, A.L., Quinn, P.D.: Development and validation of the short grit scale (grit-s). J. Pers. Assess. **91**(2), 166–174 (2009)
8. Dweck, C.S.: Test your Mindset. Ballantine, New York (2006)
9. Kohler, B., Gluchow, M., Brigge, B.: Teaching basic software engineering to senior high school students. In: Information Systems and Technology for Organizations in a Networked Society, pp. 149–166. BusinessScience (2014)
10. McCartney, R., Eckerdal, A., Mostram, J.E., Sanders, K., Zander, C.: Successful students – Strategies for getting unstuck. SIGCSE Bull. **39**, 156–160 (2007)
11. Mueller, C.M., Dweck, C.S.: Praise for intelligence can undermine children's motivation and performance. J. Pers. Soc. Psychol. **75**(1), 33–52 (1998)
12. Shepard, L.A.: Linking formative assessment to scaffolding. Educ. Leadersh. **63**(3), 66–70 (2005)
13. Vygotsky, L.S.: Mind in Society: The Development of Higher Psychological Processes. Harvard University Press, Cambridge (1978)

Author Index

Ade-Ibijola, Abejide   69

Calitz, André P.   35, 51, 115
Coetzee, Serena   143

Durrheim, Mark S.   69

Eloff, Jan H.P.   131
Ewert, Sigrid   69

Foster, Greg   123

Glaum, Arthur   115
Greyling, Jean   115

Halland, Ken   43
Hazelhurst, Scott   187

Kench, Delia   187
Koorsse, Melisa   35, 51

Machanick, Philip   104
Mahanga, Khadija M.   179
Marshall, Linda   131

Nash, Jane   123
Nel, Liezel   95

Olivier, Martin S.   3
Otulaja, Femi   187

Pieterse, Vreda   59, 160

Radebe, Fani Moses   95
Rautenbach, Victoria   143

Seymour, Lisa F.   179
Solms, Fritz   59
Suleman, Hussein   83

Taljaard, Marinda   35
Travica, Bob   22
Tsietsi, Mosiuoa   171

van Eekelen, Marko   160

Zietsman, Jaco   51